THE CATHOLIC UNIVERSITY OF AMERICA
CANON LAW STUDIES
No. 162

THE CRIME OF ABORTION IN CANON LAW

AN HISTORICAL SYNOPSIS AND COMMENTARY

by

ROGER JOHN HUSER, O.F.M., A.B., J.C.L.
Priest of the Cincinnati Province of St. John Baptist

A DISSERTATION

Submitted to the Faculty of Canon Law of the Catholic University of America in Partial Fulfillment of the Requirements for the Degree of Doctor of Canon Law

THE CATHOLIC UNIVERSITY OF AMERICA PRESS
WASHINGTON, D. C.
1942

Imprimi Potest:
ADALBERTUS ROLFES, O.F.M.,
Minister Provincialis.

337542

Nihil Obstat:
LUDOVICUS MOTRY, S.T.D., J.C.D.,
Censor Deputatus.

Imprimatur:
✠ MICHAEL J. CURLEY, D.D.,
Archiepiscopus Baltimorensis et Washingtonensis.

Baltimorae, die 19 maii, 1942.

COPYRIGHT, 1943
THE CATHOLIC UNIVERSITY OF AMERICA PRESS

Printed by
THE PAULIST PRESS
New York, N. Y.
51

"Let the little children be, and do not hinder them from coming to Me, for of such is the kingdom of heaven." (*Matthew* xix. 14.)

TABLE OF CONTENTS

CHAPTER VII

CHAPTER VIII

CHAPTER IX

CHAPTER X

CHAPTER XI

CHAPTER XII

FOREWORD

IN accordance with the divine precept "Thou shalt not kill" the Catholic Church has always condemned murder and its kindred crimes against human life, even if that life be still hidden within the sanctuary of the mother's womb. Thus, from the earliest centuries the Church has added severe penalties to her condemnations of the crime of abortion—the nefarious procedure of expelling from the womb of the mother a child still incapable of extra-uterine existence.

It is the purpose of the historical part of this study to outline ***the general ecclesiastical penal legislation against abortion***, from the first centuries down to the Code of Canon Law, ***with particular emphasis on the censure of excommunication and the irregularity***. But the censure and the irregularity for abortion as known today did not come into existence until the sixteenth and the thirteenth centuries respectively. Abortion was, of course, penalized before those times. In regard to the first twelve centuries this study aims to state what the penalties were rather than to classify them in accordance with present-day jurisprudence.

The historical study of ecclesiastical penalties against abortion is treated as follows. After a brief consideration of the laws of ancient paganism and of the Jews, there are considered the pronouncements of the Fathers, which pronouncements laid the foundation for conciliar legislation. The legislation of the early councils is stated, discussed briefly, and traced through the principal canonical collections in vogue in the various regions of the Church up to the time of Gratian. The *Decretum* of Gratian and the pre-Gregorian Decretals supply the texts against abortion that were incorporated into the Decretals of Pope Gregory IX, thereby becoming the first statutes against abortion to be found in the official universal law of the Church. The severe Constitution *"Effraenatam"* of Pope Sixtus V (1585-1590) together with its modification by Pope Gregory XIV (1590-1591) is shown to constitute the foundation for the present-day law; and the legislation of Pope Pius IX

(1846-1878) is recognized as the immediate source of the censure against abortion as now found in the Code of Canon Law.

The second part of this work comprises the canonical commentary—the study of the present-day law as contained in the Code. The scope of the commentary is limited specifically to this: *what precisely constitutes the crime of abortion* in canon law so that the person guilty thereof incurs *ipso facto* the censure of excommunication and the irregularity arising from the crime, and, if he be a cleric, becomes liable to the *ferendae sententiae* penalty of deposition. The answer is given by commenting upon those words of the Code which convey the *essential notion of the crime,* namely the words "*procurantes abortum, effectu secuto.*"

It is not the aim of the writer to discuss the morality of abortion or to treat the penalties themselves, but, it may be repeated, to consider solely those elements which are peculiar and proper to the crime of abortion as defined in the law of the Church. Moreover, in so far as the physical and obstetrical factors of abortion are relevant and necessary to a correct canonical understanding of the crime, these factors receive special attention—factors which all too frequently receive inadequate consideration in canonical treatises.

* * *

The writer wishes to take this opportunity to express sincere thanks to the Very Reverend Adalbert Rolfes, O.F.M., Minister Provincial, for the privilege of undertaking graduate study in the School of Canon Law at the Catholic University of America; to the Faculty of the School of Canon Law for their unfailing kindness and scholarly instruction; to the Very Reverend Leonard Walsh, O.F.M., Commissary of the Holy Land, Washington, D.C., for his many favors; to J. Bay Jacobs, M.D., Fellow of the American College of Obstetricians, Associate Professor of Obstetrics at Georgetown University School of Medicine, and Director of Child and Maternal Welfare of the District of Columbia, for his helpful suggestions and his kindness in reading the manuscript of the canonical commentary; and to numerous confrères and all others who in so many ways have been of assistance in the preparation of this study.

Part One

Historical Synopsis

PRELIMINARY NOTE

Before an approach is made to the historical study of the penal legislation against abortion, cognizance must be taken of a theory which had a great influence on ecclesiastical law. This theory is the distinction between the formed and the non-formed, the animated and the non-animated fetus. According to the sources used in the preparation of this study, the *formed* fetus is one that has reached a stage of development characterized by distinct physical organs and members, i. e., it has acquired human form. The *non-formed* fetus has not yet attained this development. Frequently the terms *animated* and *non-animated* are employed as synonymous for *formed* and *non-formed*. Strictly, *animated* and *non-animated* refer to the presence or absence of the human soul. According to the theory of delayed animation, the human soul cannot be present until the fetus has reached the certainty of development mentioned above, and hence the term *animated* becomes synonymous with *formed*. Sometimes the terms *vivified* and *non-vivified* are used.

This distinction is found in ancient Oriental codes, and was commonly accepted by Greek philosophers, notably Aristotle (384-322 B.C.). The Septuagint version of the Scriptures altered the Hebrew text to embody this distinction, which was acceptable even to some of the great Fathers of the Church.

The Church has always held in regard to the morality of abortion that it is a serious sin to destroy a fetus at any stage of development. However, as a *juridical norm* in the determination of penalties against abortion, the Church at various times did accept the distinction between a *formed* and a *non-formed*, an *animated* and a *non-animated* fetus.

CHAPTER I

ANCIENT LAWS

Article I. Oriental Laws

The *Sumerian Code* (c.2000 B.C.) contains the most ancient law prescribing penalties for abortion. According to this Code a fine is demanded as penalty if anyone strikes a woman and thus causes the loss of her unborn child. The fine imposed is greater for a deliberate blow than for an accidental one.[1]

The *Code of Hammurabi* (c.1800 B.C.) fines the man who destroys the fetus by striking a pregnant woman. However, the amount of the fine depends not upon the deliberation of the act, as in the Sumerian law, but upon the social status of the mother. Furthermore, if the woman thus attacked be of the highest rank and die as a result of this attack, the daughter of the guilty man must suffer death.[2]

The Assyrian Code (c.1500 B.C.) imposes a fine, the lash, and public service upon the man who causes an abortion by striking a woman with child. If the victim is another man's wife the penalties were more severe, involving even the death of the guilty person. Crucifixion and impaling were the punishments for the woman who deliberately caused an abortion to herself. In this Code the fetus is spoken of as a human life; cognizance is also taken of the stages of fetal development.[3]

[1] I, §§1-2—Text and discussion in Meisner, *Babylonien und Assyrien* (2 vols., Heidelberg: Carl Winters Universitätsbuchhandlung, 1920-1925), I, 149-150. See also Dölger, "Das Lebensrecht des ungeborenen Kindes und die Fruchtabtreibung in der Bewertung der heidnischen und christlichen Antike,"—*Antike und Christentum,* IV (1933), 1-61, especially 4-5; hereafter this article will be cited as "Das Lebensrecht" and the periodical as *AuC.*

[2] §§209-214—English translation by D. D. Luckenbill in Smith, *The Origin and History of Hebrew Law* (Chicago: The University of Chicago Press, 1931), p. 211.

[3] Part I, §§21, 49-52—Smith, *op. cit.,* pp. 226, 235, 236; Jastrow, "An Assyrian Law Code,"—*Journal of the American Oriental Society,* XLI (1921),

The Hittite Code (c.1300 B.C.), while keeping the fine proportional to the social status of the mother, prescribed a higher fine if the fetus had attained a certain stage of physical development and formation.[4]

In the *Vendidad* of ancient Persia (not older than 600 B.C.) the woman with child was admonished not to destroy the fruit of conception because of shame and human respect. Should she fail to heed this warning, both she and the father of the child were held to be guilty of wilful murder. The guilt of the crime was imputed also to the person who supplied abortifacient drugs. Fine and flogging were the penalties prescribed.[5]

Four factors in this ancient legislation are of particular significance, for down through the centuries they played an important rôle in both civil and ecclesiastical laws against the crime of abortion. The *first* factor is that the unborn child is evaluated as a human being—in the Assyrian law.[6] The *second* factor is that the penalties are gauged in relation to the stage of fetal development—in the Assyrian and in the Hittite Codes.[7] The *third* is that cognizance is taken of the deliberateness of the act—in the Sumerian

20-21, 46-48, with numbering and translation of the text differing slightly from that in the work by Smith. For detailed discussion of the Assyrian Code, cf.: Belkin, *Philo and the Oral Law,* Harvard Semitic Series, Vol. XI (Cambridge, Mass.: Harvard University Press, 1940), 131, 132, footnote 125; Smith, *op. cit.,* pp. 243, 244; Jastrow, *art. cit.,* footnotes on pages cited. Dölger ("Das Lebensrecht,"—*AuC,* IV [1933], 4) refers to only a portion of the Assyrian legislation regarding abortion.

[4] §§17-18 Sturtevant-Bechtel, *A Hittite Chrestomathy* (Philadelphia: University of Pennsylvania, 1935), p. 215. Cf. Smith, *op. cit.,* p. 250, for translation by A. Walther.

[5] *Vendidad, Fargard XV (On Sin),* II, nn. 11-14—*The Sacred Books and Early Literature of the East,* Charles F. Horne et al. editors (14 vols., New York & London: Austin, and Lipscomb, Inc., 1914), VII, *Ancient Persia,* pp. 121-122.

[6] Dölger ("Das Lebensrecht,"—*AuC,* IV [1933], 5) therefore would seem to be too severe in his criticism of these enactments of antiquity. It is to be noted that he fails to refer to the relevant sections 49-52 of the Assyrian Code.

[7] Belkin (*Philo and the Oral Law,* footnote 125, pp. 131, 132) states that the Assyrian Code "is the only prebiblical code which . . . makes a distinction between a developed foetus and one in the early stages."

enactment. The *fourth,* that the Persian law is perhaps the first to embody a clear and express application of penalties to those who *co-operate* in the destruction of the unborn child.

Article II. Greek Laws

It is very probable that statutes against abortion existed in the legal codes of ancient Greece. Although no specific law can be cited today, there is indirect evidence that abortion was forbidden and even penalized by Lycurgus (+9th century B.C.) and Solon (638-558 B.C.), lawgivers of Sparta and Athens respectively.[8] Furthermore, it is not at all unlikely that similar statutes existed among Grecian peoples down through the following centuries.[9]

On the other hand, the Greeks enjoy the dubious distinction of being the first positively to advise and even to demand abortion in certain cases.[10] Hippocrates (460-357 B.C.), in the famous Hippocratic Oath, pronounced against making abortifacients available to women who were bearing children.[11] Nevertheless, he himself is reputed to have indicated means whereby abortion could be procured by one who desired it.[12]

[8] Pseudo-Galenus, *An quod in Utero est sit Animal,* 5—*Galeni Omnia quae Exstant Opera* (7 vols., Venetiis, 1572), I, 67. Plutarch (46?-120?) relates an incident evincing Lycurgus' disapproval of abortion.—*Lycurgus,* III, 2-3, in *Plutarch's Lives,* translation by B. Perrin, Loeb Classical Library (hereafter to be abbreviated as *LCL*) (11 vols., New York: The Macmillan Co. and G. P. Putnam's Sons, 1914-1926), I, 211. See also Döllinger, *The Gentile and the Jew in the Courts of the Temple of Christ,* translated by N. Darnell (2. ed., 2 vols., London, 1906), II, 259.

[9] For detailed discussion, see Dölger, "Das Lebensrecht,"—*AuC,* IV (1933), 10-14; cf. also Belkin, *Philo and the Oral Law,* p. 131, footnote 123.

[10] Cf. Heidenreich, "Dissertatio in casum alterum Constitutionis Pii P. IX, d. d. 12. octob., 1869,"—*Archiv für katholisches Kirchenrecht,* LXIII (1890), 289-390, especially 292 (hereafter this article will be cited as "Dissertatio" and the periodical as *AKKR*); Eschbach, *Disputationes Physiologico-Theologicae* (3. ed., 3 fasc. in 1 vol., Romae: Desclée, 1913), II, 74.

[11] The Latin text of the Oath may be found in Eschbach, *op. cit.,* II, 74; the German, in Dölger, "Das Lebensrecht,"—*AuC,* IV (1933), 15. For a modern English version which avoids direct reference to abortion, see Lambert-Goodwin, *Medical Leaders from Hippocrates to Osler* (Indianapolis: The Bobbs-Merrill Co. [1929]), p. 25.

[12] A. Beugnet, "Avortement,"—*Dictionnaire de Théologie Catholique* (Paris:

Plato (427-347 B.C.), in his plan for the ideal republic, would have the law command abortion if a woman conceived after the age of forty.[13] Aristotle (384-322 B.C.) desired to limit the number of children in a family to a determined number. Should this number be exceeded, abortion was to be procured; but in order that the destruction of the fetus be lawful, it was to be effected before sensation and life were present.[14] And life was held to be present at that stage of fetal development characterized by the formation of distinct organs, the fortieth day after conception for males and the ninetieth day for females.[15]

Aristotle's distinction regarding fetal development is the lone contribution of Greek thought to later ecclesiastical legislation regarding the crime of abortion.

Article III. Jewish Laws

In the Mosaic legislation reference is made to abortion in *Exodus,* XXI, 22-23. According to the Vulgate text, if by striking a pregnant woman someone caused her to lose her child, he was required

Librarie Letouzey et Anè, 1903—), I, part 2, 2644-2652, especially 2646; Taussig, *Abortion, Spontaneous and Induced, Medical and Social Aspects* (hereafter to the cited as *Abortion*) (St. Louis: The C. V. Mosby Co., 1936), p. 33. Tertullian described an instrument employed by Greek physicians to destroy the fetus.—*De Anima,* cap. 25—*Corpus Scriptorum Ecclesiasticorum Latinorum* (hereafter to be abbreviated as *CSEL*) (Vindobonae, 1866—), XX, 342; Migne, *Patrologiae Cursus Completus, series latina* (221 vols., Parisiis, 1858-1864), II, 691-692 (hereafter this work will be cited as *MPL*).

[13] *De Republica,* lib. 5, n. 9—*The Republic,* translated by Paul Shorey, *LCL* (2 vols., New York: G. P. Putnam's Sons, 1930-1935), I, 467.

[14] *Politica,* lib. 7, cap. 16—*The Politics,* translated by H. Rackham, *LCL* (New York: G. P. Putnam's Sons, 1932), pp. 623 & 625, listing the relevant passage as Book 7, chapter 14, number 10.

[15] *Historia Animalium,* lib. 7, cap. 3—*The Works of Aristotle* (11 vols., Oxford edition, 1908-1931), IV, 583a.

Whether or not Aristotle held that the rational soul is infused at this moment is a moot question. See: A. Chollet, "Animation,"—*Dictionnaire de Théologie Catholique,* I, part 2, 1306; Stockums, "Historisch-Kritisches über die Frage: Wann entsteht die geistige Seele?"—*Philosophisches Jahrbuch,* XXXVII (1924), 225-252, especially 241; Florentinus, "Disputatio de ministrando baptismo humanis foetibus abortivorum,"—*Analecta Juris Pontificii,* VI (1863), 1280-1339, especially 1297.

to make compensation by a fine. Only if the mother died was the party who struck the blow sentenced to death.[16] In the Vulgate text reference is made only to accidental abortion.[17]

This law of Moses appears in quite different form in the Septuagint translation (between 300-200 B.C.) of the Exodus text. According to the Greek version, if the fetus dislodged from the womb by the blow was *unformed*, an indemnity was to be paid. In the event that the aborted child was *formed*, the party who struck the blow had to give life for life.[18]

As has already been noted, the theory of embryonic formation as a determinant of legal punishment for abortion was current among the Assyrians and Hittites, and also among the Greeks, even before the Septuagint translation came into being. In demanding the death penalty for the destruction of the *formed* fetus, the Septuagint evaluated the unborn child as a human being—an evaluation which very likely was discussed by Greek scholars who antedated the Septuagint.[19] The Septuagint definitely reflects the Grecian philosophical and medical thought current in Alexandria during the centuries immediately preceding the Christian era.[20]

Although it was primarily directed against accidental and indirect abortion,[21] the Septuagint law probably was the basis for the Jewish law and legal practice which held that the voluntary abortion of a developed fetus was murder, for it destroyed the life of a human

[16] In substantial agreement with the Vulgate are the Hebrew, Peshitto, Samaritan Pentateuch, Syriac, and Targumin of Onkelos. Cf. *Biblia Sacra Polyglotta*, edited by Brian Walton (6 vols., London, 1657), I, 316, 317.

[17] According to Eschbach (+1923) (*Disputationes Physiologico-Theologicae*, II, 74) this indicates that at the time of Moses (about 1500 B. C.) voluntary abortion was prevalent neither among the Jews nor among their immediate neighbors; otherwise Moses surely would have legislated against this crime. See also Heidenreich, "Dissertatio,"—*AKKR*, LXIII (1890), 292.

[18] Cf. *Biblia Sacra Polyglotta*, I, 316.

[19] See Dölger, "Das Lebensrecht,"—*AuC*, IV (1933), 10-15.

[20] Aptowitzer, "Jewish Criminal Law,"—*The Jewish Quarterly Review*, new series, XV (1924-1925), 115; Dölger, "Das Lebensrecht,"—*AuC*, IV (1933), 6-10.

[21] Eschbach, *Disputationes Physiologico-Theologicae*, II, 50; Dölger, "Das Lebensrecht,"—*AuC*, IV (1933), 9.

being.[22] This is reputed to have been the position of the Alexandrian School. For the writings of Philo of Alexandria (25 B.C.-c.41 A.D.) picture Jewish thought and the Jewish courts in Egypt as subscribing to the strict view of the Septuagint—abortion is murder.[23]

Adhering to the Massoretic text of Exodus, which made no distinction regarding fetal development, the Palestinian School and the common rabbinical teaching said nothing about murder in relation to abortion, regardless of the stage of embryonic development. Thus the accepted Talmudic law, as found in the Jerusalem *Gemara*, considered the unborn child to be but a part of the mother, at least in this matter of abortion. In cases of difficult childbirth the life of the mother could be safeguarded by destroying the child in the womb, provided that neither its head nor the greater part of its body had been delivered.[24]

A few words may be said about the position of Flavius Josephus (37-c.100). In the *Antiquitates*, the law regarding an attack upon a pregnant woman is stated essentially as given in the Vulgate. There is no reference to fetal development. A fine is prescribed, with the death penalty invoked only if the mother should be killed.[25] In *Contra Apionem*, however, he says that the law forbids a woman to

[22] Eschbach (*op. cit.*, II, 77) thinks that perhaps the translators themselves intended this law to repress deliberate abortion, which, as the existence of the law would then indicate, had become prevalent at that time. But see Eschbach's statement, *op. cit.*, II, 50.

[23] *The Special Laws*, bk. III, §§ 108-109—*Philo, LCL* (10 vols., 8 now published, Cambridge: Harvard University Press, 1929—), VII (translation by F. H. Colson, 1937), 545. Cf. Aptowitzer, "Jewish Criminal Law,"—*The Jewish Quarterly Review*, new series, XV (1924-1925), 89; Belkin, *Philo and the Oral Law*, p. 130. Goodenough maintains that Philo reflects a Palestinian tradition.—*The Jurisprudence of the Jewish Courts in Egypt* (New Haven, Conn.: Yale University Press, 1929), pp. 110-114.

[24] Aptowitzer, "Jewish Criminal Law,"—*The Jewish Quarterly Review*, new series, XV (1924-1925), 85, 86, 91-111; Belkin, *Philo and the Oral Law*, pp. 132-136.

[25] Book IV, n. 33—*Josephus, LCL* (6 of 9 vols. published, New York: G. P. Putnam's Sons, vols. 1-4, 1926-1930; Cambridge, Mass.: Harvard University Press, vols. 5-?, 1934—), IV (translated by H. St. J. Trackeray), 609 and 611.

procure abortion, and should she do so, she is a murderess.[26] As a result of these two statements, scholars dispute the position of Josephus regarding the legal aspect of abortion.[27]

Thus, current among the Jews of the early Christian era were a lenient (Palestinian) and a strict (Alexandrian) legal viewpoint of the crime of abortion. The former was based upon the Hebrew text of Exodus, XXI, 22-23; the latter, upon the Septuagint. It is significant that the Septuagint version—abortion as murder—was the one broadcast throughout the Roman world, both by the Jews and by the Apostles and early Christian missionaries. Therefore, it can be readily understood that the Septuagint-inspired aspect subsequently exerted great influence upon the laws as well as upon moral doctrines. This is demonstrated in the following chapter, which discusses the teaching of the Fathers and the enactments of the early Councils.

Article IV. Roman Laws

In Roman law the earliest legal reference to abortion is said to date from the days of the Monarchy (753-c.510 B.C.). A husband was permitted to divorce his wife if she had been guilty of deliberate abortion.[28]

However, it is commonly accepted today that abortion as a crime in its own right was not punished during the Republic (c.510-27 B.C.), nor during the early Empire (27 B.C.-305 A.D.).[29] Several

[26] Book II, n. 24—*op. cit.*, I (translated by H. St. J. Trackeray), 373, 375.

[27] Aptowitzer, in opposition to others, maintains that the text in *Contra Apionem* does not refer to *legal* punishment, but is a condemnation of abortion as *morally* wrong. Therefore Josephus, in holding that abortion would not be legally punishable as murder, reflects the position generally ascribed to the Palestinian School.—"Jewish Criminal Law,"—*The Jewish Quarterly Review*, new series, XV (1924-1925), 85-87 and footnote 117. See also Belkin, *op. cit.*, pp. 136-137.

[28] Plutarch, *Romulus*, XXII, 3—*Plutarch's Lives*, edited by B. Perrin, *LCL*, I, 161 and 163. See Mommsen, *Le Droit Pénal Romain*, translated by J. Duquesne (4 vols., Paris, 1907), II, 353. This same right was granted the husband by Justinian in C. (5. 17) 11. 2, and was later incorporated in N. (22. 16) 1; however, a later constitution, to be found in N. (117. 8), retracted the concession.

[29] Mommsen, *op. cit.*, II, 353-354; Dölger, "Das Lebensrecht,"—*AuC*, IV (1933), 38-39.

decades before the Emperors ruled the Roman State, Cicero (+43 B.C.) seems to have censured this legal laxity.[30]

After the Cornelian Law against assassins and poisoners had been passed (c.81 B.C.), abortion could have been and undoubtedly was punished, not because of the abortion itself, but because dangerous medicines and poisons were involved. Under this statute in Republican times the woman who employed these means upon herself was not punished. But the crime rested upon those who cooperated—who, by manufacture or sale, made these drugs available to the prospective mother, or who administered them to her.[31] Thus, poisoning, not abortion as such, was the immediate object of this statute.[32] And only if the mother died was the death penalty, *summum supplicium,* prescribed. Otherwise the guilty of humble rank were condemned to the mines, while the more noble were relegated to an island and deprived of a portion of their property.[33]

At the close of the second century of the Christian era Roman law punished abortion, not only on the basis provided by the Cornelian statute against poisoners, but also as a crime in itself.[34] Septimius Severus (193-211 A.D.) was probably the first Roman Emperor to punish the prospective mother who deliberately procured

[30] *Pro Cluentio,* cap. 11, n. 32—*Cicero, The Speeches,* edited by H. Grose Hodge, *LCL* (New York: G. P. Putnam's Sons, 1927), p. 255. See also Mommsen, *op. cit.*, II, 354, footnote 1; Dölger, "Das Lebensrecht,"—*AuC,* IV (1933), 39; D. (48. 19) 39.

[31] D. (48. 8) 1. 1 and 3. 1-2. Beginning with the late classical period, this woman if married would have been punished in virtue of other laws, as may be seen above.

[32] Cf. A. Beck, *Römisches Recht bei Tertullian und Cyprian,* Eine Studie zur frühen Kirchenrechtsgeschicte, Schriften der Königsberger gelehrten Gesellschaft: Geisteswissenschaftliche Klasse, 7 Jahr, Heft 2 (Halle: Max Niemeyer Verlag, 1930), p. 121, footnote 1; Perozzi, *Istituzioni di Diritto Romano* (2. ed., 2 vols., Roma: Athenaeum, 1928), I, 186, footnote 3.

[33] D. (28. 19) 38. 5.

[34] During the Empire, abortion was classed among the *crimina extraordinaria*—a category of crimes existing outside the pale of the formulary system, punished by no fixed penalty, and determined by no staple statute. Regarding crimes of this type see Sherman, *Roman Law in the Modern World* (2. ed., 3 vols., New York: Voorhis & Co., 1924), II, 489-490; Strachan-Davidson, *Problems of the Roman Criminal Law* (2 vols., Oxford, 1912), II, 161, and footnote 1.

an abortion upon herself.[35] His rescript pronounced exile upon the *wife* who thus deliberately deprived her husband of children.[36] Another imperial decree prescribed temporary exile for a *wife* who out of hatred for her divorced husband procured an abortion.[37] In a fragment attributed to Ulpian (+228) the *praeses* of the province was instructed to punish with exile the woman who employed force to cause an abortion to herself.[38]

Several significant facts may be gleaned from the foregoing consideration of Roman laws. (1) Although in these cases abortion itself was the object of the punishment, the reasons motivating the laws were not the rights of the unborn child. (2) The fragment ascribed to Ulpian did not refer expressly to married women, as did the other two.[39] (3) The three laws in the Digest imposed the penalty upon a woman who procured the abortion on herself. Another party who used drugs on the mother for this purpose was held by the Cornelian statute against poisoners in general.

The fact that no concern was evinced about the intrinsic morality of abortion or about the rights of the unborn child to life is not difficult to understand. It was an assumed legal principle in Roman law that the unborn was not a human being, a principle which betrayed the influence of the Stoic theory that the human soul was infused only at the time of birth.[40] Fragments in the Digest state that the fetal child is not a *homo*—a living, human being.[41] Rather, the fetal child is held to be a part of the maternal viscera,[42] something

[35] Mommsen, *op. cit.*, II, 354; Dölger, "Das Lebensrecht,"—*AuC*, IV (1933), 39, 42.

[36] D. (47. 11) 4.

[37] D. (48. 19) 39.

[38] D. (48. 8) 8.

[39] But see Eschbach, *Disputationes Physiologico-Theologicae*, II, 75.

[40] Cf. Beck, *Römisches Recht bei Tertullian und Cyprian*, p. 121, footnote 1; Perozzi, *Istituzioni di Diritto Romano*, I, 185-186; Dölger, "Das Lebensrecht,"—*AuC*, IV (1933), 21, 32, 37.

[41] D. (35. 2) 9. 1: ". . . partus nondum editus homo non recte fuisse dicitur."

[42] D. (25. 4) 1. 1: "Partus enim antequam edatur, mulieris portio est vel viscerum."

not yet living,[43] not *in rebus humanis,*[44] and at most only a potential person—*in spe.*[45]

While the rights of the unborn child were not considered in this penal legislation, interference with fetal development was punished for other reasons: especially as an infringement upon the right of the father,[46] but also as a danger to the mother,[47] as bad example,[48] and as a disregard of the State's rights to future citizens.[49]

Punishments prescribed in the Digest are: condemnation to the mines; [50] exile,[51] sometimes only temporary; [52] and partial forfeiture of possessions.[53] Only if the mother died was the death penalty demanded.[54]

[43] D. (38. 8) 1. 8: ". . . non dum animax [variants: *animal, animans*] fuerit."

[44] D. (1. 5) 7; (37. 9) 1 and 7; (28. 6) 10. 1.

[45] Cf. D. (11. 8) 2; (37. 9) 1.

[46] D. (47. 11) 4.

[47] D. (48. 19) 35. 5.

[48] D. (48. 19) 38. 5.

[49] D. (37. 9) 1. 15. Cicero advocated even capital punishment for deliberate abortion because of the injustice to the father, to the family name and the family's inheritance rights, to the human race, and to the State.—*Pro Cluentio,* cap. 11, n. 32—*Cicero, The Speeches,* edited by H. Grose Hodge, *LCL,* p. 255; see also D. (48. 19) 39.

[50] (48. 19) 38. 5.

[51] (48. 8) 8.

[52] (47. 11) 4; (48. 19) 39.

[53] (48. 19) 38. 5.

[54] (48. 19) 38. 5.

CHAPTER II

PATRISTIC WRITINGS AND EARLY CONCILIAR LEGISLATION

Article I. Patristic Writings

At its inception Christianity encountered a widespread practice of deliberate abortion,[1] and confronted its pagan contemporaries with the novel moral-viewpoint that abortion was a serious sin and a heinous crime. Abortion was classed by the Church as murder, because abortion effected the death of a human person, albeit unborn. In opposition to the Roman-law position that abortion violated the rights of others (especially of the father), the Church condemned abortion as a violation of the rights of the unborn.[2]

This position is revealed in the Pseudo-Apostolic and in the early patristic writings of the East and the West.

Perhaps the earliest Christian pronouncement against abortion exists in the terse commandment of the *Didache* (80-100): "Thou shalt not kill the fetus by an abortion." [3] This pronouncement against abortion was carried over into the *Pseudo-Barnabas Epistle*

[1] Lecky, *History of European Morals from Augustus to Charlemagne* (4. ed., 2 vols., London, 1880), II, 20-22; Döllinger, *The Gentile and the Jew in the Courts of the Temple of Christ,* II, 287-288. Pagan writers themselves attest to this fact; see quotations from pagan classics found in Dölger, "Das Lebensrecht,"—*AuC,* IV (1933), 39-41.

[2] Perla, "Aborto,"—*Enciclopedia Italiana di Scienze, Lettere ed Arti* (36 vols. and appendix, Milano: Istituto Giovanni Trecani, 1929-1939), I, 111; Kober, *Die Deposition und Degradation* (Tübingen, 1867), 764; M. Roberti, "Nasciturus pro iam Nato Habetur,"—*Cristianesimo e Diritto Romano,* Pubblicazioni della Università Cattolica del Sacro Cuore, serie seconda: Scienze Giuridiche, Vol. XLIII (Milano: Società Editrice "Vita E Pensiero," 1935), pp. 66-84, esp. 67-70.

[3] Cap. II, n. 2: οὐ φονεύσεις τέκνον ἐν φθορᾷ.—Funk, *Patres Apostolici* (2. ed., 2 vols., Tubingae, 1901-1913), I, 8.

(before 132),[4] and into the *Canones Ecclesiastici SS. Apostolorum* (c.300).[5]

The *Apostolic Constitutions* (c.400) not only repeated the commandment of the *Didache,* but added the observation that the formed or developed fetus possesses a God-given soul. Killing this fetus, therefore, will be avenged as murder.[6]

Athenagoras, an Apologist of the East, writing to Emperor Marcus Aurelius about 177, affirmed that the Christians considered as guilty of homicide those women who procured abortion. The guilty will have to render an account to God for the destruction of the fetus, which is an object of His care.[7]

Clement of Alexandria (+c.215) spoke of the destruction of the unborn child as a wicked and malicious means employed to conceal illicit sexual relations.[8]

In the West, perhaps the most eloquent voice raised against the crime of abortion was that of Tertullian (+c.240). He called deliberate abortion murder. Since murder is forbidden, said Tertullian, it follows that the destruction of the developing human being in the mother's womb is illicit; it is simply a *festinatio homicidii.* No distinction must be made between killing the child before or after birth; both are murder.[9] It seems, however, that Tertullian made

[4] Cap. XIX, n. 5—Funk, *Patres Apostolici,* I, 91.

[5] Can. 6—Schaff, *Teaching of the Twelve Apostles* (3. ed., New York, 1890), p. 241; also in Pitra, *Iuris Ecclesiastici Graecorum Historia et Monumenta* (2 vols., Romae, 1864-1868), I, 78.

[6] Lib. VII, cap. 2—Funk, *Didascalia et Constitutiones Apostolorum* (2 vols., Paderborn, 1905), I, 392.

The *Apostolic Constitutions* were accepted in the Eastern Church, until rejected by the Trullan Synod in 692, as a quasi-official code of ecclesiastical law; see Van Hove, *Commentarium Lovaniense,* Vol. I, Tom. I, *Prolegomena ad Codicem Iuris Canonici* (Mechliniae: H. Dessain, 1928), n. 107 (hereafter cited as *Prolegomena*).

[7] *Legatio pro Christianis,* cap. 35—Geffcken, *Zwei griechische Apologeten* (Leipzig-Berlin, 1907), p. 153; Migne, *Patrologiae Cursus Completus,* series graeca (161 vols., Parisiis, 1856-1866), VI, 969 (hereafter to be cited as *MPG*).

[8] *Paedagogus,* lib. II, cap. 10, N. 96, n. 1—*Clement,* edit. Stählin, Die griechischen christlichen Schriftsteller (3 vols., Leipzig, 1905-1909), I, 215; *MPG,* VIII, 512.

[9] *Apologeticus,* cap. 9, n. 8—*Tertullian,* translated by T. R. Glover, *LCL* (New York: G. P. Putnam's Sons, 1931), p. 48; *MPL,* I, 371-372. See also

this charge of murder only if the fetus had attained a certain stage of development and formation; for only then is the fetus a *homo*, according to Tertullian.[10]

Both Minucius Felix (+third cent.)[11] and St. Cyprian (+258)[12] stated that parents who perform abortion are guilty of parricide.

Hippolytus (+c.235), too, characterized deliberate killing of the unborn child as murder.[13]

Thus the ground work was laid for the conciliar legislation enacted at the beginning of the fourth century, which legislation consistently regarded and punished abortion as murder, as will be seen in the following article. After the Councils had taken cognizance of abortion in their penal legislation, the Fathers continued their stirring condemnations of this abominable practice. Of these Fathers brief mention will be made only of Saints John Chrysostom, Augustine, and Jerome.[14]

In one of his homilies St. John Chrysostom (+407), enumerating the crimes to which drunkenness leads, spoke of the destruction of the unborn as "murder before birth." In fact, this Saint said that he knows not what name to give this crime of preventing the birth

De Exhortatione Castitatis, cap. 12—*MPL*, II, 977. For a discussion as to whether or not Tertullian permitted the destruction of the fetal child in cases of difficult childbirth, see: Eschbach, *Disputationes Physiologico-Theologicae*, II, 185-186; Dölger, "Das Lebensrecht,"—*AuC*, IV (1933), 44-49.

[10] *De Anima*, cap. 37—*CSEL*, XX, 363. Note however that in another place (*De Anima*, cap. 27—*CSEL*, XX, 344) he maintained that the life-giving soul is present at the moment of conception. On this point see: Dölger, "Das Lebensrecht,"—*AuC*, IV (1933), 32-37; Roberti, "Nasciturus pro iam nato habetur,"—*Cristianesimo e Diritto Romano*, XLIII (1935), 75-77.

[11] *Octavius*, cap. 30, nn. 2-3—*Minucius Felix*, trans. by G. H. Rendall, *LCL* (New York: G. P. Putnam's Sons, 1931), p. 406.

[12] *Epistola*, LII (VII ad Cornelium), 2—*CSEL*, III, part 2, 619.

[13] *Refutatio Omnium Haeresium*, edit. Wendland (also known as *Philosophoumena*), lib. IX, cap. 12, n. 25—*Hippolytus*, Die griechischen christlichen Schriftsteller (3 vols., Leipzig, 1916), III, 250; *MPG*, XVI-3, 3387.

[14] St. Basil is treated in the following article on conciliar legislation; see *infra*, Article II, D.

of the conceived child—a crime which is "even worse than murder."[15]

St. Augustine (+430), in his explanation of the law of *Exodus* (according to the Septuagint reading) held that destruction of the *formed* fetus was murder, but destruction of the *non-formed* was not.[16] He did not state that the latter would not be murder before God, but only that such action would not be classed as murder befor the law. In his *De Nuptiis et Concupiscentia* he severely condemned any deliberate interference with the fetus, whether already endowed with life or not.[17] Thus St. Augustine distinguished between a formed and a non-formed fetus, between a living and a not-yet-living fetus.[18] Yet, he did not hold "formed" to be necessarily synonymous with "living," or "non-formed" with "not-yet-living."[19] In fact, he confessed ignorance of any human power to know at what time the fetal child begins to live.[20]

[15] *Commentarius in Epistolam ad Romanos, homilia* XXIV, n. 4: πρὸ τῆς γενέσεως φόνος. . . . μᾶλλον δὲ καὶ φόνου τι χεῖρον.—*MPG*, LX, 626.

[16] *Quaestiones in Heptateuchum*, lib. II, *Quaest. de Exodo*, q. 80—*CSEL*, XXVIII, part 3, 147-148; incorporated as a part of c. 8, C. XXXII, q. 2, in the *Decretum* of Gratian.

[17] Lib. I, cap. 15—*CSEL*, XLII, 230; incorporated as a part of c. 7, C. XXXII, q. 2, in the *Decretum* of Gratian.

[18] Regarding formed and non-formed, see *Quaestiones in Heptateuchum*, lib. II, *Quaest. de Exodo*, q. 80 (*CSEL*, XXVIII, part 2, 147-148) and *Enchiridion*, cap. 85 (*MPL*, XL, 272). Regarding living and not-yet-living, see *De Nuptiis et Concupiscentia*, lib. I, cap. 15 (*CSEL*, XLII, 230) and *Enchiridion*, cap. 86 (*MPL*, XL, 272).

[19] In one text he implies that the non-formed fetus has life (*Enchiridion*, cap. 85—*MPL*, XL, 272), and in another that it has not, at least in the eyes of the law (*Quaestiones in Heptateuchum*, lib. II, *Quaest. de Exodo*, q. 80—*CSEL*, XXVIII, part 2, 147-148).

[20] *Enchiridion*, cap. 86—*MPL*, XL, 272.

For further study of St. Augustine's position in this matter, cf.: M. Roberti, "Nasciturus pro iam nato habetur,"—*Cristianesimo e Diritto Romano*, XLIII (1935), 81-83; Eschbach, *Disputationes Physiologico-Theologicae*, II, 16, footnote 4; Dölger, "Das Lebensrecht,"—*AuC*, IV (1933), 57-58; Stockums, "Wann entsteht die geistige Seele?"—*Philosophisches Jarhbuch*, XXXVII (1924), 241-242. The latter two articles call particular attention to the influence of the Septuagint text of Exodus XXI, 22-23, upon St. Augustine.

St. Jerome (+420) spoke of abortion as murder and parricide.[21] He also admitted that until the fetus has attained a certain stage of development it is not considered a *homo* and therefore true homicide would not be committed by abortion procured before that time.[22]

Article II. Early Conciliar Legislation

A. Introduction

Prior to any consideration of the legislation regarding abortion enacted by the early ecclesiastical councils, several observations are not only apropos but essential.

(1) In the early centuries one does not find, and would not reasonably expect to find, detailed classification and strict terminology of sins and crimes. For example, the terms "*moechia*" and "*adulterium*" are frequently employed in the broad sense of the New Testament, to include various sins of the flesh.[23]

(2) The Church had not the highly technical and clearly defined system of penal jurisprudence known today. Therefore early legislation can not always be judged according to present-day norms and practices.

(3) Particular law would naturally be worded in keeping with *local* circumstances and exigencies. A statute condemning and punishing a certain crime would, therefore, probably not be worded to include all the many forms this crime could and perhaps would assume in the future or in some other locale.

These factors must be kept in mind when one attempts to interpret and evaluate enactments made many centuries ago, made at a time when the Church had but recently begun to flourish and develop.

[21] *Epistola XXII* (Ad Eustochium), cap. 13—*CSEL*, LIV, 160.

[22] *Epistola CXXI* (Ad Algasiam), q. 4, n. 5—*CSEL*, LVI, 16. This text is incorporated in c. 10, C. XXXII, q. 2, of the *Decretum* of Gratian.

[23] Cf. A. Vacant, "Adultère,"—*Dictionnaire de Théologie Catholique*, I, part 1, 476, and also 464, 506; Hefele-Leclercq, *Histoire des Conciles* (10 vols. in 19, Paris, 1907-1938), I, part 1, 224, footnote 1.

B. Council of Elvira

The Council of Elvira, Spain (300 [?]) is generally accepted as the first council to enact legislation in punishment of abortion. Canon 63 of this Council reads:

> "Si qua mulier per adulterium, absente marito, conceperit, idque post facinus occiderit, placuit, neque in fine dandam esse communionem, eo quod geminaverit scelus." [24]

The canon does not explicitly mention abortion, but is directed simply against the killing of "that which was conceived." Thus, the mind of the Council may well have been to include in the condemnation the destruction of the infant's life both before birth (by abortion or by any of the various operations known today as forms of embryotomy) as well as after birth (infanticide). As has been seen on preceding pages, deliberate interference with and destruction of fetal life had already merited the severe censures of the pseudo-Apostolic writings and of the early Fathers. Whatever the mind of the Fathers of Elvira may have been, it is commonly held that canon 63 of this Council was invoked in practice to punish abortion.[25] This conclusion seems justified in view of the fact that canonical collections and canonical writings down through the centuries have classed this canon with other dicta and laws which punished abortion.

Refusal of *communio* even on the death-bed was prescribed by the Council of Elvira not only for abortion, but also for many other serious sins and crimes.[26] Scholars are not agreed upon the meaning of the term *communio* as employed in the disciplinary canons of the

[24] Mansi, *Sacrorum Conciliorum Nova et Amplissima Collectio* (53 vols. in 60, Parisiis, 1901-1927), II, 16. Hereafter this work will be referred to as Mansi.

[25] Hollweck, *Die kirchlichen Strafgesetze* (Mainz, 1899), p. 250; Stockums, "Abortus und kirchliches Strafrecht,"—*Theologie und Glaube,* XV (1923), 93-100, especially 94; Dölger, "Das Lebensrechts,"—*AuC,* IV (1933), 56; Cappello, *Tractatus Canonico-Moralis de Censuris iuxta Codicem Iuris Canonici* (3. ed., Taurinorum Augustae: Marietti, 1933), n. 388 (hereafter this work will be cited as *De Censuris*); Coronata, *Institutiones Iuris Canonici* (5 vols., Vols. I-II, 2. ed., 1939, Vols. III-V, 1933-36, Taurini: Marietti), IV, 462. But see also Delmaille, "Avortement,"—*Dictionnaire de Droit Canonique* (Paris: Letouzey et Anè, 1924—), I, 1536-1561, especially 1539.

[26] See, for example, cc. 1-3, 6-8, 10, 12, 13, 17, 18—Mansi, II, 5-9.

Council of Elvira and other early councils. Some maintain that the term meant association with the faithful or sacramental absolution, but not the Holy Eucharist.[27] Others hold that only sacramental communion and not reconciliation with the body of the faithful was meant.[28] Still others say that both reconciliation with the Church and partaking of the Holy Eucharist were included under the term *communio.*[29] In any event, the legislation of the Council of Elvira against abortion was severe.

In specifically referring to the absence of the husband, the Council of Elvira perhaps was acting upon the charges of some of the Fathers that women were resorting to abortion and infanticide in order to conceal illicit relations.[30]

The text of canon 63 of the Council of Elvira clearly refers to the destruction of a child conceived in adultery. This raises the question: Would the killing of a child conceived in fornication or in lawful wedlock have gone unpunished? In other words, was the circumstance of adultery an essential element of the crime which the Council wished to punish? A strict interpretation of the text of the law would of course have demanded that the circumstance of adul-

[27] Cf. the authorities cited in Hefele-Leclercq, *Histoire des Conciles,* I, part 1, 221, footnote 5. Gabriel de l'Aubespine (+1630) says that only rarely is sacramental communion meant; generally communion with the faithful is to be understood.—*Notae in Canones Eliberini,* ad can. 1—Mansi, II, 35-36. See also Moriarty, *The Extraordinary Absolution from Censures,* The Catholic University of America Canon Law Studies, No. 113 (Washington, D. C.: The Catholic University of America, 1938), p. 21.

[28] Thus Hefele, in Hefele-Leclercq, *op. cit.,* I, part 1, 221-222, and 217; Schmitz, *Die Bussbücher und die Bussdisciplin der Kirche* (Mainz, 1883), pp. 17-19; Baronius, *Annales Ecclesiastici* (37 vols., reprint, Vols. I-XXVIII, Bar-le-Duc, 1864-1875; Vols. XXIX-XXXVII, Paris, 1876-1883), II, nn. 41, 43; Ferdinandus de Mendoza, *De Confirmando Concilio Illiberitano,* VIII, lib. II, cap. 6—Mansi, II, 118; Severinus Binius, *Notae*—Mansi, II, 28-30.

[29] D'Alès, *L'Edit de Calliste, Etude sur les origines de la pénitence chrétienne* (Paris, 1914), p. 376, footnote 2. Regarding this discussion, see also Moriarty, *op. cit.,* pp. 14-15, 20-22.

[30] Tertullian, *De Virginibus Velandis,* cap. 14—*MPL,* II, 958; *De Pudicitia,* cap. 5—*CSEL,* XX, 227. Clement of Alexandria, *Paedagogus,* lib. II, cap. 10, N. 96, n. 1—*Clement,* edit. Stählin, Die grieschischen christlichen Schriftsteller, I, 215; *MPG,* VIII, 512. See also Balsamon, *Commentaria* (in Canones Synodi Ancyranae, can. 21)—*MPG,* CXXXVII, 1185.

tery be verified; nevertheless, it seems unlikely that it was the intention of the Fathers of Elvira thus to restrict the application of the law. The primary object of this canon was the protection and vindication of infant life, and not the punishment or penalization of marital infidelity. Therefore it appears reasonable to suppose that in practice the other cases mentioned above would have been punished.

The Council of Elvira's rigorous enactment which demanded life-long punishment for the crimes of abortion and infanticide reflects a severity characteristic of the early Spanish Church.[81] But in keeping with the growing trend away from extreme rigorism in disciplinary laws, less stringent penalties for the crime of abortion followed very soon in the enactments of other councils.

C. Council of Ancyra

The Council of Ancyra (capital of Galatia, Asia Minor), held in 314, was the first Eastern Council to legislate against abortion. Canon 21 in its English translation reads:

> Women who prostitute themselves, and who kill the children thus begotten, or who try to destroy them when in their wombs, are by ancient law excommunicated to the end of their lives. We, however, have softened their punishment, and condemned them to the various appointed degrees of penance for ten years.[82]

Unlike the legislation of the Council of Elvira, this canon makes no reference to the destruction of a child which was conceived in an *adulterous* union, but is directed against any woman who was guilty of killing her infant. Furthermore the Fathers of Ancyra expressly include the killing of the child while still in the mother's womb.

[81] As to the extent in the early Church of the rigorous discipline enforced by the Council of Elvira, see Schroeder, *Disciplinary Decrees of the General Councils, Text, Translation, and Commentary* (St. Louis: B. Herder Book Co., 1937), p. 36, footnote 79; and Moriarty, *op. cit.*, pp. 20-22.

[82] Hefele, *A History of the Councils of the Church from the Original Documents*, Vol. I, translated by William R. Clark (2. ed., Edinburgh, 1883), 220. Περὶ τῶν γυναικῶν τῶν ἐκπορνευουσῶν, καὶ ἀναιρουσῶν τὰ γεννώμενα, καὶ σπουδαζουσῶν φθόρια ποιεῖν· ὁ μὲν πρότερος ὅρος μέχρις ἐξόδου ἐκώλυσεν, καὶ τούτῳ· συντίθενται· φιλανθρωπότερον δέ τι εὑρόντες, ὡρίσαμεν δεκαέτη χρόνον κατὰ τοὺς βαθμοὺς τοὺς ὡρισμένους πληρῶσαι.—Mansi, II, 520.

And again, the very wording implies that perhaps even the attempt to destroy the fetus was punished.[33]

Noteworthy also is the fact that the distinction between the formed and the non-formed fetus is mentioned neither by the Council of Elvira nor by the Council of Ancyra. Both Councils, moreover, spoke of punishment for women only, and specifically for those who cause the abortion to themselves.[34]

The *ancient law* by which the guilty were placed outside the pale of the Church even unto their death is not identified by the Council of Ancyra. By *ancient law* reference may have been made to canon 63 of the Council of Elvira, as is maintained by some,[35] or, as seems much more likely, to an earlier and more severe general discipline in the Church.[36]

In lessening the penalty for abortion and infanticide the Coun-

[33] The Greek term σπουδαζουσῶν means a *voluntary trying* and was so understood by various translators. Thus, Dionysius Exiguus (+c.540) even though using the less accurate expression *secum agere,* "to intend" (Mansi, II, 526 [giving the canon as number 20]), a rendering accepted by Pitra (+1889) (*Iuris Ecclesiastici Graecorum Historia et Monumenta,* I, 447). Gentian Hervet (+1584) gives a far better translation in *dant operam,* which was reproduced successively by Beveridge (+1708) (*Synodicon sive Pandectae Canonum et Conciliorum* [2 vols., Oxford, 1672], I, 398) and Migne (+1875) (*MPL,* CXXXVII, 1186). So too Hefele (+1893): ". . . und die Leibesfrucht abzutreiben *suchten* . . ." (*Conciliengeschichte,* I [2. ed., Freiburg im Breisgau, 1873], 240) and his English translator, Clark: ". . . try to destroy . . ." (cf. quotation given in text above).

[34] Routh interprets the Greek text of this canon so as to include under the penalty those who cooperate in the crime, but commentaries and canonical collections generally do not have even an allusion to cooperation.—*Reliquiae Sacrae* (5 vols., 2. ed., Oxonii, 1846-1848), IV, 168. Cf. Hefele-Leclercq, *Histoire des Conciles,* I, part 1, 323-324. Schmitz (+1899) (*Die Bussbücher und die Bussdisciplin der Kirche,* pp. 280-281) says that canon 24 of *Poenitentiale Valicellanum I* shows that penitential practice interpreted canon 21 of the Council of Ancyra to include *helpers* in the crime. See *infra,* Section F. of this Article, for the legislation of St. Martin of Braga (+580), based on this canon.

[35] V. g., Hefele, in Hefele-Leclercq, *Histoire des Conciles,* I, part 1, 240; Van Espen, *Commentarius in Canones Juris Veteris, in Jus Novum Canonicum, Novissimum,* III, 119; and implied in Delmaille, "Avortement,"—*Dictionnaire de Droit Canonique,* I, 1539.

[36] Thus, Leclercq, in Hefele-Leclercq, *op. cit.,* I, part 1, 323, footnote 2; Eschbach, *Disputationes Physiologico-Theologicae,* II, 78.

cil had no intention of palliating the viciousness of the crimes. The Church, in punishing crimes, acts now severely, now leniently, as conditions of time, persons, and places require, and as the salvation of souls therefore demands.[37]

The public penance of ten years required by the Council of Ancyra was to be performed "according to the various appointed degrees of penance." In the third and fourth centuries it was the practice in the East to group penitents into "stations" or grades according to the type or degree of penance to be performed. At the time of the Council of Ancyra only three grades were known, namely, those of the *audientes,* of the *substrati,* and of the *consistentes;*[38] but at the time of St. Basil (+379) there was recognized a fourth group, that of the *flentes,* who occupied the lowest rank among the various classes of public penitents.[39]

The influence of canon 21 of the Council of Ancyra was great, and appears to have been basic for the majority of the ecclesiastical enactments against abortion down to the middle ages. If not the exact wording, at least the substance of the canon (particularly the ten-year penalty) is contained in subsequent legislation. The canon itself appears in all important canonical collections. Its influence may be partially explained by the fact that this Council was a *concilium quasi-plenarium,* at which were represented the Churches of Asia Minor and Syria. Furthermore, the Council's disciplinary decrees gained prestige and authority by being placed in the *corpus* of ancient canons recognized and ratified by the Council (Fourth Ecumenical) of Chalcedon in 451.[40]

[37] See, for example, the explanation given by Pope Innocent I (402-417) in a letter written in 405 to Exsuperius, Bishop of Toulouse.—Jaffé, *Regesta Pontificum Romanorum ab condita Ecclesia ad annum post Christum natum MCXCVIII* (hereafter to be cited as *Regesta*), n. 90; text of the letter in *MPL,* XX, 498; see also Schroeder, *Disciplinary Decrees of the General Councils,* p. 43; Van Espen, *op. cit.*, III, 111.

[38] Only three grades are referred to by the Council of Nice (325), canon 11 —Mansi, II, 673.

[39] St. Basil, *Epistola Canonica II,* can. 22—*St. Basil, The Letters,* translated by Deferrari, *LCL* (4 vols.), Vol. III (New York: G. P. Putnam's Sons, 1930), 112-114; *MPG,* XXXII, 723; and *Epistola Canonica III,* can. 56, 57—*St. Basil, The Letters,* III, 246-248; *MPG,* XXXII, 797.

[40] Canon 1—Mansi, VII, 357.

D. Canons of St. Basil

St. Basil the Great (+379) in his *Three Canonical Letters*, written in 374 and 375, gave solutions to many canonical questions presented to him by Amphilochius, Bishop of Iconium (373-394). These *canons* or replies of St. Basil were considered as official ecclesiastical legislation, or on a par with conciliar enactments in the Eastern Church, and were not without influence in the West.[41] Hence St. Basil's pronouncements regarding abortion, as contained in these letters, are placed in this article on conciliar legislation rather than in the article dealing with the teachings of the Fathers.

The legislation of St. Basil contained in *canon 2* is the following:

> A woman who deliberately destroys a foetus is answerable for murder. And any fine distinction as to its being completely formed or unformed is not admissible amongst us. For in this case not only the child which is about to be born is vindicated, but also she herself who plotted against herself, since women usually die from such attempts. And there is added to this crime the destruction of the embryo, a second murder—at least that is the intent of those who dare these things. We should not, however, prolong their punishment until death, but should accept the term of ten years; and we should not determine the treatment according to time but according to the manner of repentance.[42]

At St. Basil's time a dispute had arisen in Asia Minor regarding the theory of fetal formation and non-formation in relation to abortion. Certain parties contended that killing a non-formed uterine

[41] Cf. Van Hove, *Prolegomena*, n. 52; Pitra, *Iuris Ecclesiastici Graecorum Historia et Monumenta*, I, 576 ff, especially 613 ff.

[42] Φθείρασα κατ' ἐπιτήδευσιν, φόνου δίκην ὑπέχει. ἀκριβολογία δὲ ἐκμεμορφωμένου καὶ ἀνεξεικονίστου παρ' ἡμῖν οὐκ ἔστιν. ἐνταῦθα γὰρ ἐκδικεῖται οὐ μόνον τὸ γεννηθησόμενον, ἀλλὰ καὶ αὐτὴ ἡ ἑαυτῇ ἐπιβουλεύσασα· διότι ὡς ἐπὶ τὸ πολὺ ἐναποθνήσκουσι ταῖς τοιαύταις ἐπιχειρήσεσιν αἱ γυναῖκες. πρόσεστι δὲ τούτῳ καὶ ἡ φθορὰ τοῦ ἐμβρύου, ἕτερος φόνος, κατά γε τὴν ἐπίνοιαν τῶν ταῦτα τολμώντων. δεῖ μέντοι μὴ μέχρι τῆς ἐξόδου παρατείνειν αὐτῶν τὴν ἐξομολόγησιν, ἀλλὰ δέχεσθαι μὲν τὸ μέτρον τῶν δέκα ἐτῶν· ὁρίζειν δὲ μὴ χρόνῳ, ἀλλὰ τρόπῳ τῆς μετανοίας τὴν θεραπείαν. —*St. Basil, The Letters*, translated by Deferrari, *LCL*, III, 20-23; *MPG*, XXXII, 672.

child did not merit the punishments for murder.[43] Basis for this contention could well be had from the Septuagint and from contemporary Greek thought, both of which, as has been seen, held to the distinction between the formed and the non-formed fetus.[44] Since the Council of Ancyra had made not the slightest reference to the fetal formation theory, Bishop Amphilochius sought a solution from St. Basil, who definitely excluded any consideration of this theory in determining the canonical guilt for abortion.

The penance of ten years mentioned by St. Basil had been previously prescribed by the Council of Ancyra. This penance was undoubtedly apportioned in accordance with the four stations or grades.

In reference to the emphasis on the manner rather than on the duration of the penance, Balsamon observed that if the penance were seriously and diligently performed, the time might be lessened; on the contrary, if the party contemned the penance, the time could be protracted beyond the stipulated ten years.[45]

St. Basil stated in *canon 2* that those who were guilty of abortion incurred the penalties for murder. And the punishment for voluntary murder, according to the Saint, was twenty years of public penance; for involuntary murder, ten years.[46] But the ten-year penalty for abortion is no indication that it was not considered to be voluntary murder. The commentators on Oriental ecclesiastical discipline explained that in the case of abortion the lesser penalty was justified because mitigating circumstances commonly attended

[43] Cf. Balsamon, *Commentaria, In Epistolam S. Basilii Canonicam I,* ad can. 2—*MPG,* CXXXVIII, 588; Dölger, "Das Lebensrecht,"—*AuC,* IV (1933), 56.

[44] Zonaras, in discussing canon 2 of St. Basil, expressly refers to the Septuagint version of Exodus XXI, 22-23—*Commentaria, In Epistolam S. Basilii Canonicam I,* ad can. 2—*MPG,* CXXXVIII, 592. See Blastares, *Syntagma Canonum,* T, cap. 28—*MPG,* CXLIV, 1209. See also Dölger, "Das Lebensrecht," —*AuC,* IV (1933), 56-58.

[45] *Commentaria, loc. cit.*—*MPG,* CXXXVIII, 588. See Moriarty, *The Extraordinary Absolution from Censures,* p. 11, regarding the remission of public penance in general.

[46] *Epistola 217* or *Ad Amphilochium III Canonica,* can. 56 and can. 57—*St. Basil, The Letters,* translated by Deferrari, *LCL,* 246-248; *MPG,* XXXII, 797.

and influenced the commission of this crime, for example, grave fear caused by threats of parents, masters, and others.[47]

In *canon 8* the following observation is made by St. Basil: "And so women who give drugs that cause abortion are themselves also murderers as well as those who take the poisons that kill the foetus." [48]

This is the first time (so far as this writer can determine) that ecclesiastical penal law against abortion condemned beyond doubt co-operation in the crime.[49]

Canon 8, dealing *ex professo* with the distinction between voluntary and involuntary murder, does not state the precise punishment incurred by co-operators, other than that they are guilty of voluntary murder. It seems, however, that they were subject to the same ten-year term of public penance, as were those who actually committed the crime upon themselves, rather than to the standard twenty-year penalty for voluntary murder.[50]

According to St. Basil, therefore, the following (women) were guilty of murder and subject to ten years of public penance: (1) those who actually destroyed the fetus in their womb; (2) those who gave or made available to others drugs capable of killing the fetus; (3) those who accepted or held these poisons in their possession, even though the child was not actually destroyed.[51]

[47] Balsamon, *Commentaria, loc. cit.—MPG,* CXXXVIII, 588 and 590; Blastares, *Syntagma Canonum,* Γ, cap. 28—*MPG,* CXLIV, 1210. See also St. Basil himself, *Epistola 217* or *Ad Amphilochium III Canonica,* can. 52—*St. Basil, The Letters,* translated by Deferrari, *LCL,* III, 244; *MPG,* XXXII, 796.

[48] Καὶ αἱ τοίνυν τὰ ἀμβλωθρίδια διδοῦσαι φάρμακα φονεύτριαί εἰσι καὶ αὗται, καὶ αἱ δεχόμεναι τὰ ἐμβρυοκτόνα δηλητήρια.—*St. Basil, The Letters,* translated by Deferrari, *LCL,* III, 34; *MPG,* XXXII, 677.

[49] But see *supra,* p. 20, footnote 34. Cooperators were held to be equal with the actual perpetrators of the crime under the Roman law statute against assassins and poisoners.—D. (48. 8) 3. 1-2 (see *supra,* p. 9) and under the Persian law (*supra,* p. 3).

[50] Balsamon, *Commentaria, loc. cit.—MPG,* CXXXVIII, 588, and *In Concilium in Trullo,* ad can. 91—*MPG,* CXXXVII, 825.

[51] Regarding this third class, Balsamon thus expressly interprets the legislation of St. Basil: οὐ μόνη ἡ φθείρασα τὸ ἔμβρυον ὑπόκειται τῷ κανονικῷ τοῦ φονέως ἐπιτιμίῳ, ἀλλὰ καὶ ἡ διδοῦσα ἐμβρυοκτόνα δηλητήρια, καὶ ἡ

E. Council of Lerida

In keeping with the chronological treatment of the conciliar legislation, attention must now be directed to the Council of Lerida (524), in the Province of Tarragona, Spain.

Canon 2 of this Council reads:

> Hi vero qui male conceptos ex adulterio foetus vel editos necare studuerint, vel in uteris matrum potionibus aliquibus colliserint, in utroque sexu adulteris, post septem annorum curricula, communio tribuatur: ita tamen, ut omni tempore vitae suae fletibus et humilitati insistant. Si vero clerici fuerint, officium eis ministrandi recuperare non licet; attamen in choro psallentium a tempore receptae communionis intersint. Ipsis veneficis in exitu tantum, si facinora sua omni tempore vitae suae defleverint, communio tribuatur.[52]

The penalties were pronounced against the destruction of the child both while it was still in the womb and after it had been born, but, as in the earlier Spanish Council of Elvira, only against children conceived in adultery. Nevertheless, as already explained in the discussion on the Council of Elvira, this canon was undoubtedly so interpreted in practice as to imply punishment for any abortion.

Even the attempt to commit these crimes was punished, if *studuerint* be interpreted strictly. Surely, the precise position of the word *studuerint*—seek after or attempt—in the text of the canon is not to receive such emphasis as to restrict the penalties solely to the attempted killing of a child already born, and thus to exclude from punishment an attempted abortion.[53]

Subject to the penalty were both or either of the adulterers who

ἔχουσα, καὶ ἡ λαβοῦσα, κἂν μὴ φονεύσῃ τὸ ἔμβρυον.—*Commentaria, loc. cit.*—*MPG*, CXXXVIII, 588.

[52] Mansi, VIII, 612.

[53] "If anyone should *seek to* put to death his child begotten in adultery whether after its birth or in its mother's womb. . ."—Hefele, *A History of the Councils of the Church from the Original Documents*, IV, translated by William R. Clark (Edinburgh: T. & T. Clark, 1895), 133. Doubt on this score perhaps would have been clarified by St. Martin of Braga's canon against abortion.—Cf. *infra*, Section F. of this Article. In so far as the writer has been able to determine, no other commentator or author (except perhaps St. Martin of Braga) even hints at this conclusion. But, besides the fact that the very wording of the text leads to this conclusion, it may be held to be highly probable.

resorted to killing the child already born or still in the mother's womb.[54]

Moreover, for the first time in ecclesiastical legislation, clerics are mentioned expressly in connection with the penalties for abortion and kindred crimes of infant murder. But even before the Council of Lerida clerics who were guilty of abortion would have incurred the varied and severe penalties for homicide, since abortion was commonly held to be a form of murder, as has been pointed out in the writings of the Fathers and in other conciliar enactments.[55]

After the seven years' exclusion from communion had expired, the guilty party was required nevertheless to practice penance and humility for the remainder of his life.[56] A cleric, while not subjected to the foregoing public penance,[57] lost whatever ecclesiastical office he had, and was perpetually disqualified from regaining it.

that the Fathers of Lerida knew St. Augustine's teaching on sin. Then the inclusion of *attempt* under the same penalty would be a logical and necessary consequence of the christian concept of sin, as fundamentally opposed to the formal legalism of the Jewish law.

[54] In the version of this canon found in the collection of Regino of Prüm (+915) an explanatory phrase is inserted, as indicated by the italics in the following excerpt: ". . . in utroque sexu adulteris, *id est patri vel matri. . .*"—*De Disciplinis Ecclesiasticis,* lib. II, cap. 64—F. G. A. Wasserschleben, *Reginonis Abbatis Prumiensis Libri duo de Synodalibus Causis et Disciplinis Ecclesiasticis* (Lipsiae, 1840), p. 239 (hereafter this work will be cited simply as *Reginonis Libri Duo*); *MPL,* CXXXII, 297-298. Cf. *infra,* footnote 34 of Chapter III.

[55] See Kober, *Die Deposition und Degradation,* p. 596. Regarding legislation in the early centuries against clerics guilty of capital crimes, see Schroeder, *Disciplinary Decrees of the General Councils,* pp. 20-21, 37-38, and the *Decretum Gratiani,* cc. 1-12, D. L.

[56] Eschbach (*Disputationes Physiologico-Theologicae,* II, 78) holds in this regard: ". . . ut recepti in communionem fidelium quarto poenitentiae gradui per omnem vitam insisterent." It seems very unlikely that the words of the canon *fletibus et humilitati insisterent* refer to the penitential station of *flentes,* for these stations were restricted to the Eastern Church, and only at the beginning of the middle ages were they perhaps known in a few places in the West. Cf. Schroeder, *op. cit.,* p. 40, footnote 90; E. Amann, "Pénitence-Sacrement,"—*Dictionnaire de Théologie Catholique,* XII, part 1, 804.

[57] It was a principle of the discipline both in the East and in the West that members of the clergy were not admitted to public penance.—See, Amann, *art. cit.,* 803.

Perhaps this provision may be designated as a form of deposition.[58] While it was more severe than a mere deprivation, since it included a perpetual disqualification, it had not the extreme provision of the degradation known today, for the guilty man remained in the ranks of the clergy.[59] The cleric could again take part in the choral recitation of the Divine Office, which was commonly considered a part of the public worship.

The insertion of legislation against poisoners in the same canon which dealt with the penalties enacted against abortion and infanticide was due no doubt to the fact that these crimes were so frequently associated in actual practice, abortifacient drugs being employed as the usual means for procuring abortion.[60] Under the term *poisoners* were included all who were engaged in manufacturing, selling, or otherwise making these drugs available to the public.[61] These individuals were readmitted to communion only in the hour of death.

F. Canons of St. Martin of Braga

St. Martin (+c.580) Bishop of Dumia and later Metropolitan of Braga, Galicia (Portugal), was the author of a canonical collection known by such titles as *Collectio Martini Bracarensis, Liber Capitulorum, Excerpta Martini,* and *Capitula Martini Papae.*[62] His purpose was to give a correct and clear translation particularly of the Greek canons already known in the West. In so doing he fre-

[58] Thus Kober (*Die Deposition und Degradation,* p. 119) mentions this canon as an example of partial deposition.

[59] Cf. Kober, *op. cit.*, pp. 130-131; Wernz, *Ius Decretalium,* VI (Romae et Prati, 1913), n. 118.

[60] Drugs as means for effecting abortion are mentioned in the following: Roman law, D. (48. 19) 38. 5; *Canones Ecclesiastici SS. Apostolorum*—Pitra, *Iuris Ecclesiastici Graecorum Historia et Monumenta,* I, 78; Athenagoras, *Legatio pro Christianis,* cap. 35—Geffcken, *Zwei griechische Apologeten,* p. 153 or *MPG,* VI, 969; Tertullian, *De Exhortatione Castitatis,* cap. 12—*MPL,* II, 977, and *De Pudicitia,* cap. 5—*MPL,* II, 1039; St. Jerome, *Epistola XXII* (Ad Eustochium), cap. 13—*CSEL,* LIV, 160; St. Basil (cf. *supra,* p. 24).

[61] Regarding this trafficking in poisons, see Roman law (*supra,* p. 9); Canons of St. Basil (*supra,* p. 24); Trullan Synod (*infra,* p. 29).

[62] Cf. Maassen, *Geschichte der Quellen und der Literatur des canonischen Rechts* (Gratz, 1870), pp. 802-806 (hereafter to be cited as *Geschichte der Quellen*); Cicognani, *Canon Law,* authorized English version by J. M. O'Hara and F. Brennan (2. ed., Philadelphia: The Dolphin Press, 1935), p. 218.

quently altered the texts, even in essential elements, with a view to accommodating the canons of the East to the customs and circumstances of the Spanish Church.[63]

Thus, St. Martin of Braga so modified the legislation of the Council of Ancyra on abortion that he practically became the author of a new law. Subsequent canonical collections place his legislation relevant to abortion on a par with related enactments of Church councils. Therefore, the law in St. Martin's collection merits consideration in this article on conciliar laws.

The pronouncement of St. Martin regarding abortion is contained in *canon 77* of his collection, and reads as follows:

> Si qua mulier fornicaverit, et infantem qui exinde fuerit natus occiderit; et quae studuerit abortum facere, et quod conceptum est necare; certe, ut non concipiat, elaborat, sive ex adulterio sive ex legitimo conjugio; has tales mulieres nec in morte recipere communionem priores canones decreverunt. Nos tamen pro misericordia, sive tales mulieres, sive conscias scelerum ipsarum, decem annis agere poenitentiam judicamus.[64]

As has been said, this canon is an amplified version of *canon 21* of the Council of Ancyra. *Canon 77*, in addition to punishing abortion and infanticide as the Fathers of Ancyra had done, punished contraceptive practices. Noteworthy also is the fact that this canon prescribed punishment for attempted abortion. Moreover, in so far as the penalty for abortion is concerned, the canon does not distinguish between a fetus conceived in adultery or in legitimate wedlock.[65] And for the first time in Western legislation there is a clear indication that the penalty for abortion was incurred also by cooperators in the crime—*conscias scelerum ipsarum*. As penalty for these crimes, St. Martin retains the ten-year penance previously prescribed by the Council of Ancyra and by St. Basil.

G. Trullan Synod

The Trullan Synod, or *Concilium Quinisextum*, held at Constan-

[63] Maassen, *op. cit.*, pp. 804-805; "Observatio Garsiae Loasiae"—Mansi, IX, 845.

[64] Mansi, IX, 858.

[65] Cf. *supra*, Section B. of this Article, *in re* the Council of Elvira, the text of which clearly refers to adulterous conception.

tinople in 692, pronounced against abortion simply by repeating St. Basil's *canon 8* against co-operators in the crime.[66]

While St. Basil stated that co-operators (traffickers in poisons) were voluntary murderers, this Synod expressly pronounced them to be *subject to the penalties for murder.* What these penalties were is not stated in *canon 91.* However, as was true in the similar circumstances attending *canon 8* of St. Basil, the ecclesiastical penalty undoubtedly was the ten-year public penance prescribed in *canon 2* of St. Basil for actual perpetrators of abortion.[67]

Conclusion

With the Trullan Synod the deposit of ecclesiastical laws pertaining to abortion was complete. That is to say, whenever a particular Church or region (other than the regions discussed above) legislated against abortion, from the period of the councils here discussed up to the twelfth century, no law was proclaimed which was entirely new, or which differed basically from the provisions contained in this deposit of conciliar legislation.

Ordinarily the legislation of regional or particular councils was not restricted to the territory of its origin. Strictly considered these particular laws would have had no binding force in places outside the jurisdiction of the respective councils. But up to the twelfth century there was little concern about the distinction between general and particular laws. Statutes enacted in one region, as long as they did not conflict with decrees of ecumenical councils, very often were adopted as law in other regions. Thus, in practice, disciplinary measures of particular councils constituted in the main the universal disciplinary law of the Church up to the twelfth century, not by the official declaration of the Church but through the medium of accepted common usage.[68] The following chapter illustrates this with regard to the laws enacted against abortion.

[66] Trullan Synod, can. 91: Τὰς τὰ ἀμβλωθρίδια διδούσας φάρμακα καὶ τὰς δεχομένας τὰ ἐμβρυοκτόνα δηλητήρια τῷ τοῦ φονέως ἐπιτιμίῳ καθυποβάλλομεν.—Mansi, XI, 981.

[67] Cf. Balsamon, *Commentaria, In Concilium in Trullo,* ad can. 91—*MPG,* CXXXVII, 825-828.

[68] See Van Hove, *Prolegomena,* n. 99; Cicognani, *Canon Law,* p. 173.

CHAPTER III

CANONICAL COLLECTIONS UP TO THE TWELFTH CENTURY

In the early centuries many enactments of regional councils were accepted and observed as quasi-common law in other territories. This diffusion of particular law was effected by *canonical collections,* which may be defined as "codes and books drawn up exclusively, or at least primarily, for the purpose of gathering together and coordinating ecclesiastical laws." [1] In short, *collections* were accumulations of particular law.

The deposit of conciliar laws against abortion closed with the Trullan Synod (692). The purpose of the present chapter is to trace briefly the acceptance and the influence of this legislation relative to abortion, as found in several of the more important collections down to the twelfth century.

This chapter is divided into three articles: I. Collections in the Eastern Church. II. Collections in the Western Church through the ninth century. III. Collections in the Western Church from the tenth to the twelfth century.

Article I. Collections in the Eastern Church

A. Greek Collections

Only the outstanding canonical collections in the Eastern Church after the time of Photius (c.815-897) will be considered. It is to be noted that none of the Eastern collections includes Western legislation regarding the crime of abortion.

Most of the disciplinary canons of the Eastern councils, including the canons dealing with abortion, were incorporated into the Photian Collection (883). The canons on abortion enacted by the Council of Ancyra, by the Trullan Synod and by St. Basil are

[1] Thus quoted by Cicognani, *Canon Law,* p. 132.

quoted in that part of the *Photian Collection* which is known as the *Syntagma Canonum.*[2] These same enactments are merely cited in the section called the *Nomocanon,* which was simply a revision of the *Nomocanon of Fourteen Titles,* published in the first half of the seventh century.[3]

In 920 the Collection of Photius was accepted as the official law throughout the Eastern Church, which position has been retained for it ever since. Hence the canons on abortion from the Trullan Synod, from the Council of Ancyra, and from the canonical letters of St. Basil are found in the *Pedalion*[4] and in *The Sacred Canons,*[5] both of which constitute collections of the official law in the dissident Greek Church of today.

In the twelfth century the Eastern law, as found in the Collection of Photius, was discussed in the commentaries of the Oriental canonists, John Zonaras (+c.1120), Alexis Aristenus (+c.1160), and Theodore Balsamon (+c.1195), the Schismatic Patriarch of Antioch. Detailed explanation was given of the statutes against abortion contained in the earlier Greek conciliar law.[6] These explanations or *scholia* clarified obscurities and solved apparent contradictions, as has already been pointed out in the previous chapter.[7] The Greek Orthodox Church today recognizes as authoritative the *scholia* of Zonaras and of Balsamon, the two greatest of the Byzantine commentators.[8]

After the Photian Collection was accepted as official law in the

[2] Tit. XIII, cap. 10—*MPG,* CIV, 920-924. See p. 19, for the Council of Ancyra; p. 29, footnote 66, for Trullan Synod; p. 22, for St. Basil.

[3] Tit. XIII, cap. 10—*MPG,* CIV, 1200.

[4] Agapios and Nicodemus, Πηδάλιον, ἤτοι ἅπαντες οἱ ἱεροὶ καὶ θεῖοι κανόνες (5. ed., Athens: J. N. Kesisoglou, 1908), pp. 569, 573.

[5] A. S. Alivizatos, Οἱ ἱεροὶ Κανόνες (Athens: "O. Prometheus," 1923), pp. 124 (Trullan Synod), 155 (Ancyra), 362 and 365-366 (St. Basil).

[6] For the *Commentaria* of these three canonists on the Council of Ancyra, see *MPG,* CXXXII, 1185-1188; on the Trullan Synod, *MPG,* CXXXVII, 825-828; on St. Basil, *MPG,* CXXXVIII, 588-592.

[7] See especially *supra,* pp. 23, 24, 29.

[8] The commentators of the *Pedalion* (Preface, p. 6, and footnotes 1-2) base their interpretation on the commentary of Zonaras and on the commentary of Balsamon. Regarding the Byzantine commentators, see Cicognani, *Canon Law,* pp. 205-206; Lijdsman, *Introductio in Jus Canonicum,* I, n. 74.

tenth century, it was synopsized to facilitate its use in the courts. The Eastern laws on abortion are found in abbreviated form in the tenth century work of Symeon Metaphrastes; [9] in the *Synopsis Canonum Omnium* attributed to Alexis Aristenus; [10] in the *Syntagma Alphabeticum Canonicum* of Matthew Blastares (+c.1335); [11] and in the *Epitome* of Constantine Harmenopulos (+c.1350).[12]

An interesting canon, and quite apropos, appears in the Collection of Arsenius Monachus (+c.1255). This work, however, apparently was little known and therefore of questionable influence. According to this canon the administering of drugs to destroy the fetus carried the following penalties: for one in sacred orders, the expulsion from the ranks of the clergy; for a layman, the prohibition ever to enter the priesthood, and ten years' segregation.[13]

B. Armenian and Syrian Collections

In a collection of canons (of uncertain date) used in the Armenian Church, penalties of nine and of three years' penance are prescribed for abortion.[14]

The *Nomocanon* of Gregory Bar-Hebraeus (+1286), the most famous of the collections of the Syrian Monophysite Church, designates as voluntary murderers those who offer abortifacient poisons to women. Abortion caused by bodily violence is punished by monetary fine, the amount of which is determined by attending circumstances.[15]

[9] *Epitome Canonum—MPG,* CXIV, 253 (Ancyra), 276 (St. Basil), 292 (Can. 91 of Trullan Synod as can. 79).

[10] *MPG,* CXXXIII, 76 (Ancyra), 105 (Trullan Synod as can. 83 and St. Basil as can. 5).

[11] Γ, cap. 28—*MPG,* CXLIV, 1209.

[12] Sect. VI—*MPG,* CL, 165. Regarding these abbreviators, see Cicognani, *Canon Law,* pp. 205-206; Van Hove, *Prolegomena,* n. 115.

[13] *Epitome Canonum,* can. 129: Δεῖ . . . τοὺς τὰ ἐμβρυοκτόνα φάρμακα διδόντας . . . εἰ μὲν ἱερωμένοι εἶεν, καθαιρέσει ὑποβάλλειν· εἰ δὲ λαϊκοί, εἰς ἱερωσύνην μὴ ἔρχεσθαι, ἀλλ' ἀφορίζεσθαι . . . ἐπὶ χρόνους δέκα. —— *MPG,* CXXXIII, 55.

[14] *Canones et Constitutiones Ordinis Ecclesiae Nersetis Armeniorum Catholici,* cap. 27, 30—Mai, *Scriptorum Veterum Nova Collectio* (10 vols., Romae, 1825-1838), X, part 2, 313. Cardinal Mai states (*op. cit.,* X, part 2, 312, footnote 2) that these cannot be ascribed to Nerses the Great (fourth century).

[15] Cap. 34, sect. I, directio 7 et 10—Mai, *op. cit.,* X, part 2, 217-218.

Article II. Collections in the Western Church Through the Ninth Century

A. Italian Collections

The *Versio Prisca* or *Itala* (c.450), one of the early versions of the Oriental councils as known in the West, embodied the legislation of the Council of Ancyra against abortion. And the Fathers of Ancyra demanded ten years' penance. Since an early Western council, the Council of Elvira, (c.300), had previously demanded lifelong penance for this crime, a mitigated penalty for abortion may have been introduced into the West by the *Prisca*, or by an earlier Roman collection which it represented.

This milder penalty was certainly popularized by the widely circulated and highly renowned collection of Dionysius Exiguus (+c.540), which contained the canon of the Council of Ancyra.[16] Although not published with papal authority, this collection was used in Rome and throughout the entire Western Church.[17]

The enactment of the Council of Ancyra is likewise found in the *Collectio Quesnelliana* (500-550), a Roman collection contemporary with the Dionysian collection but less influential.[18]

B. African Collections

The legislation of the Council of Ancyra relative to abortion is epitomized in the *Breviatio Canonum* (c.546) of Fulgentius Ferrandus of Carthage,[19] and quoted, according to the version of Dionysius Exiguus, in the *Concordia Canonum Cresconii*, written probably by an African bishop about 600.[20]

[16] *Liber (Codex) Canonum*, can. 40—*MPL*, LXVII, 155.

[17] Cf. Fournier-Le Bras, *Histoire des Collections Canonique en Occident* (2 vols., Paris: Recueil Sirey, 1931-1932), I, 36-37, especially 94-98 (hereafter this work will be cited as *Histoire des Collections*); Pitra, *Iuris Ecclesiastici Graecorum Historia et Monumenta*, I, pp. LI, 423; Van Hove, *Prolegomena*, n. 126.

[18] *MPL*, LVI, 441. Regarding this collection, see Zeiger, *Historia Iuris Canonici* (2 vols., Romae: Apud Aedes Universitatis Gregorianae, 1939-1940), I, 40.

[19] Num. 152—*MPL*, LXVII, 957. Regarding this collection, see Fournier-Le Bras, *op. cit.*, I, 34-35.

[20] Can. 103—*MPL*, LXXXVIII, 881. Cf. Fournier-Le Bras, *op. cit.*, I, 35.

C. Spanish Collections

The canonical collection of St. Martin of Braga (+580) was discussed in the chapter on conciliar legislation. It was then noted that St. Martin's version of the canon of the Council of Ancyra against abortion was amplified to include contraceptive practices, attempted abortion, and co-operation in the crime.[21]

The *Collectio Hispana* (c.633[?]), the most important of the Spanish collections, was the first to embody legislation on abortion from other councils in addition to that which was derived from the Council of Ancyra. Together with canon 21 of this Eastern Council, the *Collectio Hispana* incorporated the laws against abortion that were found in the earlier Spanish sources—the Council of Elvira, the Council of Lerida, and the Collection of St. Martin of Braga.[22]

D. Frankish Collections

Mention must again be made of the *Collectio Dionysiana* (c.500), a product of the Roman Church. This collection, embodying only the Ancyra statute against abortion, became the quasi-official law of the Church in the Frankish Kingdom in 774, when it was sent to Charlemagne by Pope Hadrian I (772-785). Hence it is known as the *Hadriana* or *Dionysio-Hadriana*.[23]

The deposit of conciliar laws on abortion, enlarged and put into general circulation by the *Collectio Hispana* was afforded even wider diffusion by being included in the *Pseudo-Isidorian Collection* (847-

[21] Cf. *supra*, p. 28.

[22] *MPL,* LXXXIV, 108 (Ancyra and Elvira), 322-323 (Lerida), 584-585 (St. Martin); cf. also the *Excerpta Canonum,* lib. IV, tit. X—*MPL,* LXXXIV, 76.

This chronological collection, falsely ascribed to St. Isidore of Seville (+636), was accepted in Spain as an authentic legal code and officially recognized as such by Pope Alexander III (1159-1181), as is stated in a letter of Pope Innocent III to the Archbishop of Compostella in 1199.—*Epistola CXXXIII*—*MPL,* CCXIV, 686. The *Collectio Hispana* was also accepted outside the Spanish Church, particularly in the Frankish Kingdom.—See Fournier-Le Bras, *Histoire des Collections,* I, 68-70, 100-102.

[23] Can. 40—*MPL,* LXVII, 155. See Fournier-Le Bras, *op. cit.,* I, 96-98; Van Hove, *Prolegomena,* n. 126.

857). The latter collection broadcast the legislation of Elvira, Ancyra, Lerida, and St. Martin not only throughout the Frankish Church, but throughout the entire Western Church.[24]

From these collections the conciliar statutes against the crime of abortion found their way into the Capitularies, the Penitentials, and the Synodal canons of both the Frankish and the Germanic Church.

The *Capitulare* of Theodulphus, Bishop of Arles (+c.821), mentions the legislation of the Council of Ancyra.[25] The Septuagint version of the Exodus text relating to abortion is included in the *Capitularia* of Benedict the Levite, a product of the Isidorian Forgers (847-857).[26] In the *Capitula* of Radulf, Archbishop of Bourges (+866), written about 850, there is an exact restatement of the canon of St. Martin of Braga.[27]

The *Penitential* of Halitgar, Bishop of Cambrai (+831), composed about the year 829, includes only the legislation of the Council of Ancyra.[28] In addition to the canon of Ancyra the related canons of the Councils of Elvira and Lerida are incorporated by Bl. Rabanus Maurus (+855 or 856) in his *Poenitentium Liber*,[29] and in his *Poenitentiale*.[30]

[24] Hinschius, *Decretales Pseudo-Isidorianae et Capitula Angilramni* (Lipsiae, 1863), pp. 263 (Ancyra), 343 (Elvira), 346-347 (Lerida), 432 (St. Martin); *MPL*, CXXX, 266, 419, 427, 587. Regarding this collection, see Fournier-Le Bras, *op. cit.*, I, 125-233, esp. 171-187, 223-233.

[25] *MPL*, CV, 212.

[26] Lib. II, cc. 12-13—*MPL*, XCVII, 754.

[27] Cap. 41—*MPL*, CXIX, 723.

[28] Lib. IV, cap. 3—*MPL*, CV, 681. This work was composed at the request of the Archbishop of Rheims to correct abuses which accompanied the administration of the private penitential discipline.—See Fournier-Le Bras, *op. cit.*, I, 108-112.

[29] Cap. 11—*MPL*, CXII, 1410-1411. This work was written while Bl. Rabanus was still Abbot of Fulda (before 847).

[30] Cap. 8-9—*MPL*, CX, 474. Written when Bl. Rabanus was Archbishop of Mainz (847-855 or 856).

The works of Halitgar and of Bl. Rabanus, as also the works of certain others, are true canonical collections—collections of law. Although they are called *Penitentials*, they differ greatly from the *Penitentials* strictly so-called. The latter are not concerned about laws, but with gauging and enumerating *private* penances or tariffs for sins, and as such do not come within the scope of this study. May it suffice to say that their many contradictory and varied

When Bl. Rabanus took possession of the Archiepiscopal See of Mainz in 847, he heeded the request of King Louis the German (829-876) and convoked the I Provincial Synod of Mainz.[81] As the Synod's canon against abortion, the legislation of the Council of Ancyra was accepted, without, however, a citation of its source. But the same canon cited and quoted the statutes of the Councils of Elvira and Lerida.[82]

The Council of Worms (868) stated that women who voluntarily destroyed their unborn children were, beyond all doubt, to be adjudged as murderers.[83]

Article III. Collections in the Western Church from the Tenth to the Twelfth Century

In the tenth century the statutes against abortion, as found in the canonical collections, are no longer derived exclusively from the deposit of the earlier conciliar legislation, as was the case with the collections which appeared through the ninth century. After the ninth century new enactments made their appearance. These were later incorporated in the *Decretum* of Gratian and in the Decretals of the Popes.

A. Regino of Prüm

Regino, Abbot of Prüm (+915), at the request of Archbishop Ratbod of Trier [Treves], composed a collection of canons to facilitate the problem of disciplinary procedure. His work, *De Disciplinis Ecclesiasticis,* included the canons against abortion previously enact-

tariffs for abortion run the gamut of penance from twenty years to forty days. Moreover, cognizance was taken of fetal development and of animation, which factors were not admitted in conciliar legislation. See the collections of Schmitz, *Die Bussbücher und die Bussdisciplin der Kirche,* p. 841, *index.* Although the tariffs were sometimes based upon laws, particularly conciliar statutes, there is little or no evidence that laws were influenced by these tariffs. When there are indications that private penitential practice may have influenced law or its interpretation, this will be noted.

[81] Cf. Hefele-Leclercq, *Histoire des Conciles,* IV, part 1, 132.

[82] Can. 21—*Monumenta Germaniae Historica, Legum Sectio II, Capitularia Regum Francorum,* Tom. II, pars I (Ed. Alfredus Boretius et Victor Krause, Hannoverae, 1890), p. 181.

[83] Cap. 35—Mansi, XV, 876.

ed by the Councils of Ancyra, Elvira, and Lerida.[34] These canons Regino took from the *Poenitentiale* of Bl. Rabanus Maurus.[35] But in addition to these conciliar statutes, Regino incorporated into his collection the following canon:

> Si aliquis causa explendae libidinis, vel odii meditatione, ut non ex eo soboles nascatur, homini aut mulieri aliquid fecerit, vel ad potandum dederit ut non possit generare aut concipere, ut homicida teneatur.[36]

After making its first appearance in Regino's collection, this canon found its way through succeeding collections into the Decretals of Pope Gregory IX. The source from which Regino took this statute has not been determined.[37]

B. *Burchard of Worms*

The conciliar laws against abortion found in the collection made by Regino were incorporated in the famous *Decretum* of Burchard, Bishop of Worms (+1012).[38] The canon *Si aliquis,* which first appeared in Regino's collection without an inscription, was accepted and labeled by Burchard as canon 30 of the Council of Worms (860). The inscription employed by Burchard evidently rests upon a false and non-historical basis.[39] The *Decretum* of Burchard,

[34] Lib. II, cap. 62-64—F. G. A. Wasserschleben, *Reginonis Libri Duo,* p. 239, and *MPL,* CXXXII, 297. It is to be noted that the canons of Regino quoted in this study are advanced one number in *MPL,* using Baluzius' edition of Regino; thus, canons 62, 63, 64 of the Wasserschleben edition are given in *MPL* as canons 63, 64, 65 respectively. Regarding Regino's addition to the canon from the Council of Lerida, see *supra,* p. 26, footnote 54.

[35] H. Wasserschleben, *Beitraege zur Geschichte der vorgratianischen Kirchenrechtsquellen* (Leipzig, 1839), p. 11 (hereafter to be cited as *Beitraege*); F. G. A. Wasserschleben, *Reginonis Libri Duo,* p. 239, footnotes *t, u,* and *v.*

[36] *De Disciplinis Ecclesiasticis,* lib. II, cap. 89—F. G. A. Wasserschleben, *Reginonis Libri Duo,* p. 506; *MPL,* CXXXII, 301.

[37] F. G. A. Wasserschleben (*Reginonis Libri Duo,* p. 248, note *u*) says that the canon is not found in the sources of Roman law, "neque alibi inventum." Hereafter this canon will be referred to as the canon *Si aliquis.*

[38] Lib. XVII, cap. 51-52, 54—*MPL,* CXL, 931.

[39] Lib. XVII, cap. 57—*MPL,* CXL, 933. Regarding the inscription, see Friedberg's note 1 to c. 5, X, *de homicidio voluntario vel casuali,* V, 12—*Corpus*

written about 1012 as a manual for the clergy, was an important source-book for subsequent collections.

Before and during the time of Regino and Burchard, fetal development and the time of animation constituted decisive factors in the gauging of tariffs for private penance. For example, according to a penitential canon incorporated in Regino's collection, if a fetus of less than forty days was destroyed, one year's penance was to be performed; if a fetus of more than forty days, three years' penance. But if animation had taken place (the precise time is not determined), the penance was to be that which was incurred by a murderer,[40] and this penance was of ten years' duration.[41]

From the so-called *Poenitentiale Romanum* Burchard quoted a canon which prescribed three years' penance for a woman guilty of voluntary abortion.[42] In his famous penitential work called the *Corrector* or *Medicus*, he has many and varied prescriptions regarding abortion, one of which demands a penance of one year if animation has not taken place, and a penance of three years if the soul has been infused.[43]

After the time of Burchard canons of private penitential discipline regarding abortion do not appear in important canonical collections.

C. Ivo of Chartres

Ivo, Bishop of Chartres (+c.1116), in his *Decretum* repeated the penalties for abortion which had been stated by the Councils

Iuris Canonici (ed. Lipsiensis 2. post Aemilii Richteri curas . . . instruxit Aemilius Friedberg, 2 vols., Lipsiae: Tauchnitz, 1879-1881; editio anastatice repetita, Lipsiae: Tauchnitz, 1928), II, 794; Binterim, *Pragmatische Geschichte der deutschen Concilien* (7 vols., Mainz, 1851-1852), III, 163. See also footnote 37 of this chapter.

[40] *De Ecclesiasticis Disciplinis*, lib. II, can. 65—F. G. A. Wasserschleben, *Reginonis Libri Duo*, p. 240; *MPL*, CXXXII, 298 (as can. 66).

[41] *Op. cit.*, lib. II, cans. 66, 67—F. G. A. Wasserschleben, *op. cit.*, p. 240; *MPL*, CXXXII, 298 (as cans. 67, 68).

Canons 65 and 66 are identical with canon 14 of the *Poenitentiale Darmstadiensis*, quoted in H. Wasserschleben, *Beitraege*, p. 133. See also *Poenitentiale Bedae*, C. III, 12, and *Poenitentiale Egberti*, C. VII, 9—Schmitz, *Die Bussbücher und die Bussdisciplin der Kirche*, pp. 560 and 580 respectively.

[42] *Decretum*, lib. XVII, can. 60—*MPL*, CXL, 934.

[43] *Decretum*, lib. XIX, can. 5—*MPL*, CXL, 972.

of Ancyra and Lerida, and by St. Martin of Braga,[44] but omitted the canon *Si aliquis*, which had been accepted by both Regino and Burchard. Ivo also included certain statements made by the Fathers relative to abortion, which statements had not been published in canonical collections before his time. Thus, none of the following statutes in Ivo's *Decretum* is to be found in the collections of Regino and Burchard.

Two canons quote St. Augustine: The one embodies St. Augustine's condemnation of interference with fetal life; the other contains his distinction between a formed and non-formed fetus (made in interpreting the Septuagint text of Exodus on abortion), namely, that the law considers as murder solely the destruction of a formed fetus.[45] A third canon accepts a pseudo-Augustinian text which maintains that animation of the fetus takes place only after it has attained a certain stage of development or formation.[46] A fourth canon quotes a text from St. Jerome to show that there is no question of murder in the matter of fetal destruction unless the fetus is formed.[47] The remaining canon embodies a letter of Pope Stephen V in which the Pope presupposes that one guilty of abortion is a murderer.[48]

The two texts from St. Augustine and the one from St. Jerome are in Ivo's *Panormia*,[49] but the five canons of the *Decretum* are all included in his *Collectio Tripartita*.[50]

Conclusion

The collections from the tenth to the twelfth century served as

[44] Pars X, cap. 181-183—*MPL*, CLXI, 744-745.

[45] *Decretum*, pars X, cap. 55-56—*MPL*, CLXI, 706-707.

[46] *Decretum*, pars X, cap. 57—*MPL*, CLXI, 707.

[47] *Decretum*, pars X, cap. 58—*MPL*, CLXI, 707.

[48] *Decretum*, pars X, cap. 27—*MPL*, CLXI, 699; Jaffé, *Regesta*, n. 2642 (as Stephen VI [885-891]), but given as Stephen V in *Corpus Iuris Canonici*, c. 20, C. II, q. 5.

[49] Lib. VIII, cc. 12-14—*MPL*, CLXI, 1307-1308.

[50] Pars III, tit. XX, cc. 9, 15-18—cf. H. Wasserschleben, *Beitraege*, p. 55. Regarding the interdependence and authorship of the *Decretum*, *Panormia*, and *Collectio Tripartita*, see Fournier-Le Bras, *Histoire des Collections*, II, 55-105, especially, 91-94, 99-105; H. Wasserschleben, *Beitraege*, pp. 47-77, especially 77; Van Hove, *Prolegomena*, n. 181.

important sources for Gratian's *Decretum* and for the subsequent Decretals. Thus, the canon *Si aliquis* of Regino and Burchard was received into the Decretals of Pope Gregory IX, and Ivo's five canons on abortion were accepted by Gratian. The important contribution of this period is Ivo's introduction into canonical collections of the distinction between fetal formation and non-formation. St. Basil's canons expressly rejected this distinction, and no conciliar enactments admitted it. It figured, however, in the application of *private* penitential tariffs. Having now appeared in the work of Ivo of Chartres, it was to assume a major rôle in the Church's penal legislation on abortion, even down to the present century.

CHAPTER IV

LEGISLATION FROM GRATIAN TO POPE GREGORY IX

ARTICLE I. GRATIAN AND THE DECRETISTS

A. The Decretum *of Gratian*

THE appearance of Gratian's *Decretum* about the year 1140 marked the beginning of a new era in the field of canon law. Previous canonical collections were little more than heterogeneous collections of commonly-quoted canons that frequently were contradictory. Attempting to solve difficulties and reconcile contradictions, Gratian himself interpreted and evaluated these texts. Thus he played a double rôle: that of a collector and also that of an author. Former laws and ancient authorities were selected with discriminating care to substantiate and explain his own teaching on a particular point.[1]

1. Gratian's Teaching Regarding Abortion

Regarding abortion, the earlier canonical collections had simply collected the ancient texts. There was little or no interpretation of these texts. Gratian, too, gathered the authoritative expressions dealing with abortion, but he did so in order to substantiate his position regarding this crime, namely, that *abortion is not murder if the soul has not been infused into the fetus.*

In discussing the status of persons who marry only for sexual pleasure, Gratian quotes St. Augustine's condemnation of those who in any way destroy their unborn children.[2] This prompts Gratian to ask: "Are those who procure abortion to be judged as murderers?" His answer: "He is not a murderer who brings about abortion before the soul is infused into the body." [3]

[1] Cf. Kuttner, "The Father of the Science of Canon Law,"—*The Jurist,* I (1941), 2-19.

[2] C. 7, C. XXXII, q. 2.

[3] Ad c. 8, C. XXXII, q. 2.

As proof he offers three texts from the writings of the Fathers—statements which appeared in the collections of Ivo of Chartres. The first is St. Augustine's statement that the law does not consider as murder the destruction of a non-animated fetus.[4] The second, a pseudo-Augustinian text, maintains that, as in the case of Adam, the body must be formed, that is, developed, before the soul can be and is present.[5] A third canon embodies the text from St. Jerome stating that murder is not involved unless the fetus is formed.[6]

There are two other references to abortion in the *Decretum*. While treating matter not directly related to abortion, Gratian happens to quote sources which refer to this crime. Thus, in discussing responsibility for deliberate and accidental homicide, he inserts a canon which states that accidental abortion does not merit punishment.[7] In another place Gratian embodies a letter ascribed to Pope Stephen V. This letter, outlawing proof by ordeal for parents whose infant died under suspicious circumstances, clearly assumes that abortion is murder.[8]

This, then, is Gratian's position regarding the crime of abortion: abortion is murder if the fetus at the time of its destruction is already animated; if the fetus is not yet animated, murder is not involved. Gratian does not indicate the *time* of animation. Neither does he indicate the precise penalties which abortion merits, but the abortion of a formed or animated fetus, in as much as it is murder, naturally involved the penalties for homicide.

2. Gratian's Teaching Regarding Homicide

Gratian's treatment of homicide revolves principally about clerics and aspirants to the clerical state who have been guilty of homicide.

[4] C. 8, C. XXXII, q. 2.

[5] C. 9, C. XXXII, q. 2. Regarding the authenticity of this text, see Richter-Friedberg, *Corpus Iuris Canonici*, I, 1122, note 84; Berardi, *Gratiani Canones Genuini ab Apocryphis Discreti* (2. ed. Veneta, 3 vols. in 4, Venetiis, 1783), III, 220.

[6] C. 10, C. XXXII, q. 2.

[7] C. 48, D. L. This canon is falsely inscribed as a papal letter; cf. Richter-Friedberg, *Corpus Iuris Canonici*, I, 198, note 743; Berardi, *op. cit.*, II, 364.

[8] C. 20, C. II, q. 5; Jaffé, *Regesta*, n. 2642.

As stated in a letter of Pope John VIII (872-882), a priest who is guilty of murder cannot continue to exercise his priesthood.[9] In fact, no cleric thus guilty may continue to exercise orders, much less be promoted,[10] and even though penance be done, he cannot be readmitted to the sacred ministry.[11] Even one who simply counsels homicide is not to be ordained. Should anyone gain admission to orders by concealing his guilt, he is to be deposed.[12]

Gratian, however, maintains that these canons bind only when there is a case of voluntary murder which could have been avoided. If the killing was unavoidable, for example, in necessary self-defense, the cleric could be reinstated after doing adequate penance.[13] In cases of accidental homicide a dispensation will permit the penitent cleric to continue the exercise of the Orders already received.[14]

B. The Decretists

The *Summa* of Roland Bandinelli, disciple of Gratian and later Pope Alexander III (1159-1181), written before 1148, contains little more than a summation and confirmation of Gratian's position regarding abortion.[15] Paucapalea,[16] writing before Bandinelli, and Stephen of Tournai (+1203),[17] writing after 1160, say nothing about abortion.

[9] C. 4, D. L.; Jaffé, *Regesta*, n. 2588.

[10] C. 5, D. L. (letter of Pope Nicholas I [858-867]); Jaffé, *Regesta*, n. 2160.

[11] C. 6, D. L. (letter of Pope Nicholas I); Jaffé, *Regesta*, n. 2164.

[12] C. 8, D. L. (St. Martin of Braga).

[13] Cf. dictum ante c. 36, D. L. Can. 36 prescribes a two-year penance in such cases.

[14] C. 37, D. L. (Pope Urban II [1088-1099]), and *dictum* before this canon; Jaffé, *Regesta*, n. 4090.

See also cc. 8, 39, 41, 49, D. L., and c. 17, C. VI, q. 1. For detailed discussion, cf. Rudolf R. v. Scherer, "Die Irregularitas ex Delicto Homicidii,"—*AKKR*, XLIX (1883), 37-73, especially 34-43; Kuttner, *Kanonistische Schuldlehre von Gratian bis auf die Decretalen Gregors IX*, Studi e Testi, n. 64 (Città del Vaticano: Bibliotheca Apostolica Vaticana, 1935), pp. 187 ff.

[15] Ad *Quod vero* of c. 8, C. XXXII, q. 2—Thaner, *Die Summa Magistri Rolandi nachmals Papstes Alexander III* (Innsbruck, 1874), p. 167.

[16] Schulte, *Die Summa des Paucapalea* (Giessen, 1890).

[17] Schulte, *Die Summa des Stephanus Tornacensis* (Giessen, 1891). Note, however, that this work is only a partial edition.

Rufinus (+c.1190), however, in his *Summa Decretorum*, written about 1157-1159, gives a lengthy commentary on Gratian's canons relating to abortion, and on canons not mentioned by Gratian. The teaching of Rufinus regarding abortion may be summarized as follows.[18] Both the one who accidentally—*non sponte*—causes abortion to another, and the woman herself who involuntarily suffers an abortion, although not guilty of crime,[19] should perform some little penance *ad cautelam*.[20] In cases of voluntary abortion, either by the mother herself or by another upon her, a distinction must be made: if the fetus is *non-formed*, three years' penance must be undertaken; [21] if *formed*, the guilty party is a murderer, and as such incurs the penalties for murder.

According to Rufinus,[22] if murder be deliberate, a layman is to do penance according to the norms established by Burchard of Worms. And these norms vary from seven years to a lifetime, according to circumstances.[23] A cleric guilty of deliberate homicide is to be deposed and is never to be reinstated.[24] In an entirely different passage, Rufinus adds that in the case of deliberate homicide, which is manifest, there can be no question of reinstatement, even though most perfect penance has been performed. If the homicide was occult and adequate penance has been sincerely completed, the

[18] Ad *Aliquando* of c. 7, C. XXXII, q. 2—Singer, *Die Summa Decretorum des Magister Rufinus* (Paderborn, 1902), pp. 482-483.

[19] Rufinus here refers to c. 48, D. L. For discussion of the Decretists regarding this canon, cf. Kuttner, *Kanonistische Schuldlehre*, pp. 236-237. See also, *supra*, footnote 7 of this Chapter.

[20] Rufinus here refers to c. 6, C. XXXIV, q. 2. The amount or duration of the penance was very likely determined by the priest with whom the penitent was dealing; cf. *infra*, footnote 37 of this Chapter.

[21] Reference here to Burchard, *Decretum*, lib. XVII, can. 60 (*MPL*, CXL, 934).

[22] Ad *Casu quoque* of the *dictum* ante c. 37, D. L.—Singer, *op. cit.*, p. 125.

[23] Cf. Burchard, *Decretum*, lib. VI, cc. 1-9, 12-14, 17-18—*MPL*, CXL, 763-769. When discussing the penance for those who procure sterility or impede conception, Rufinus (referring to the canon *Si aliquis*, as found in Burchard) states that the *usual* penance of *seven years for homicide* is not to be imposed in these cases, but a lesser penance, according to the judgment of the priest.—Ad *Aliquando* of c. 7, C. XXXII, q. 2—Singer, *op. cit.*, p. 482.

[24] Rufinus here cites the *dictum* ante c. 37, D. L.

cleric can again exercise his ministry, yet it would be better and safer if he never did so.[25]

C. The Glossa Ordinaria

The *Glossa Ordinaria* on the *Decretum* of Gratian was assembled by John Teutonicus (+1245-1246) about the years 1215-1217, and with but few changes was put into its final form by Bartholomew of Brescia (+1258) about 1245. In a chronological study, the Gloss (as found in the printed editions) should be considered after the Decretals of Pope Gregory IX. But since the Gloss' position regarding abortion was little, if at all, influenced by the Gregorian decretals and is properly the work of the Decretists, it will be summarized here.

The Gloss maintains consistently that one who commits abortion is guilty of murder. It insists, however, upon the distinction based upon the more or less advanced stages of fetal development. That is, there can be no murder unless the soul is present; and the soul is not infused until the body has been properly formed or developed in the mother's womb.[26] But in referring to this distinction the terminology of the Gloss varies. One finds *formed* and *non-formed,* as used in the early centuries.[27] The expressions vivified,[28] and *animatum* and *non-animatum* are sometimes used.[29] Despite the varying terminology, the idea is the same: only when the soul is present, that is, after the fetus is *formed,* can abortion be reckoned as murder.

The Gloss distinguishes between voluntary and accidental murder.[30] Huguccio (+1210), writing about 1188, and John Teutonicus hold that if a cleric commits voluntary murder he may not be granted a dispensation to exercise his orders. And this rule obtains even if

[25] Ad *Ex praemissis* of *dictum* ante c. 1, D. L.—Singer, *op. cit.,* p. 115.

[26] C. 8, C. XXXII, q. 2 ad v. *nec animatum.*

[27] C. 20, C. II, q. 5 ad v. *per abortum.*

[28] Ad *de his* ante c. 8, C. XXXII, q. 2.

[29] C. 9, C. XXXII, q. 2 ad v. *det animam.*

[30] The distinction of the Gloss regarding murder also includes necessary homicide; however, this classification is not discussed by the Gloss in relation to abortion.

the crime is occult and penance has been performed. Bartholomew of Brescia writes, about 1240, that at his time this opinion of Huguccio regarding occult homicide was prevalent, although others held that in cases of occult homicide which had been expiated by penance no dispensation would be required to exercise the orders already received.[31]

When the killing is accidental but results from an illicit action, the cleric engaged in this action cannot exercise even the order which he has received.[32] Another gloss, however, implies that the lack of diligence or due care is the foundation for the punishment, even though the action was licit in itself.[33] In short, unless some guilt accompanies the accidental death, the cleric incurs no penalty and can even be promoted to higher orders.[34]

Article II. The Decretals Before Gregory IX

To the legislation on abortion found in the *Decretum* of Gratian must be added the enactments that appeared in the *Quinque Compilationes Antiquae*. These Compilations or Collections contain statutes which were passed over in Gratian's *Decretum,* and also papal letters that appeared after the *Decretum* was written (c.1140).

A. Compilatio I

The *Compilatio I,* also called *Breviarium,* was compiled by Bernard of Pavia (+1216) between 1188 and 1192. This work incorporated two old texts regarding abortion which had been omitted by Gratian. First there is the text of Exodus, xxi, 22-23, in the Vul-

[31] C. 6, D. L. ad v. *de his* and *CASUS*; see also c. 5, D. L. ad v. *clericum.* The legislation was not so strict for crimes other than homicide; see c. 6, D. XXV, ad v. *primum.*

[32] C. 6, D. L. ad v. *de his.*

[33] C. 37, D. L. ad v. *clerico.*

[34] C. 42, D. L. ad v. *sed casu.* See also *CASUS* of c. 48, D. L. For detailed treatment of the Decretists' teaching regarding homicide, cf. Kuttner, *Kanonistische Schuldlehre,* pp. 189-222; Kuttner, "Ecclesia de Occultis non Iudicat,"—*Acta Congressus Iuridici Internationalis* (5 vols., Romae, 1935-1937), III, 225-246, especially, 234-243; Rudolph R. v. Scherer, "Die Irregularitas ex Delicto Homicidii,"—*AKKR,* XLIX (1883), 43-44.

gate version, which makes no reference to fetal formation.[35] Secondly there is the canon *Si aliquis*, which was introduced to canonical collections by Regino of Prüm and accepted by Burchard of Worms. It will be recalled that this canon prescribes that he is to be held *as a murderer* who does anything to another party which results in the prevention of the conception, the gestation, or the birth of children.[36]

Bernard of Pavia explains this legislation. He calls attention to the fact that although the text of Exodus quoted in the *Compilatio I* does not distinguish between a formed and a non-formed fetus, this distinction is made by Gratian. Therefore, if a *formed* child dies as a result of abortion, it is a case of murder, the varying penalties for which will depend upon the degree of deliberation in the act. If the fetus is *non-formed*, a penalty *"as for"* homicide (implying that real murder is not involved) is to be imposed in the discretion of the judge.[37] According to Bernard the penalty for voluntary homicide (and therefore for the abortion of a formed fetus) is deposition for clerics, and excommunication for laymen.[38] In cases of accidental homicide guilt is incurred only if the action which resulted in the death was illicit or if due care was not exercised.[39] In this case the

[35] Lib. V, tit. 10, c. 2—Friedberg, *Quinque Compilationes Antiquae* (Lipsiae, 1882), p. 57.

[36] Lib. V, tit. 10, c. 13—Friedberg, *op. cit.*, p. 58. The text of this canon is given *infra*, p. 51, footnote 2.

[37] *Casus Decretalium*, lib. V, tit. 10, c. 2—Laspeyres, *Bernardi Papiensis Summa Decretalium* (Ratisbonae, 1860), pp. 348-349.

Regarding the implication that *real* murder is not involved in the abortion of a *non-formed* fetus: (1) in this case Bernard says that the judge is to determine the penalty, but in cases of true murder the penalty is determined by law (cf. the three following footnotes); (2) in another canon (*Casus Decretalium*, lib. V, tit. 10, c. 3—Laspeyres, *op. cit.*, p. 359) he clearly distinguishes between one who is *reus homicidii* and one upon whom *tamquam de homicidio poenitentia imponenda*. Bernard's meager comment on the canon *Si aliquis* throws no light upon the matter.—*Casus Decretalium*, lib. V, tit. 10, c. 13—Laspeyres, *op. cit.*, p. 352. Regarding this matter, see the similar teaching of Rufinus (*supra*, p. 44, footnote 23) and of St. Raymond of Pennafort (*infra*, pp. 52-53).

[38] *Summa Decretalium*, lib. V, tit. 10, § 7 *in fine*—Laspeyres, *op. cit.*, p. 223. Bernard here refers to cc. 8, 44, D. L.

[39] *Summa Decretalium*, lib. V, tit. 10, § 5—Laspeyres, *op. cit.*, p. 22. As

penalty for a layman is five years' penance; for a cleric, deposition, unless a dispensation intervene (*nisi dispensative toleretur*).[40] No dispensation, according to Bernard's knowledge, is given from the deposition which attaches to *voluntary* homicide.[41]

B. Compilatio IV

The *Compilatio IV*, composed about 1215-1217, contains but one canon relative to abortion—a letter written in 1211 by Pope Innocent III (1198-1216) to a Carthusian Prior and his confrères. The Pope wrote that a priest who had accidentally, albeit not without some guilt, caused an abortion could continue to exercise the sacred ministry if the fetus had not yet been vivified (*vivificatus*); otherwise he was to refrain from exercising the ministry.[42]

In his Gloss (before 1218) on this letter of Pope Innocent III, John Teutonicus points out that one of Gratian's canons (the letter of Pope Stephen V which makes no distinction regarding fetal formation) is to be understood in the light of other canons which clearly distinguished between a formed and a non-formed fetus.[43]

Conclusion

Gratian, the Decretists, and the Decretal Letters before Pope Gregory IX all accepted the distinction between the formed and

authority, Bernard refers to cc. 49-51, 42-44, D. L. See also *Casus Decretalium*, lib. V, tit. 10, c. 8—Laspeyres, *op. cit.*, p. 351.

[40] *Summa Decretalium*, lib. V, tit. 10, § 7—Laspeyres, *op. cit.*, p. 223. Bernard cites cc. 9, 37, 42-44, D. L.

This dispensation may be one of three kinds: *magna, maior, maxima*. The first of these obtained when the one who had received higher orders could later exercise only inferior orders; the second, when the cleric could again exercise all the orders he had received; the third, when the cleric could in addition be promoted to still higher orders.—*Summa Decretalium*, lib. V, tit. 10, § 8—Laspeyres, *op. cit.*, p. 223.

[41] *Summa Decretalium*, lib. V, tit. 10, § 8—Laspeyres, *op. cit.*, p. 224.

[42] Lib. V, tit. 6, c. 4—Friedberg, *Quinque Compilationes Antiquae*, p. 148; Potthast, *Regesta Pontificum Romanorum inde ab a. post Christum natum MCXCVIII ad a. MCCCIV* (2 vols., Berolini, 1874-1875). This text is given, *infra*, footnote 1 of Chapter V.

[43] Lib. V, tit. 6, c. 4, ad v. *vivificatus*—Antonius Augustinus, *Antiquae Collectiones Decretalium cum Antonii Augustini Episcopi Ilerdensis notis* (Ilerdae [Lerida], 1576).

the non-formed (animated and non-animated) fetus. They agreed, moreover, that abortion involving a formed fetus was true murder, and penalties for this abortion followed the general norms of penalties for homicide. The Decretists, notably Rufinus and Bernard of Pavia, indicated that abortion of a non-formed fetus was considered quasi-homicide, that is, the penalties were *similar* to but not so severe as those for true homicide.

CHAPTER V

FROM THE DECRETALS OF GREGORY IX UP TO THE COUNCIL OF TRENT

Article I. The Decretals of Pope Gregory IX

The Decretals of Pope Gregory IX (1227-1241), an authentic collection of laws for the universal Church, were promulgated in 1234. In this collection two canons are found which refer to the crime of abortion, both of which were taken by St. Raymond of Pennafort (+1275), the compiler of the Decretals, from the *Compilationes Antiquae.*

One canon dealing with abortion is the letter written in 1211 by Pope Innocent III to the Carthusians. It had earlier been incorporated in the *Compilatio IV.* The case concerned a priest "qui quandam mulierem praegnantem . . . per zonam arripuit, quasi ludens," and thereby according to the woman's statement caused her to sustain an abortion. Heeding the advice of others, the priest refrained from exercising his sacred ministry. When he was asked to intervene in this case, Pope Innocent replied that the sacred ministry could be exercised if the conceived child had not yet been animated; otherwise not.[1]

The second canon is the canon *Si aliquis,* which, after having been handed down from Regino of Prüm (+915), now becomes official law. This statute, of dubious origin, states in effect that

[1] "Sicut ex litterarum vestrarum tenore accepimus quum quidam presbyter vestri ordinis, qui prius fuerat niger monachus, quandam mulierem praegnantem, cum qua contraxerat consuetudinem inhonestam, et quae asserebat, se concepisse ex eo, per zonam arripuerit, quasi ludens, ipsa *mulier postmodum* per hoc sic se asseruit esse laesam, quod occasione huiusmodi abortivit; propter quod idem presbyter, proborum virorum usus consilio, se ipsum duxit ab altaris ministerio sequestrandum. +*Quare nobis humiliter supplicastis, ut cum eo agere misericorditer dignaremur.* Nos vero devotioni vestrae insinuatione praesentium respondemus, quod, si nondum erat vivificatus conceptus, ministrare poterit; alioquin debet ab altaris officio abstinere."—C. 20, X, *de homicidio voluntario vel casuali,* V, 12; Potthast, *Regesta,* n. 4312.

anyone who *does* anything to a man or to a woman or *gives* them anything to drink which has for its effect the prevention of conception, or gestation, or the birth of a child is to be held as a murderer.[2]

Thus the Decretals of Pope Gregory IX brand the following as murder: abortion, sterilization, contraception, and, in short, any prevention of or effective interference with human procreation. But are all these crimes to be understood as *true murder?* Or is it merely the abortion which involves an animated fetus that constitutes *true murder,* so that the other crimes here mentioned can not be considered as implying more than *quasi-murder.* The letter of Pope Innocent III to the Carthusians implies that a negative answer be given to the first query and an affirmative reply to the second. A definitive answer must be sought in the writings of the Decretalists, who interpreted and applied in practice the legislation of the Gregorian Decretals.

Before considering the Decretalists, one may say a word about the law of the Decretals regarding homicide in general. The guilt and punishment for voluntary homicide are incurred by him who effectively co-operates, by physical assistance, counsel, etc., as well as by the one who actually performs the deed.[3] To these persons the ranks of the clergy are closed—they are in effect irregular. And if they already are clerics, they not only are not to be promoted to higher orders,[4] but must be deposed from the sacred ministry and do penance in a monastery.[5] The basic principle of the Gregorian Decretals on accidental homicide is to be found in this *summary*: "Homicidium casuale imputatur ei qui dabat operam rei illicitae vel etiam licitae, secundum alium intellectum, si non adhibuit omnem diligentiam, quam debuit." [6]

[2] "Si aliquis causa explendae libidinis vel odii meditatione homini aut mulieri aliquid fecerit, vel ad potandum dederit, ut non possit generare, aut concipere, vel nasci soboles, ut homicida teneatur."—C. 5, X, *d homicidio voluntario vel casuali,* V, 12. For the early history of this canon cf. *supra,* pp. 37, 47.

[3] C. 6, X, *de homicidio voluntario vel casuali,* V, 12.

[4] C. 11, X, *de homicidio voluntario vel casuali,* V, 12.

[5] C. 6, X, *de homicidio voluntario vel casuali,* V, 12.

[6] Ante c. 8, X, *de homicidio voluntario vel casuali,* V, 12.

Article II. Teaching of the Decretalists

A consideration of several of the outstanding authorities who followed Pope Gregory IX will show that only the abortion which involved an animated fetus was held to be true murder in the eyes of the law, and as such merited all the penalties for murder. The abortion of a non-animated fetus and crimes of sterilization and contraception constituted what may be called quasi-homicide. The teaching of the Decretalists will be considered A. regarding abortion; B. regarding homicide.

A. Regarding Abortion

St. Raymond of Pennafort (+1275), in his *Summa* written between 1223 and 1238, asks this question: How is the perpetrator of the actions which are proscribed by the canon *Si aliquis* (that is, sterilization, contraception, abortion) to be judged regarding homicide and irregularity? The Saint replies that one who causes an abortion is truly guilt of murder and incurs the consequent irregularity if the fetus is already animated (formed), for then a human being is killed. If the fetus has not been animated, then the party responsible for the abortion is not to be considered guilty of murder, which in its canonical effects would also entail the incurring of the irregularity, but is to be accounted as guilty of murder only in so far as his action constitutes the basis for a *penance* which is identical with the penance entailed by real murder. The same is to be said of the one who gives a poison or does anything which has for its effect the prevention of conception or the impeding of gestation—that is to say, such a party will be held merely to the performance of the penance that results from the sin of murder.[7]

It seems, therefore, that St. Raymond makes a distinction between real or actual homicide, on the one hand, and quasi- or fictitious homicide on the other. The former begets the irregularity inasmuch as a human being has been killed *de facto*. The latter, since no human life is actually taken, does not give rise to the

[7] *Summa* (2. ed., Avenione, 1715), lib. II, tit. 1, § 6. St. Raymond cites both canons referring to abortion in the Gregorian Decretals, i. e., cc. 5, 20.

irregularity, but does demand that the usual *penance* for homicide be imposed.[8] A similar distinction had been made by Rufinus, by Bernard of Pavia, and, as the following pages reveal, by other Decretalists following St. Raymond.

Bernard de Bottone (+1266) states that no irregularity is contracted unless true homicide has been committed, that is, unless an *animated* fetus dies through abortion. Procuring sterility, impeding conception, and causing the abortion of a *non-animated* fetus is not true homicide and may be accounted as such only in its relation to the subsequent *spiritual* penalty. Irregularity is not incurred in these cases.[9] In his *Casus,* Bernard likewise insists that the letter of Pope Stephen V, which simply states that abortion is homicide, is to be understood in the light of the formation-animation distinction.[10]

Cardinal Hostiensis (+1271) maintains in his *Commentaria* that in the application of the canon *Si aliquis* cognizance must be taken of the animation question, as was done by Pope Innocent III in his reply to the Carthusians, and as outlined in the *Decretum* of Gratian. If the fetus is formed, abortion is true murder and gives rise to the irregularity for murder; if the fetus is non-formed, no irregularity is incurred and the crime is not true but rather interpretative homicide.[11] In his *Summa,* written about 1253, Hostiensis calls the abortion of a non-formed fetus (as well as sterilization and contraceptive measures) *homicidium conditionaliter,* for which no irregularity results but a *penitentia spiritualis* must be imposed.[12]

Ioannes Andreae (+1348) agrees substantially with what has been said and offers little more than a paraphrase of the Gloss of Bernard de Bottone. Abortion is homicide more properly—*verius*—if the fetus has been animated; it is only interpretative homicide if the fetus has not yet been animated.[13]

[8] Cf. also *Summa,* lib. II, tit. 1, §§ 2, 4.

[9] Glossa ad c. 5, X, *de homicidio voluntario vel casuali,* V, 12, v. *ut homicida.*

[10] C. 20, X, *de homicidio voluntario vel casuali,* V, 12, *CASUS.*

[11] Ad c. 5, X, V, 12, v. *nasci.*

[12] *Summa Aurea* (Venetiis, 1580), lib. V, *de homicidio voluntario vel casuali,* n. 1.

[13] *Novella Commentaria* (6 vols. in 5, Venetiis, 1578), ad c. 5, X, *de homicidio voluntario vel casuali,* V, 12, n. 1, v. *homicida.*

Panormitanus (Nicholaus de Tudeschis), also known as Abbas Siculus (+1453), claims to follow the opinion of Godfrey of Trani (+1245), namely, that the irregularity is never contracted in cases of abortion unless the fetus is already animated.[14]

B. Regarding Homicide

The abortion of an animated fetus, being true murder, is subject to all the penalties for murder.

St. Raymond of Pennafort expressed the generally accepted penalty for *voluntary* homicide, that is, deposition and irregularity, from which a dispensation is not to be given.[15] Both Hostiensis[16] and Parnormitanus[17] adhere to the common teaching that the Pope has the power to grant this dispensation, but in practice he will most rarely use this power, since it is not normally expedient to do so. Only by way of extraordinary exception will he do so.

Following the norms of the Gregorian legislation the Decretalists hold that if guilt (due either to an action illicit in itself or to negligence) precedes accidental homicide, the cleric is to be deposed, and the contracted irregularity prevents the exercise of any and all orders.[18] According to Panormitanus, only the Pope can dispense to permit the exercise of sacred orders, but the bishop may do so regarding minor orders.[19]

[14] *Commentaria* (5 vols. in 7, Venetiis, 1588), ad c. 5, X, *de homicidio voluntario vel casuali,* V, 12, n. 3; ad c. 20, X, *de homicidio voluntario vel casuali,* V, 12, nn. 1, 2.

[15] *Summa,* lib. II, tit. 1, §§ 4, 5.

[16] *Summa Aurea,* lib. V, tit. *de homicidio voluntario vel casuali,* n. 7.

[17] *Commentaria,* ad c. 6, X, *de homicidio voluntario vel casuali,* V, 12, n. 12.

[18] St. Raymond of Pennafort, *Summa,* lib. II, tit. 1, §4; Hostiensis, *Summa Aurea,* lib. V, tit. *de homicidio voluntario vel casuali,* n. 4; Panormitanus, *Commentaria,* ad c. 7, X, *de homicidio voluntario vel casuali,* n. 2, where he states that the cleric is to be deposed, but see *additio b* to n. 2.

[19] *Commentaria,* ad c. 7, X, *de homicidio voluntario vel casuali,* V, 12, n. 2; ad c. 8, X, *de homicidio voluntario vel casuali,* V, 12, nn. 2, 4.

The three types of dispensation—*magna, maior, maxima*—from the irregularity of accidental homicide mentioned by Bernard of Pavia (cf. *supra,* footnote 40 of Chapter IV)) remained in vogue.—St. Raymond of Pennafort, *Summa,* lib. II, tit. 1, § 5; Hostiensis, *Summa Aurea,* lib. V, tit. *de homicidio voluntario vel casuali,* n. 7.

In addition to the above penalties for clerics, a spiritual penance is to be performed. For voluntary homicide, the penance is ordinarily to last seven years; [20] for accidental homicide, five years.[21]

Article III. The Time of Animation

It has been seen that the formation-animation theory was adopted by Gratian as a juridical norm for judging whether abortion did or did not constitute homicide. The Decretists, the Gloss on the *Decretum* of Gratian, and the *Compilationes Antiquae* likewise accepted it. In the Decretals of Pope Gregory IX the distinction between a formed and a non-formed (animated and non-animated) fetus was admitted for the first time into an official collection of universal ecclesiastical law. Yet in all these texts on the question of abortion it is not stated at which precise moment one may judge that animation has taken place. The same is true of the early Decretalists, such as Bernard de Bottone, St. Raymond of Pennafort, and Cardinal Hostiensis.

A norm regarding the time of animation could have been deduced from the gloss of John Teutonicus on a *dictum* of Gratian, which however did not deal with abortion. This gloss stated that the male fetus is without life for forty days before the soul is infused, and the female fetus for eighty days.[22] The Gloss of Joannes Andreae on a text (in no way related to abortion) in the *Constitutiones* of Pope Clement V (1305-1314), promulgated in 1317, stated that the soul is not infused until the fetus has been organized and developed to receive it. The Gloss said that some hold this infusion to take place either on the fortieth or on the eightieth day after conception, in relative association with the male or female fetus.[23]

[20] St. Raymond of Pennafort, *Summa,* lib. III, tit. 34, § 41. Hostiensis (*Summa Aurea,* lib. V, tit. *de homicidio voluntario vel casuali,* n. 4) mentions both five and seven years, and excommunication if the penance is contemned.

[21] St. Raymond of Pennafort, *Summa,* lib. III, tit. 34, § 43. Regarding the duration of this penance, see also Hollweck, *Die kirchlichen Strafgesetze,* § 162, footnote 8.

[22] Ad *principium,* D. V. v. *quadraginta.*

[23] Ad c. un., *de summa trinitate et fide catholica,* I, 1, in Clem., v. *simul unitas.*

The Gloss of Accursius (+1260) on the Digest of Justinian stated that before forty days the fetus is not a human being—*homo*—but that after such time any one who commits abortion is accountable for homicide.[24]

It is certain that many and varied were the *times* advanced as norms, yet the 40-80 day norm, as found in the Gloss, seems to have been commonly accepted. Thus Panormitanus refers only to the latter.[25] And according to Barbosa (1589-1649) the 40-80 day calculation was the commonly accepted one after the time of Andrea Alciati (1492-1550).[26]

Summary of Decretal Law

The following conclusions may be advanced as summarizing the doctrine of the decretal law and the common teaching of the decretalists.

1. Abortion is a serious sin, whether the fetus is animated or not.

2. The distinction between an animated and a non-animated fetus is admitted in order to determine whether or not the *legal* penalties for homicide are incurred by the one who causes the abortion.

3. The voluntary abortion of an animated fetus is voluntary murder and begets both the irregularity and also the penalties decreed against voluntary homicide by the law.

4. The accidental abortion (not without some guilt) of an animated fetus, like an accidental homicide, begets the irregularity, but a dispensation is more readily obtainable. It is generally admitted, however, that no irregularity is incurred if no guilt has preceded the accidental abortion.

[24] Ad D. (47. 11) 4, v. *exilium*.

[25] *Commentaria,* ad c. 5, X, *de homicidio voluntario vel casuali,* V, 12, n. 3.

[26] *Vota Decisiva et Consultativa Canonica* (Venetiis, 1710), lib. I, vot. 12, n. 27, and see nn. 19-26 for varied norms of various authorities; and *Collectanea Doctorum tam Veterum quam Recentiorum in Ius Pontificium Universum* (6 vol. in 3, Lugduni, 1716), ad c. 8, C. XXXII, q. 2, n. 1, and ad *principium,* D. V., n. 1. See also Paul Borgasius (+1541), *Tractatus de Irregularitatibus et Impedimentis* (Venetiis, 1574), pars IV, tit. *de veneficiis,* n. 15.

5. The abortion of a non-animated fetus, as well as the acts of sterilization and contraception is not true homicide; therefore no irregularity is incurred and there is no question of the need of a dispensation for the exercise or reception of orders. Yet these crimes constitute quasi-homicide, i. e., they are considered to be equivalent to homicide in so far as they require the same *penance* to be done as that which is required for true homicide; there is need of an absolution from the sin, but there is no need of a dispensation from irregularity, for the latter is not present in such cases.

6. The precise time at which animation may be judged to have taken place is variously estimated, but the lapse of forty or eighty days respectively after the conception of a male or a female fetus was the generally accepted norm.

Article IV. Conciliar Laws

A. Particular Councils

Numerous particular councils and diocesan synods from the thirteenth century upward to the Council of Trent provided severe penalties against abortion, some of them being more severe than the general law of the Church as found in the Decretals.

The Synod of Riez, in 1285, penalized both abortion and murder with excommunication to be incurred *ipso facto,* from which absolution was reserved to the Holy See. So broad was the scope of this statute that hardly any one effectively associated with the commission of these crimes could escape the penalty. The excommunication was incurred by all who knowingly co-operated by assisting, advising, or suggesting, by selling, or otherwise providing deadly drugs to effect the abortion or the murder.[27]

The same Synod stated that a cleric thus implicated in the crime was *ipso facto* deprived of any benefice he held. In addition he was to be degraded and given up to the civil authorities. If one's reputation was tainted by a prudent and founded probability that he had

[27] Can. 14—Mansi, XXIV, 581. One may well question by what authority a *particular* synod reserved a censure to the Holy See.

been involved in the procuring of abortion or of murder, he could receive no ecclesiastical honor or dignity.[28]

These provisions of the Synod of Riez (which make no mention of the animation distinction) were adopted almost verbatim by the Councils held at Avignon in 1326 [29] and in 1337,[30] and by the Synod of Lavaur in 1368.[31]

As a precautionary measure against abortion and murder the Synod of Riez demanded that apothecaries and all those who gave, sold, or otherwise administered dangerous drugs and poisons had to inform the civil authorities before these products could be dispensed to their clients or customers. Those who neglected this requirement, together with those who counseled or consented to this neglect, were to be excommunicated (i. e., by sentence) and sent to the Holy See for absolution.[32]

The two above-mentioned Councils of Avignon accepted also this ruling of the Synod of Riez, but with a slight modification. The report of the apothecaries was to be made to the episcopal curia rather than to the secular authorities.[33]

The Council of Avignon in 1326 listed among the cases—*casus*—which for absolution were reserved to the bishop the procuring of abortion on oneself or on another.[34] There was nothing exceptional, however, about constituting abortion as a reserved sin from which absolution had to be obtained either from the bishop or from his delegate. Numerous examples are found in the councils and synods held from the mid-thirteenth century onward.[35]

[28] Synod of Riez, can. 14—Mansi, XXIV, 581.

[29] Can. 18—Mansi, XXV, 754-755.

[30] Can. 22—Mansi, XXV, 1094.

[31] Can. 116—Mansi, XXVI, 537.

[32] Can. 13—Mansi, XXIV, 580.

[33] Council of 1326, can. 17—Mansi, XXV, 754; Council of 1337, can. 21—Mansi, XXV, 1094.

[34] Can. 22—Mansi, XXV, 757-758.

[35] Council of Frisia (1246), can. 4—Hartzheim, *Concilia Germaniae* (11 vols., Coloniae Augustae Agrippinensium, 1759-1790), III, 573 (all citations in this footnote are from this source); Synod of Liege (1287), cap. 4, n. 11—III, 687; Council of Breslau (1290)—III, 587; Synod of Würzburg (1298), stat. 21—IV, 36; Council of Utrecht (1310), stat. 3—IV, 168; Council of Mainz (1310)—IV, 221 (this canon adds as a reserved sin the procuring of sterility);

B. The Council of Trent

The Council of Trent (1545-1563) did not legislate specifically about the crime of abortion. However, the Council's statutes regarding iregularity and other vindictive penalties for homicide applied to the abortion of an *animated* fetus, for this kind and only this kind of abortion was commonly admitted to constitute true homicide.[86]

The Council of Trent held that one who was guilty of voluntary homicide was irregular, even if the crime was occult and not proved by judicial process; and it was forbidden to confer upon him any ecclesiastical benefice, even a simple benefice, that is, one without the *cura animarum*. Such a person, moreover, was perpetually excluded from every ecclesiastical order, benefice and

Council of Utrecht (1343), n. 3—IV, 344; Synod of Breslau (1446)—V, 295; Synod of Würzburg (1446)—V, 350; Council of Eichstaett (1447)—V, 369; Synod of Tournai (1481), cap. 4—V, 527; Council of Constance (1463)—V, 566; Synod of Bamberg (1491), tit. 58—V, 630; Synod of Schwerin (1492), stat. 55—V, 651; Provincial Council of Magdeburg (1503?)—V, 721; Synod of Ratisbon (1512)—VI, 111; Synod of Tournai (1520), cap. 7—VI, 155; Synod of Hildesheim (1539), cap. 50—VI, 338; Synod of Cambrai (1550), tit. 5—VI, 695 (if one in danger of death has been absolved by a priest without recourse to the bishop, the penance must be performed within a month under pain of reincurrence in the sin [sic]); Synod of Constance (1567), tit. 12, cap. 9—VII, 491 (only when the sin of abortion is occult, is the case not reserved to the bishop).

[86] Cf. teaching of the Decretalists, *supra*, Article III of this Chapter. See also Suarez, who expressly excludes the abortion of a non-animated fetus from the irregularity of the Council of Trent.—*De Censuris in Communi et in Particulari de Excommunicatione, Suspensione, et Interdicto, ac Praeterea de Irregularitate*, disputatio XLIV, sect. II, n. 13—*Opera Omnia* (26 vols., ed. nova a Carole Berton, Parisiis: Apud Ludovicum Vives, 1856-1866), XXIII-2, 432 (hereafter this work will be cited as *De Censuris*); De Graffiis, *Decisiones Aureae Casuum Conscientiae* (Venetiis, 1596), lib. II, cap. 62, n. 13.

Maiolus (+1597?) states: ". . . videtur homicida esse, et irregularis, etiamsi foetus occisus nondum formatus, nec animatus esset. . ." He adds that if the fetus was animated only the Pope can dispense, while if it was not animated the bishop can do so; if any doubt exists about the animation, then a dispensation must be obtained from the Pope, not only for the reception but also for the exercise of orders.—*Tractatus de Irregularitate et Aliis Canonicis Impedimentis* (Romae, 1619), lib. V, cap. 48, § 1, n. 4. Maiolus, however, was expressing an opinion—note his *videtur*—peculiarly his own.

office.[37] These provisions pertained to *voluntary* homicide, whether directly or indirectly voluntary.[38]

The law relative to the *accidental* abortion of an animated fetus followed the norms decreed for accidental homicide, i. e., *homicidium casuale,* which inflict the irregularity similarly as for voluntary homicide.[39] The Council stated that if homicide is committed not on set purpose, but accidentally (*ex casu*) or in self-defense, the matter was to be referred to the local ordinary, who must take cognizance of the case to verify the facts involved before a dispensation could be granted.[40] It was maintained by many that this statement of the Council does not of itself give the bishop the faculty to dispense, but that it refers to a necessary measure which must take place before the Holy See will commission the bishop to dispense. This matter refers only to the case of *public* homicide *ex casu.*[41]

[37] Sess. XIV, *de ref.,* c. 7: "Cum etiam qui per industriam occiderit proximum suum et per insidias, ab altari avelli debeat, qui sua voluntate homicidium perpetraverit, etiam si crimen id nec ordine judiciario probatum, nec alia ratione publicum, sed occultum fuerit, nullo tempore ad sacros ordines promoveri possit; nec illi aliqua ecclesiastica beneficia, etiam si curam non habeant animarum, conferri liceat; sed omni ordine, ac beneficio et officio ecclesiastico perpetuo careat."

[38] See, v. g., Laymann, *Theologia Moralis* (2 vols., Venetiis, 1719), lib. III, tract. III, pars III, cap. 10; P. Gasparri, *Tractatus Canonicus de Sacra Ordinatione* (2 vols., Parisiis, 1893-1894), n. 413.

[39] For the text of the Council of Trent, see footnote 40, immediately following. Cf. Laymann, *Theologia Moralis,* lib. III, tract. III, pars III, cap. 10, assert. I; Suarez, *De Censuris,* disp. XLV, sect. I, nn. 1-2, and especially sect. II, n. 5—*Opera Omnia,* XXIII-2, 425-426, and 429 respectively.

[40] Sess. XIV, *de ref.,* c. 7: "Si vero homicidium non ex proposito, sed casu, vel *vim vi repellendo, ut quis se a morte defenderet,* fuisse commissum narretur; quam ob causam etiam ad sacrorvm Ordinum et altaris ministerium, et beneficia quaecumque ac dignitates, jure quodammodo dispensatio debeatur; committatur loci Ordinario, aut ex causa metropolitano, seu viciniori episcopo; qui non nisi causa cognita, et probatis precibus ac narratis, nec aliter, dispensare possit."

[41] Cf. Suarez, *De Censuris,* disp. XLV, sect. 1, n. 2—*Opera Omnia,* XXIII-2, 448; Reiffenstuel, *Ius Canonicum Universum* (7 vols., Parisiis: Apud Ludovicum Vives, 1864-1870), lib. V, tit. 12, nn. 221-222; Schmalzgrueber, *Ius Ecclesiasticum Universum* (5 vols. in 12, Romae, 1843-1845), lib. V, tit. 12, n. 251; Barbosa seems to state that the Council gives the local ordinary this

Another reform chapter in the Council of Trent dealt expressly with the matter of dispensation from the irregularity of homicide. This canon gave bishops the faculty to dispense from all occult irregularities, except from voluntary homicide.[42] Hence, in virtue of this canon the bishops had the power to dispense from irregularity in cases of occult accidental homicide,[43] but not in cases of voluntary homicide, even though it was occult.[44] Still authors maintained as probable that the bishop could dispense from irregularity in cases of *occult* homicide when the death was not directly intended, but only indirectly and *in causa,* constituting *homicidium mixtum ex voluntario et casuali.* It was held that when the Council of Trent excepted voluntary homicide from the faculty of the bishops, it probably did not except this type of homicide.[45] In fact, it was maintained that in cases of homicide indirectly and *in causa* intended, the bishop could dispense to allow the exercise of at least minor orders even though the crime was public.[46]

power.—*De Officio et Potestate Episcopi* (Lugduni, 1628), alleg. 39, n. 54. Regarding this dispute, see Boenninghausen, *Tractatus Iuridico-Canonicus de Irregularitatibus* (3 fasc. in 1 vol., Monasterii, 1863-1864), II, 62-67.

42 Sess. XXIV, *de ref.,* c. 6: "Liceat episcopis in irregularitatibus omnibus et suspensionibus ex delicto occulto provenientibus, excepta ea quae oritur ex homicidio voluntario, et exceptis aliis deductis ad forum contentiosum dispensare. . ." For detailed commentary see: Lega, *Praelectiones in Textum Iuris Canonici de Delictis et Poenis* (2. ed., Romae, 1910), nn. 244 and 362 (hereafter this work will be cited as *De Delictis et Poenis*).

43 Cf. De Graffiis, *Decisiones Aureae Casuum Conscientiae,* lib. II, cap. 62, n. 10.

44 Laymann, *Theologia Moralis,* lib. III, tract. III, pars III, cap. 12, n. 1, assert. I.

45 "Probabile est, Episcopum dispensare posse cum homicida occulto, qui tamen hominis necem directe non intenderat, sed solum indirecte, et in causa. Exempla habes; Si quis mulierem gravidam incaute percussit, et abortum procreavit. . . Nam ejusmodi homicidia, cum non sint ex proposito directo, ac formali, non sunt simpliciter ac perfecte voluntaria, sed veluti mixta ex voluntario et casuali. . ."—Laymann, *op. cit.,* lib. III, tract. III, pars III, cap. 12, n. 2, assert. IV. Laymann cites authorities who uphold this opinion and some who disagree. See also Lega, *De Delictis et Poenis,* n. 362.

46 Cf. Laymann, *op. cit.,* lib. III, tract. III, pars III, cap. 12, n. 3, assert. VI.

CHAPTER VI

FROM SIXTUS V (1588) TO THE CODE OF CANON LAW

Pope Sixtus V (1585-1590) in his Constitution *"Effraenatam"* of October 29, 1588, pronounced very severe penalties against the crime of abortion.[1] Three years later, in 1591, Pope Gregory XIV (1590-1591) issued another Constitution dealing with abortion, the *"Sedes Apostolica."*[2] The legislation of these two papal constitutions remained in effect down to the promulgation of the Code of Canon Law in 1918 in so far as the irregularity and vindictive penalties were concerned, but was modified in part by the Constitution *"Apostolicae Sedis"* of Pope Pius IX in 1869 regarding the censure for abortion.

Article I. From Sixtus V to Pius IX

The details of the legislation to be considered in this article were enacted by Pope Sixtus V in the celebrated Constitution *"Effraenatam,"* but several important modifications were made by the Constitution *"Sedes Apostolica"* of Pope Gregory XIV. Because of the mutual inter-relation of the two Constitutions of Popes Sixtus and Gregory, and because of the short interval between the dates of their promulgation, they can best be treated as a single enactment. However, two dissimilarities must be emphasized.

Pope Gregory XIV modified the Constitution of Pope Sixtus V on two points.

(1) The legislation of Pope Sixtus had been sweeping. It penalized the abortion of a non-animated as well as of an animated fetus, thus effecting a radical change in the common law which had prevailed from the time of Gratian; it invoked the same penal sanctions

[1] *Codicis Iuris Canonici Fontes cura Emi. Petri Card. Gasparri Editi* (9 vols., Romae [postea Civitate Vaticana]: Typis Polyglottis Vaticanis, 1923-1939, [Vols. VII, VIII et IX *ed. cura et studio Emi. Iustiniani Card. Serédi*]), n. 165; hereafter this work will be cited as *Fontes.*

[2] *Fontes,* n. 173.

against whatever was studiously perpetrated either through the ministering of potions or poisons to render women sterile, or through the placing of obstacles or hindrances to prevent conception; it branded the evil counsellors and the scheming accomplices as well as the actual perpetrators.[3] The legislation of Pope Gregory restricted the comprehensive application of the penalties to the case which involved the abortion of an *animated* fetus. Punishments for the abortion of a non-animated fetus were to be determined as they had been before the Sixtine Constitution was issued.[4]

(2) An excommunication *ipso facto* incurred and reserved to the Holy See (except in *articulo mortis*) was one of the penalties of the Sixtine Constitution.[5] Gregory XIV altered this so as to reserve the absolution to the local ordinary.[6] In all matters other than these two drastic changes Gregory XIV confirmed the legislation of Pope Sixtus V.

The following pages present the law of the combined Constitutions of Pope Sixtus V and Gregory XIV. Briefly stated, this is the Sixtine-Gregorian law relative to abortion: all who procure, in any way whatsoever, the abortion of an animated fetus, and all who effectively co-operate in this crime, are liable to the following penalties. (1) All the penalties enacted by both civil and ecclesiastical law against voluntary homicide. (2) Excommunication reserved to the local ordinary. (3) Irregularity. (4) Incapacity for the obtaining of any ecclesiastical office, dignity, or benefice. (5) For clerics, the deprivation of clerical privileges and of every ecclesiastical office, dignity, or benefice. (6) For clerics, deposition and degradation, followed by commitment to the secular authorities for the punishments of civil law.

This legislation will be discussed under three heads: A. *Object* of the crime: what was the crime to be punished? B. *Subject* of the crime: who incurred the punishment? C. *Penalties* for the crime: what punishments awaited the offender?

[3] Const. "*Effraenatam,*" 29 oct. 1588—*Fontes,* n. 165.

[4] Const. "*Sedes Apostolica,*" 31 maii 1591, §3—*Fontes,* n. 173. Cf. *supra,* p. 57.

[5] "*Effraenatam,*" 29 oct. 1588, § 6—*Fontes,* n. 165.

[6] Const. "*Sedes Apostolica,*" 31 maii, 1591, § 2—*Fontes,* n. 173.

A. Object of the Crime

The object of the crime was the *abortion of an animated fetus.* Abortion is defined by Pope Sixtus V as *eiectio fetus immaturi.*[7] This definition, in sense if not in the exact terminology, became the standard,[8] even to the present day. Peculiarly, before Pope Sixtus V abortion was not expressly defined either in the ecclesiastical laws against the crime, or in the interpretation of these laws by the authors.

The abortion punished by this legislation is the abortion of an *animated* fetus. Pope Gregory XIV did not define the precise moment of animation, and the authors, with great unanimity, held to the common norm: the fortieth day after conception for males, the eightieth for females. That this was the commonly accepted norm is stated by Laymann (+1635),[9] Barbosa (+1649),[10] Reiffenstuel (+1703),[11] Viva (+c.1710),[12] Sporer (+1714),[13] Elbel (+1756),[14] and St. Alphonsus Liguori (+1787).[15] The Sacred Congregation of the Council referred to it as the more common and

[7] Const. "*Effraenatam,*" 29 oct. 1588, § 1—*Fontes,* n. 165.

[8] See, v. g., Francesco Bordoni of Parma (+1671), writing before 1641, who says that all commentators on the Constitution of Sixtus V thus define abortion.—*Variae Resolutiones seu Consilia Regularia* (Venetiis, 1641), resolutio XLV, n. 1; Barbosa, *Vota Decisiva et Consultativa Canonica,* lib. I, votum XII, nn. 2, 9; Sporer, *Theologia Moralis,* Supplementa by K. Kazenberger (3 vols., Venetiis, 1731), tom. III, pars IV, n. 696 (unless otherwise stated, this edition of Sporer's work will be quoted and cited); Elbel, *Theologia Moralis* (edidit Bierbaum, 2. ed., 3 vols., Paderbonae, 1895), pars X, n. 462; Jos. Pauwels, *Tractatus Theologicus de Casibus Reservatis,* tom. I, n. 140—Migne, *Theologiae Cursus Completus* (28 vols., Parisiis, 1837-1845), XVIII, 987 (hereafter Pauwel's work will be cited as *De Casibus Reservatis,* and Migne's will be abbreviated as *MTCC*).

[9] *Theologia Moralis,* lib. III, tract. III, pars III, cap. 4, n. 2.

[10] *Vota Decisiva et Consultativa Canonica,* lib. I, votum XII, n. 27, and *De Officio et Potestate Episcopi,* alleg. 51, n. 137.

[11] *Theologia Moralis* (Mutinae, 1737), tract. IX, dist. 3, n. 34.

[12] *Damnatae Theses* (12. ed., Patavii, 1732), ad prop. 34 Innoc. XI, n. 18.

[13] *Theologia Moralis,* tom. III, pars IV, n. 698.

[14] *Theologia Moralis,* pars X, n. 470.

[15] *Theologia Moralis* (ed. Gaudé, 4 vols., Romae, 1905-1912), lib. III, n. 394, q. 3°, and in n. 396 he says: "at least in the internal forum."

the accepted opinion.[16] In cases of doubt regarding the sex of the fetus, the norm of eighty days was accepted.[17]

It was pointed out by Pope Sixtus V that the abortion really had to follow—*effectu secuto*—that is, mere intention or an unsuccessful attempt was not the object of the penalties.[18] And the *effectu secuto* element had to be verified before any of the penalties were incurred. This restrictive feature applied not merely to the excommunication, but to other penalties and punishments as well.[19]

It may be noted here that the qualifying condition inherent in the phrase "*effectu secuto*" did not have to be verified to bring about the reservation of sin, a reservation which the major superiors of religious could constitute in their religious community.[20] Diocesan and provincial synods sometimes reserved the *sin* of abortion *effectu etiam non secuto*.[21]

B. Subject of the Crime

The penalties for abortion are pronounced against: (1) those who by any means whatsoever, whether physical or moral, procure

[16] *Sancti Marci Irregularitatis*, 8 iunii 1771.—*Thesaurus Resolutionum Sac. Congregationis Concilii*, XXXX (1771), 117. Cf. Pallottini, *Collectio Omnium Conclusionum et Resolutionum* (18 vols., Romae, 1868-1895), I, v. *abortus*, n. 38.

[17] Cf. St. Alphonsus Liguori, *Theologia Moralis*, III, n. 396.

[18] Const. "*Effraenatam*," 29 oct. 1588, § 1—*Fontes*, n. 165.

[19] Sporer, *Theologia Moralis*, tom. III, pars IV, nn. 714, 718, 722; Elbel, *Theologia Moralis*, pars X, n. 468; Porpora, *Theologia Moralis* (2 vols., Neapoli, 1855), I, tract. V, n. 507; Joannes Clericatus, *Erotemata Ecclesiastica* (4. ed., Venetiis, 1710), cap. 59, q. 4; Thesaurus, *De Poenis Ecclesiasticis* (ed. Giraldi, Romae, 1831), pars II, v. *abortus*; Pauwels, *De Casibus Reservatis*, tom. I, n. 159—*MTCC*, XVIII, 991; Sinistrari, *De Delictis et Poenis Tractatus Absolutissimus* (Romae, 1754), tit. VII, §1, nn. 33-34, 39, 75.

[20] Clemens VIII, decr. "*Sanctissimus*," 26 maii 1593, §1, n. 4: "Procuratio, auxilium, seu consilium ad abortum faciendum post animatum foetum, etiam effectu non sequuto."—*Fontes*, n. 177. For detailed commentary regarding this *casus*, cf. Pauwels, *De Casibus Reservatis*, tom. II, pars I, nn. 207-239—*MTCC*, XVIII, 1296-1307.

[21] Synod of Hildesheim (1652)—Hartzheim, *Concilia Germaniae*, IX, 803. Cf. also Bonacina, *Opera de Morali Theologia* (3 vols., Venetiis, 1687), tom. III, disp. II, q. II, puct. 10, nn. 4-6, and tom. II, disp. II, q. ult., sect. I, punct. 7, n. 6.

abortion, either by their own personal action or through the instrumentality of others; (2) those who assist or co-operate in the crime, again in any effective way whatsoever.

1. To Procure Abortion

To procure—*procurare*—abortion, while not explained by Pope Sixtus V, was understood as to effect intentionally or designedly and directly. Thus he incurred the penalties who brings about the abortion which was intended (expressly, or virtually by employing apt and efficacious means), and directly intended, that is, the abortion was desired as an end in itself or as means to an end. Thus is the term "*procurare*" explained by most authors, in fact by all who give an explanation of the term.[22] Others state simply that the penalties of this legislation were incurred for direct and indirect abortion, but offer no elucidation of the statement.[23]

2. To Co-operate in Abortion

Regarding complicity and co-operation in the crime of abortion, many authors are satisfied with the simple statement that co-operators incur all the penalties.[24] Sporer, however, gives a detailed discussion regarding co-operators in the crime of abortion. The general principle is that all who morally or physically give assistance incur the penalties.[25] The *mandans*, who strictly considered belongs to

[22] For example, De Graffiis (+1620) says the abortion must be effected "data opera, et ex proposito"; no censure is incurred when the abortion results "ex quadam imprudentia."—*Decisiones Aureae Casuum Conscientiae*, lib. II, cap. 63, n. 9. See also Thesaurus, *De Poenis Ecclesiasticis*, pars II, v. *abortus*; Sporer, *op. cit.*, tom. III, pars IV, nn. 714, 718, 743; Elbel, *op. cit.*, pars X, nn. 481-482; Joan. Antonelli, *Tractatus Posthumus de Juribus et Oneribus Clericorum* (Romae, 1669), lib. I, pars IV, cap. 56, n. 27.

[23] V. g., Reiffenstuel, *Ius Canonicum Universum*, lib. V, tit. 10, nn. 17, 19; Schmalzgrueber, *Ius Ecclesiasticum Universum*, lib. V, tit. 10, n. 31; Ferraris, *Bibliotheca* (9 vols., Romae, 1885-1899), v. *abortus*, n. 5.

[24] Reiffenstuel, *op. cit.*, lib. V, tit. 10, n. 19; Porpora, *Theologia Moralis*, I, tract. V, n. 507; Thesaurus, *De Poenis Ecclesiasticis*, pars II, v. *abortus*; Boenninghausen, *Tractatus Iuridico-Canonicus de Irregularitatibus*, II, 81. See also De Angelis, *Praelectiones Iuris Canonici* (5 tomes in 8 vols., Romae, 1877-1891), tom. IV, 222; Teodori, "Abortus,"—*Apollinaris*, V (1932), 252.

[25] *Theologia Moralis*, tom. III, pars IV, n. 724. Note that Bierbaum's edi-

the *procurantes,* the *consulens,* and the *consentiens,* incur all the penalties for abortion provided that they really influence the commission of the crime.[26] The common opinion considers as irregular one who tacitly consents, that is, one who says nothing, does nothing, offers no contradiction to one who is about to commit abortion, at least if the crime is considered as a favor to the one thus consenting. But this surely does not suffice, says Sporer, to incur the excommunication pronounced by Pope Sixtus V against abortion.[27]

The more common and acceptable opinion, followed earlier by Diana (+1633),[28] Laymann,[29] and De Lugo (+1660),[30] holds anyone excused from all the penalties of the Sixtine-Gregorian legislation if he merely ratifies, commends, approves, or even pays a remuneration for the abortion already committed, although the abortion be done for his own personal benefit or favor.[31] This opinion is founded upon the principle that no censure and no irregularity is *ipso facto* incurred by the mere subsequent ratification of a crime, unless this fact be expressly stated in the law.[32]

The position regarding co-operation as explained by Sporer is this. The irregularity and particularly the excommunication requires some *positive* co-operation. To co-operate only negatively (for example, by not impeding the crime although one be bound in justice to do so) does not involve the incurring of the penalties, for this is not real but interpretative co-operation. And it is a positive co-operation that is demanded by the Constitution of Pope Sixtus V.[33]

tion of Sporer's work (3 vols., Paderborn, 1901) omits the section "Abortus Moraliter Causatus" which appears in the Venice edition used in this study.

[26] *Op. cit.,* tom. III, pars IV, nn. 725, 726, 732.

[27] *Op. cit.,* tom. III, pars IV, n. 732.

[28] *Omnium Resolutionum Moralium Tomi Decem* (10 vols. in 5, Venetiis, 1728), tom. V, tract. VI, resolut. 29.

[29] *Theologia Moralis,* lib. III, tract. III, pars III, cap. 4, n. 6.

[30] *Disputationes Scholasticae et Morales* (8 vols., Parisiis, 1891-1894), *De Justitia et Jure,* disp. XIX, sect. II, n. 24.

[31] Sporer, *op. cit.,* tom. III, pars IV, n. 734; Ferraris, *Bibliotheca,* v. *abortus,* n. 8; St. Alphonsus Liguori, *Theologia Moralis,* lib. VII, n. 375; Felix Potestas (+1702), *Examen Ecclesiasticum* (Venetiis, 1751), tom. I, n. 2128.

[32] Suarez, *De Censuris,* disp. XLIV, sect. III, nn. 24-25—*Opera Omnia,* XXIII-2, 442-443.

[33] *Theologia Moralis,* tom. III, pars IV, nn. 735-737.

C. Penalties for the Crime

As not relevant to the purpose of this study the *ferendae sententiae* penalties of deposition and degradation, and the penalties of incapacitation for and the deprivation of privileges, offices, benefices, etc., are not considered on the following pages. This study is concerned with the irregularity and the excommunication for abortion.

1. Irregularity

All who procured the abortion of an animated fetus or cooperated [34] in the crime were *ipso facto* irregular. This irregularity prevented both the exercise and the reception of orders. As has been stated, after the Constitution of Pope Gregory XIV no irregularity was incurred for the abortion of a *non-animated* fetus.[35] And as a legal norm to determine the time of animation, the fortieth day after conception for males and the eightieth day for females was commonly admitted after the time of Pope Gregory XIV, just as it had been under the previous law. And even after the Constitution *"Apostolicae Sedis"* of Pope Pius IX, in 1869, abolished this dis-

[34] Lega, *Praelectiones in Textum Iuris Canonici de Iudiciis Ecclesiasticis* (2 books in 4 vols., Romae, 1896-1901), IV, n. 55 (hereafter to be cited as *Praelectiones de Iudiciis*); Lehmkuhl, *Theologia Moralis* (12. ed., 2 vols., Friburgi Brisgoviae, 1914), II, n. 1015. See also *supra*, pp. 66, 67.

[35] The Constitution was almost universally so understood. See, v. g., Thesaurus, *De Poenis Ecclesiasticis*, pars II, v. *abortus*, limitata 2; Sporer, *Theologia Moralis*, tom. III, pars IV, n. 714; Reiffenstuel, *Ius Canonicum Universum*, lib. V, tit. 10, n. 19; Ferraris, *Bibliotheca*, v. *abortus*, n. 4; St. Alphonsus Liguori, *Theologia Moralis*, lib. III, n. 395; Potestas, *Examen Ecclesiasticum*, tom. I, n. 2126; Barbosa, *De Officio et Potestate Episcopi*, alleg. 51, n. 136; Blundus, *Opus de Censuris et Irregularitate* (Romae, 1636), disp. VIII, art. III, dico 4; Sinistrari, *De Delictis et Poenis*, tit. VII, §X, n. 30; Heidenreich, "Dissertatio,"—*AKKR*, LXIII (1890), 377, 389. See also Gasparri, *Tractatus Canonicus de Sacra Ordinatione*, n. 405; and citations in immediately following footnotes 36 and 37.

Pennacchi (+1898) maintains that after the Constitution of Pope Gregory XIV irregularity for the abortion of a non-animated fetus remained in virtue of the legislation of the Council of Trent.—*De Abortu et Embryotomia seu Commentarium in Caput II. Sect. III. Const. "Apostolicae Sedis" Procurantes Abortum Effectu Sequuto* (Romae, 1884), pp. 27-28 (hereafter this work will be cited as *De Abortu*).

tinction as far as excommunication was concerned, both the distinction itself and the norm of forty and eighty days was still maintained regarding the irregularity, in accordance with the well-nigh universal teaching of the authors.[36] In cases of doubt the fetus was presumed to be female—that is, no irregularity was incurred until after the eightieth day following conception.[37] Pope Sixtus V reserved the dispensation from the irregularity contracted in consequence of an abortion to himself and his successors, even in occult cases, as authors admit.[38]

The irregularity for the crime of abortion, as established by the Sixtine-Gregorian legislation, remained in effect till the advent of the Code of Canon Law in 1918.

2. Excommunication

The penalties for procuring and for co-operating in securing the abortion of an animated fetus included an *ipso facto* incurred excommunication.[39] Absolution from this excommunication, which Pope Sixtus had reserved to the Holy See, was reserved to local ordinaries

[36] See, v. g., Göpfert, "De Excommunicatione et Irregularitate ex Abortu Oriunda,"—*Theologisch-praktische Quartalschrift* (Linz), XXXIX (1886), 374-375 (hereafter this periodical will be cited as *ThPrQs*); Bucceroni, *Institutiones Theologiae Moralis* (2. ed., 2 vols., Romae, 1893), II, n. 1204; Sägmüller, *Lehrbuch des katholischen Kirchenrechts* (3. ed., 2 vols., Freiburg im Breisgau, 1914), I, 227, footnote 2; and all the authors cited in the following footnote.

For the contrary opinion see: Boenninghausen, *Tractatus Iuridico-Canonicus de Irregularitatibus,* II, 83, footnote 8; Hinschius, *Das Kirchenrecht der Katholiken und Protestanten in Deutschland* (6 vols., Berlin, 1869-1897), V, 798, footnote 7.

[37] V. g., Heiner, *Die kirchlichen Censuren* (Paderborn, 1884), p. 249; Heidenreich, "Dissertatio,"—*AKKR,* LXIII (1890), 389-390; Hollweck, *Die kirchlichen Strafgesetze,* §163, note 8; Noldin, *De Poenis Ecclesiasticis* (6. ed., Oeniponte, 1907), n. 137; Wernz, *Ius Decretalium,* VI, 370, footnote 60; Lehmkuhl, *Theologia Moralis,* II, n. 1294.

[38] Const. *"Effraenatam,"* 29 oct. 1588, §8—*Fontes,* n. 165. Cf. Laymann, *Theologia Moralis,* lib. III, tract. III, pars III, cap. 12, n. 6; Sporer, *Theologia Moralis,* tom. III, pars IV, nn. 714-716; Elbel, *Theologia Moralis,* pars X, nn. 472-473.

[39] Sixtus V, const. *"Effraenatam,"* 29 oct. 1588, §7—*Fontes,* n. 165.

by Pope Gregory XIV, so that for the forum of conscience absolution could be given by any priest, secular or regular, who had been specially deputed by the local ordinary for these cases.[40]

Did this concession of Pope Gregory restrict the jurisdiction of the local ordinary to the *internal* forum, so that recourse to the Holy See was still required for absolution in the *external* forum? The text of Gregory's Constitution thus restricts the power of the local ordinary's delegate, but it is not equally clear regarding the power of the ordinary himself. Most commentators say nothing about this matter other than that the absolution which had formerly (under Pope Sixtus V) been reserved to the Holy Father was now conceded to the local ordinary, implying thereby that his power applied to the external as well as to the internal forum. But some state expressly that, when the crime was public, recourse still had to be made to the Holy See for absolution from the censure in the external forum—thus Diana,[41] Sporer,[42] Pauwels (+after 1759), [43] and De Angelis (+1881).[44]

Authors do not agree as to what kind of delegation was required for the priest to absolve from the censure. Some maintained that Pope Gregory's stipulation—*ad hos casus specialiter per loci Ordinarium deputatus*—was verified in the priest who had general faculties to absolve from cases reserved to the ordinary.[45] Others de-

[40] Const. "*Sedes Apostolica,*" 31 maii 1591, §2: ". . . quilibet Presbyter, tam saecularis, quam cuiusvis Ordinis regularis ad Christifidelium confessiones audiendas, et ad hos casus specialiter per loci Ordinarium deputatus, plenam, et liberam in foro conscientiae tantum, absolvendi habeat facultatem, eamdem prorsus, quam idem Sixtus Praedecessor, sibi ac suis successoribus reservavit."—*Fontes,* n. 173.

[41] *Omnium Resolutionum Moralium Tomi Decem,* tom. V, tract. IV, resolut. 7, n. 1.

[42] *Theologia Moralis,* tom. III, pars IV, n. 720.

[43] *Tractatus Theologicus de Casibus Reservatis,* tom. II, pars I, n. 236—*MTCC,* XVIII, 1306.

[44] *Praelectiones Iuris Canonici,* tom. IV, 221. Thus understood also by Lega, *Praelectiones de Iudiciis,* IV, n. 55. See also Hinschius, *Das Kirchenrecht der Katholiken und Protestanten in Deutschland,* V, 799, footnote 1; Giraldi, *Expositio Juris Pontificii iuxta Recentiorem Ecclesiae Disciplinam* (3 vols. in 2, Romae, 1829-1830), II, 758.

[45] V. g., Bonacina, *Opera de Morali Theologia,* tom. III, disp. II, q. II,

manded a special deputation which expressly mentioned the censure incurred for abortion.[46]

Article II. From Pius IX to the Code of Canon Law

The Constitution *"Apostolicae Sedis,"* promulgated by Pope Pius IX on October 12, 1869, reorganized to a great extent the penal legislation regarding censures, particularly the censures which are incurred *ipso facto*. The enactment in this Constitution concerning the crime of abortion replaced the legislation of Popes Sixtus V and Gregory XIV relating to the *censure;* however, no change was effected as to the irregularity.[47]

In the Constitution "Apostolicae Sedis," under the title *Excommunicationes Latae Sententiae Episcopis sive Ordinariis Reservatae,* is found the following enactment: *"Procurantes abortum, effectu secuto.*[48]

Since the text of this statute was incorporated into the Code of Canon Law, detailed discussion and interpretation thereof will be given in the second part of this study, the canonical commentary. At this point it will suffice to indicate the essential notions contained in the succinct text of Pius IX. Several factors peculiar to the law immediately preceding the Code are treated in more detail.

A. *"Procurantes"*

Relative to the word *"procurantes"* both the term and its concept were borrowed from the Constitution *"Effraenatam"* of Pope Sixtus V. Therefore the censure enacted by Pope Pius IX was in-

punct. 10, n. 16; Elbel, *Theologia Moralis,* pars X, n. 471; Porpora, *Theologia Moralis,* tom. I, n. 511. St. Alphonsus Liguori says that usage has interpreted it thus.—*Theologia Moralis,* lib. III, n. 397.

[46] V. g., Diana, *Omnium Resolutionum Moralium Tomi Decem,* tom. VII, tract. V, resolut. 15, 19; Sporer, *Theologia Moralis,* tom. III, pars IV, n. 720; Pauwels (*Tractatus Theologicus de Casibus Reservatis,* tom. I, nn. 162-164—*MTCC,* XVIII, 992-993) gives a detailed refutation of the contrary opinion; Salmanticenses, *Cursus Theologiae Moralis* (6 vols. in 4, Venetiis, 1728), tom. III, tract. XIII *de restitutione,* cap. II, punct. IV, §II, n. 72.

[47] Heidenreich, "Dissertatio,"—*AKKR,* LXIII (1890), 389; Pennacchi *De Abortu,* p. 27; Lehmkuhl, *Theologia Moralis,* II, n. 1294.

[48] §III, n. 2—*Fontes,* n. 552.

curred by those whom the Sixtine Constitution designated as *procuring* abortion, namely, "omnes et quicumque . . . qui . . . per se aut per interpositas personas, abortus, seu foetus immaturi . . . eiectionem procuraverint." [49] Although it was universally agreed that the term "*procurantes*" was to be understood and interpreted in the light of this parent legislation,[50] there was by no means a universal agreement regarding all the implications of meaning contained in the concept of the term "*procurantes*." This term will be discussed by way of an answer to two questions. 1. What is the essential notion of *procurare?* 2. What persons are called *procurantes?*

1. Notion of "*Procurare*"

Commentators agree that *procurare* means *aliquid studiose et ex industria quaerere.* This is further explained to mean that, in order to incur the censure for abortion, the abortion itself must be a *voluntarium directum seu in se.* A *voluntarium indirectum seu in causa* does not suffice. In a directly voluntary act the will is directed to the abortion either as an *end* in itself (v. g., the riddance of the fetus), or as a *means* to another end (v. g., the preservation of the mother's life). In an indirectly voluntary act the abortion is not of itself intended; it is intended only in so far as it follows as the result of some other act, even illicit, which is the true object of the will. Thus, one who strikes a pregnant woman out of anger but honestly does not intend the abortion, although perhaps he foresees that it will follow, does not incur the censure. And this holds true despite the fact that in his anger he may have been guilty of serious sin. On this principle and its explanation in relation to abortion authorities agreed.[51]

[49] §1—*Fontes,* n. 165.

[50] See, v. g., Pennacchi, *De Abortu,* p. 13; Parchalis de Siena, *Commentarius in Constitutionem Apostolicae Sedis* (3. ed., Romae, 1902), p. 163; D'Annibale, *In Constitutionem Apostolicae Sedis qua Censurae Latae Sententiae Limitantur Commentarii* (5. ed., Romae, 1909), n. 161 (hereafter this work will be referred to as *In Constitutionem A. S.*).

[51] V. g., D'Annibale, *In Constitutionem A. S.,* n. 159; Lega, *Praelectiones de Iudiciis,* n. 55; Noldin, *De Poenis Ecclesiasticis,* n. 93, 2; Wernz, *Ius Decretalium,* VI, n. 370 II; De Varceno, *Compendium Theologiae Moralis* (4. ed., 2 vols., Augustae Taurinorum, 1876), II, 494; Genicot, *Theologiae Moralis*

Furthermore, it is agreed that one can procure abortion either physically, that is, by blows, drugs, etc., or morally, for example, by terrorizing a woman to such an extent that abortion will ensue therefrom as an effect.[52]

2. What Persons Are Called "*Procurantes*"?

There is absolutely no doubt, except in the case of the mother herself,[53] that the censure is incurred by the person who wants the abortion and then apart from any intermediary effects it. Such a person's act of itself brings about the abortion, and hence this party certainly belongs to the class of the *procurantes*. But other persons, who may or who may not belong to this category, must be considered. They are comprised under the heads, (a) *Mandantes,* and (b) *Cooperatores et Mandatarii.*

(a) Mandantes

The crime of abortion can be effected by a person not only *per se* but also *per interpositas personas*—that is, through intermediary persons. The *mandans* is that person who intends an abortion but commissions or commands *(iubens)* another person who actually carries out the evil commission. Authors were almost unanimous in holding that the *mandans* incurs the excommunication.[54]

This position was supported by the following reasons. (1) Pope Sixtus V said that they procure abortion who effect the ejection of

Institutiones (2. ed., 2 vols., Lovanii, 1898), II, n. 608; Mocchegiani, *Iurisprudentia Ecclesiastica* (3 vols., Quaracchi, 1905), II, n. 527.

[52] See any commentator on the Constitution "*Apostolicae Sedis,*" v. g., those cited in the preceding footnote.

[53] The question whether the guilty mother herself incurred the censure of excommunication is discussed *infra,* Chapter XI, Article I.

[54] Only two of all the authors used in this study as commenting upon the legislation of Pope Pius IX excuse the *mandans.* Thus, Daris, *Tractatus de Censuris,* n. 241 (same idea as that expressed by Bucceroni, *infra*)—cited and quoted in Pennacchi, *De Abortu,* p. 14, footnote 1. Bucceroni (*Institutiones Theologiae Moralis,* II, n. 1204) maintains that he who gives no physical assistance but merely cooperates with his mandate is excused, for the law of Pius IX does not employ the phrase, "*per se aut per interpositas personas,*" as did the Constitution of Pope Sixtus V.

the fetus, either *per se* or *per interpositas personas,* and the *mandans* (and *iubens*) certainly does that very thing. (2) "Qui per alium facit, per seipsum facere videtur." (3) The *mandans* as the principal (moral) cause of the abortion properly comes under the designation *procurantes.* (4) No one maintains that *procurare* connotes only a physical action.[55]

(b) Cooperatores et Mandatarii

Just as almost all of the authors included the *mandans* under the censure as a *procurans,* so with almost the same unanimity they excluded those who co-operate in the crime as *consulentes* (advising and instructing), *faventes* (fostering and approving), and *opem praestantes* (e. g., preparing drugs).[56] They do so for this reason: Pope Sixtus V distinguished between *procurantes* and *cooperantes.* Although Pope Sixtus excommunicated the latter, Pope Pius IX speaks only of *procurantes,* and since the *cooperantes* are not mentioned in the law, they are not excommunicated.[57]

Closely associated with co-operators are the *mandatarii*—those who execute the commission of another. They, not wishing the abortion themselves, act not for themselves but *for another* and in the *name of another.* Thus, a physician may effect the abortion merely in obedience to the commission of a husband. Unquestionably the common opinion was that the *mere executors (mandatarii)* are included in the class of co-operators and hence are free from the excommunication.[58]

[55] Thus enumerated by Pennacchi, *De Abortu,* pp. 13-14. Regarding reason (4) it was shown that Bucceroni (see preceding footnote) requires some physical assistance on the part of the *mandans.*

[56] See authorities cited in footnotes 58 and 59 following.

[57] V. g., Pennacchi, *De Abortu,* p. 13; De Siena, *Commentarius in Const. A. S.,* p. 163; Ballerini-Palmieri, *Opus Theologicum Morale* (3. ed., 7 vols., Prati, 1898-1901), VII, n. 320.

[58] Lega, *Praelectiones de Iudiciis,* IV, n. 55; Heiner, *Die kirchlichen Censuren,* p. 247; D'Annibale, *In Constitutionem A. S.,* n. 161; De Varceno, *Compendium Theologiae Moralis,* II, 494; Ballerini-Palmieri, *Opus Theologicum Morale,* VII, n. 320; Gury, *Compendium Theologiae Moralis* (5. ed. in Germania, Ratisbonae, 1874), p. 901, col. 2, footnote 2; Cornelisse, *Compendium Theologiae Moralis* (3 vols., Quaracchi, 1908-1909, I, n. 589; Heidenreich,

Several authorities, however, while holding ordinary co-operators excused, said that the *mandatarii* are excommunicated. The proponents of this opinion said that the executors of the commission, although acting not for themselves, are really *procurantes,* because they actually effect the abortion. Pope Sixtus said that *procurantes* includes those who *per se* bring about the abortion, and he did not require that it be performed *pro se.*[59]

While the latter opinion surely seems to be intrinsically the more probable one, the weight of external authority rendered the milder viewpoint sufficiently probable for observance in actual practice.

B. "*Abortum*"

The concept of abortion—*eiectio foetus immaturi*—formulated by Pope Sixtus V continued to be accepted after the Constitution of Pius IX as the basis for a definition of this term. The essential notion conveyed by almost all the authors who define abortion is that it is "the ejection or expulsion from the womb of the mother of an immature fetus," namely, of a fetus not yet capable of extra-uterine existence.[60]

According to Pope Gregory XIV the abortion of only an *animated* fetus was punished by excommunication, but the Constitution of Pope Pius IX took no cognizance of the animation question. Therefore, in so far as the *censure* was concerned, no distinction was to be made between an animated and a non-animated fetus. On this

"Dissertatio,"—*AKKR,* LXIII (1890), 383, 378; Pennacchi, *De Abortu,* pp. 13, 15-17, but see also p. 23.

[59] Téphany, *Constitution "Apostolicae Sedis" Commentaire* (Tours, 1883), n. 410; Mocchegiani, *Iurisprudentia Ecclesiastica,* II, n. 522 (c), and n. 523 (d); *Commentator Patavinus,* n. 350—cited and quoted in Heidenreich, "Dissertatio,"—*AKKR,* LXIII (1890), 382; *NRT,* XI (1879), 325, n. 25.

[60] Cf., v. g., Heidenreich, "Dissertatio,"—*AKKR,* LXIII (1890), 376; D'Annibale, *In Constitutionem A. S.,* n. 159; Ballerini-Palmieri, *Opus Theologicum Morale,* II, n. 910; Pennacchi, *De Abortu,* p. 12; Genicot, *Theologiae Moralis Institutiones,* I, n. 374; Lega, *Praelectiones de Iudiciis,* IV, n. 55; Noldin, *De Poenis Ecclesiasticis,* n. 93, 1; see *supra,* p. 64.

all the authors were in agreement.[61] The distinction was still maintained, however, as a norm for determining the irregularity.[62]

C. "*Effectu Secuto*"

The abortion must actually take place, and must result from the causes or means employed to secure the abortion. Attempted abortion, therefore, was not punished by censure; nor was the penalty incurred if the abortion certainly or even probably resulted from causes other than those intentionally employed to secure the abortion.[63]

[61] As exemplifying this position, see: Pennacchi, *De Abortu*, p. 11; D'Annibale, *In Constitutionem A. S.*, n. 160; Lega, *Praelectiones de Iudiciis*, IV, n. 55; Mocchegiani, *Iurisprudentia Ecclesiastica*, II, n. 522 (a); Ballerini-Palmieri, *Opus Theologicum Morale*, VII, n. 320.

[62] Cf. *supra*, pp. 68, 69, and *infra*, p. 104.

[63] There is common agreement upon these points. See, v. g., De Varceno, *Compendium Theologiae Moralis*, II, 494; Gury, *Compendium Theologiae Moralis*, p. 901, col. 2, footnote 3; Pennacchi, *De Abortu*, pp. 23-24; D'Annibale, *In Constitutionem A. S.*, n. 161; Lega, *Praelectiones de Iudiciis*, IV, n. 55; Mocchegiani, *Iurisprudentia Ecclesiastica*, II, n. 526; Lehmkuhl, *Theologia Moralis*, II, n. 1247; Heidenreich, "Dissertatio,"—*AKKR*, LXIII (1890), 388.

GENERAL HISTORICAL SUMMARY

The early Fathers of the Church vigorously condemned abortion as murder, and thus laid the foundation for early conciliar legislation, which consistently regarded and punished abortion as murder.

The Council of Elvira (300[?]) demanded lifelong penance for any destruction of fetal life. Less stringent penalties, however, were enacted by later councils. Thus the Council of Ancyra (314) required ten years of public penance. St. Basil the great (+379), while accepting the ten-year penalty, definitely ruled out any consideration of the theory of delayed animation; moreover, he expressly included co-operators in the penalty for abortion. The Council of Lerida (524) stipulated a seven years' penance, and in addition for clerics perpetual deprivation and exclusion from ecclesiastical offices. St. Martin of Braga's (+c.580) modification of the statute of the Council of Ancyra placed under a ten year's penalty not only abortion but also any practices which aimed at preventing conception. The Trullan Synod of 692 repeated the canon of St. Basil which dealt with co-operators.

This conciliar legislation, particularly the statute of the Council of Ancyra, was accepted into the important canonical collections, both in the East and in the West, from the fifth century to the twelfth.

On the basis of Patristic statements, which had been incorporated in the works of Ivo of Chartres, Gratian formally introduced into ecclesiastical law the theory of delayed animation. Gratian maintained that abortion was murder only if it was perpetrated after the fetus has been animated.

This position was maintained by the Decretals of Pope Gregory IX, which embodied a letter of Pope Innocent III that admitted the presence of the irregularity only in consequence of the abortion of an animated fetus. Although several particular councils enacted an *ipso facto* incurred excommunication for abortion, and many local synods made abortion a reserved sin, no censure was found in the general law until the time of Pope Sixtus V.

The Sixtine Constitution "*Effraenatam*" of October 29, 1588, established the penalties of an *ipso facto* incurred excommunication reserved to the Holy See, of irregularity, of incapacitation for and deprivation of all ecclesiastical dignities, offices, and benefices. Clerics, moreover, were to be deposed, degraded and committed to the secular authorities. These penalties held not only for procuring the abortion either of an animated or of a non-animated fetus, but also for inducing sterilization and impeding conception. Pope Gregory XIV modified this legislation to apply only to abortion, and only to an abortion of an *animated* fetus. He likewise altered the reservation of the censure, so that priests especially delegated by the local ordinary could absolve from the censure in the internal forum. The irregularity established by Pope Sixtus V was confirmed and maintained down to the advent of the Code of Canon Law.

Pope Pius IX, in the Constitution "*Apostolicae Sedis,*" stated simply that those who successfully procured abortion *ipso facto* incurred excommunication reserved to ordinaries. Co-operators in abortion were excluded from incurring the censure. Cognizance was not taken of the theory of delayed animation.

Part Two

Canonical Commentary

INTRODUCTION TO COMMENTARY

The canons in the Code of Canon Law about which this commentary is primarily concerned are the following:

> **Canon 985.—Sunt irregulares ex delicto: . . . 4° Qui voluntarium homicidium perpetrarunt aut fetus humani abortum procuraverunt, effectu secuto, omnesque cooperantes;**
>
> **Canon 2350.—§ 1. Procurantes abortum, matre non excepta, incurrunt, effectu secuto, in excommunicationem latae sententiae Ordinario reservatam; et si sint clerici, praeterea deponantur.**

As indicated in the foreward to this study, the commentary aims solely to point out what in canon law precisely constitutes the crime of abortion, the results of which are *ipso facto* the censure of excommunication and the irregularity *ex delicto.* Although the irregularity is not strictly a canonical penalty, in this commentary both irregularity and excommunication are frequently referred to simply as the penalties for abortion.

Unless express exception is made or unless it is apparent from the context, the explanations and discussions which appear on the following pages apply equally to the incurring of censure and to the incurring of irregularity. For the canon which establishes the irregularity contemplates the identical crime of abortion as does the canon which inflicts the censure. That is to say, the crime of abortion in canon law is of one kind only; it results in the incurring of irregularity and censure, and for that matter, makes a cleric who is guilty of the crime liable to the *ferendae sententiae* penalty of deposition.[1] When a distinction is to be made between the censure and the irregularity this will be expressly noted.

[1] Cf. Vermeersch, *Theologiae Moralis Principia, Responsa, Concilia* (3. ed.,

This study presupposes the norms and fundamental principles of ecclesiastical law which apply to censures and to irregularities in general. Thus, when it is stated that in this or that particular instance of abortion excommunication or irregularity is incurred, it is presumed that the general requirements for crime as defined in canon law have been verified. For example, since every censure presupposes a *delictum*, the canonical notion of *delictum* is presumed, i. e., "an external, morally imputable violation of a law to which a sanction has been attached." [2]

Again, an absolutely essential postulate, if abortion is to give rise to a censure and an irregularity, is mortal sin. In a given case abortion may be seriously sinful without the notion of crime being verified, hence without involving a censure or an irregularity. On the other hand, both the irregularity and the censure of excommunication presuppose the grave sin of abortion—grave both internally (intention) and externally (action), i. e., subjectively and objectively, formally and materially.[3] Hence, whatever excuses from the serious sin of abortion excuses both from the irregularity and from the censure.[4] In this study of the *crime* of abortion the verification of mortal sin is presupposed.

4 vols., Romae: Università Gregoriana, 1933-1937), II, n. 584 (hereafter this work will be cited as *Theologiae Moralis Principia*).

[2] Canon 2195, §1.

[3] Cf. canons 986; 2195, §1; 2241, §1. "Ex ipsa delicti definitione . . . requiritur . . . peccatum grave, etiam qua externum est."—Vermeersch-Creusen, *Epitome Iuris Canonici* (3 vols., Vol. I, 6. ed., 1937, Vols. II-III, 5. ed., 1934-1936, Mechliniae: H. Dessain), III, n. 438 (hereafter this work will be cited as *Epitome*); Noldin-Schönegger, *De Censuris* (30. ed., Oeniponte: F. Rauch, 1936), n. 20; Cappello, *Tractatus Canonico-Moralis de Sacramentis* (3 vols. in 6), Vol. II, pars III, *De Sacra Ordinatione* (Taurinorum Augustae: Marietti, 1939), nn. 454, 2 and 455 (hereafter this volume will be cited as *De Sacra Ordinatione*); Sipos, *Enchiridion Iuris Canonici* (4. ed., Pécs: "Haladás R. T.," 1940), p. 984; Roberti, *De Delicti et Poenis*, Vol. I (altera impressio, Romae: Libraria Pontificii Instituti Utriusque Iuris, 1938), n. 75.

[4] Cf. canon 2218, §2; Cappello, *De Sacra Ordinatione*, n. 454, 1; Noldin-Schönegger, *De Censuris*, n. 20; Vermeersch-Creusen, *Epitome*, II, n. 254, 3. It may at times be difficult to prove this excuse in the external forum to the satisfaction of ecclesiastical superiors.

CHAPTER VII

EXPLANATION OF "TO PROCURE" ABORTION

ARTICLE I. THE TECHNICAL MEANING OF "TO PROCURE"

The term *procurare* has been associated with ecclesiastical legislation relative to abortion since the sixteenth century. In papal pre-Code laws it is employed by Popes Sixtus V (1585-1590),[1] Gregory XIV (1590-1591),[2] Clement VIII (1592-1605),[3] and Pius IX (1846-1878).[4] In the Code of Canon Law this term is used in reference both to the censure and to the irregularity incurred for abortion.[5]

In the two canons under consideration the term *procurare* has a specific and technical meaning. The expression does not mean merely the performance or commission, the doing, effecting, or bringing about of an abortion. Abortion may be effected without being procured, in the technical sense of the term. It is important, therefore, to understand the technical import of the expression "*to procure* abortion."

Both before and after the Code, there is general agreement among authors as to the essential notions contained in the phrase "to procure" as it is employed in relation to the crime of abortion.

It may be said that he procures an abortion who *intends* it and *designedly* or *purposely* brings it about by employing *means in themselves efficacious* for the purpose. This is the form commonly employed by authors in defining the procuring of an abortion. In fact almost every definition or explanation employs some, if not all, of the terms italicized in the above statement. Certainly all adequate explanations will contain these two elements as essential

[1] Const. "*Effraenatam,*" 29 oct. 1588, §1.—*Fontes,* n. 165.

[2] Const. "*Sedes Apostolica,*" 31 maii 1591, §1.—*Fontes,* n. 173.

[3] Decr. "*Sanctissimus,*" 26 maii 1593, §1, 4.—*Fontes,* n. 177.

[4] Const. "*Apostolicae Sedis,*" 12 oct. 1869, §III, n. 2.—*Fontes,* n. 552.

[5] Canons 2350, §1, and 985, 4°, respectively.

to the concept of procuring abortion: (1) intention (direct), and (2) deliberate use of efficacious means.[6]

Abortion which begets censure and irregularity is variously labeled by authors as *voluntarium in se*, or *voluntarium directum*, or "directly procured," or simply "direct abortion." On the other hand, abortion not subject to censure and irregularity is designated as abortion which is *voluntarium in causa*, or *voluntarium indirectum*, or "indirectly procured," or simply "indirect."[7]

It is essential to note the particular sense in which the various terms are employed by individual authors. Sometimes these respective terms are used interchangeably; sometimes not. Particularly with reference to the terms direct and indirect, the authors frequently stress the element of *means*. The effecting of the abortion is viewed from the aspect of strict physical causality of the means employed to produce the abortion. Thus the abortion is designated direct abortion when the means touch the fetus itself. At other times reference is made primarily to *intention*, and the abortion is called direct abortion when it is intended, indirect when it is not intended. In view of these facts the writer considers the terms mentioned in the preceding paragraph neither essential nor particularly helpful in correctly understanding the crime (not the sin) of abortion in canon law. In so far as the notion of *procuring* abortion is concerned, it appears sufficient to state that the crime is

[6] See, for example, Cappello, *De Censuris*, n. 384; Vermeersch-Creusen, *Epitome*, III, n. 551; Coronata, *Institutiones*, IV, p. 459, n. 2015; Noldin-Schönegger, *De Censuris*, n. 92, 2; Chelodi, *Ius Poenale* (4. ed., recognita et aucta a Vigilio Dalpiaz, Tridenti: Ardesi, 1935), n. 80; I. Teodori, "Abortus,"—*Apollinaris*, V (1932), 352.

[7] V. g., Cappello, *De Sacra Ordinatione*, n. 506, 6, and *De Censuris*, n. 384; Vermeersch-Creusen, *Epitome*, III, n. 551; Loiano, *Institutiones Theologiae Moralis ad Normam Iuris Canonici*, II (Taurini: Marietti, 1935), nn. 389-394 (hereafter this work will be cited as *Institutiones Theologiae Moralis*); Salucci, *Il Diritto Penale* (2 vols., Subiaco: Tipografia dei Monasteri, 1926-1930), II, 221; Ayrinhac-Lydon, *Penal Legislation* (New York: Benziger Brothers, 1936), pp. 30, 240; Brys, "De Poenis Latae Sententiae,"—*Collationes Brugenses*, XXXIII (1933), 188, and "De Poena in Procurantes Abortum,"—*Collationes Brugenses*, XXXIV (1934), 43.

committed when the abortion (1) is intended (not merely permitted) and (2) results from the means employed for this purpose.[8]

Article II. Intention and Efficacious Means

Before any discussion of the elements of intention and means, it may be in place again to emphasize the impossibility of the existence of the crime of abortion which begets censure and irregularity unless the abortion itself be seriously sinful as regards both the internal and the external acts. That is, there must be present both the formal and the material sin of abortion: the internal act of intending abortion must be a serious sin, and the external action effecting the ejection of the fetus must be a serious sin of abortion. If either internally (subjectively) or externally (objectively) the abortion is not a mortal sin, there is no crime in the concept of canon law—hence no censure or irregularity.

A. Intention

Only the element of intention is here considered. The crime requires that the abortion be intended, that is, the ejection of the fetus must be willed either as an end in itself or as a means to some other end. Thus the pregnancy may be interrupted simply to rid the prospective mother of an unwanted child, or on the plea of safeguarding the health of the mother. In both cases the abortion is the object which is willed; hence, on the score of intention, the crime exists. Abortion thus intended, as an end in itself or as means to an end, is frequently designated directly intended abortion.

Eliminated from the category of procured abortion—therefore, from the realm of crime—is what is technically known as *permitted* abortion. Although often referred to as indirectly intended, strictly considered the abortion in this case is not intended at all, but is

[8] Cipollini: "*Procurantes abortum:* sunt qui abortum intendunt et efficaciter causant. . ."—*De Censuris Latae Sententiae* (Taurini: Marietti, 1925), n. 77, p. 173; Vermeersch: "*Procurant* abortum quicumque actione physica vel morali, efficaci et directa intentione, efficiunt ut expellatur fetus. . ."—*Theologiae Moralis Principia,* II, n. 584. Regarding confusion due to terminology, see *infra,* pp. 86-88.

merely permitted. It is permitted to follow as the perhaps even foreseen effect of some other action, this other action being intended for a purpose independent of abortion. This permitted abortion may sometimes be licit in accordance with the well-known principles which involve the double effect. But even in the event that it be seriously sinful, it does not constitute the crime of procuring abortion, for the abortion is not intended but only permitted. The classic example given by authors is that of a man who motivated by anger or hatred strikes a woman with child, intending harm to the woman only. Even though he foresees the abortion which actually follows from his attack upon the woman, he does not intend the abortion; he intends harm to the woman and only permits the abortion. Consequently, despite serious sin, he does not commit the crime of abortion.[9]

To summarize: Considered solely from the aspect of intention, in order that the crime of abortion be verified, hence in order that the censure and irregularity be incurred, it is required and it also suffices that the abortion be intended, willed either as an end in itself or as a means to some other end.

B. Efficacious Means

Intention of itself suffices for the sin but not for the crime of abortion. The second essential element in the notion of *procured* abortion is that it be brought about by deliberate use of means in themselves (*de* or *in se*) efficacious.

Deliberate use—The external action (use of means) causing abortion must be motivated by the intention of obtaining the effect of abortion. Thus, if one who has in mind to commit abortion, accidentally or unknowingly places an act which results in the ejection of the fetus, he is not guilty of the crime of abortion. This is true

[9] Cf., v. g., Coronata, *Institutiones,* IV, 459; Vermeersch-Creusen, *Epitome,* III, n. 551; Cappello, *De Censuris,* n. 385; Noldin-Schönegger, *De Censuris,* n. 92, 2; Bouuaert-Simenon, *Manuale Juris Canonici* (3 vols., Vols. I, III, 3. ed., Gandae et Leodi: H. Dessain, 1931), III, 381; Farrugia, *Commentarium in Censuras Latae Sententiae Codicis Juris Canonici* (2. ed., Melitae: Ex Typographia "Malta" Fortunati Mizzi, 1921), n. 68 (hereafter this work will be cited as *Commentarium*).

even though serious sin is committed, for example, if the abortion results from gross carelessness.

Means—The means employed to effect abortion may be either *physical* (v. g., drugs) or *moral* (v. g., psychic trauma, as terror inflicted upon the mother). The abortion may be caused by a *single* means (v. g., the use of drugs alone) or the cause may be *multiple,* consisting of a combination of means (v. g., the use of drugs and x-rays). The means may be *simple,* i. e., *simplex,* consisting of a single individual act (v. g., curettage); or it may be *complex,* a series of acts following naturally and necessarily one from another and ultimately resulting in the expulsion of the fetus (v. g., certain drugs produce abortion by their primary toxic effect upon the intestines or kidneys).

In themselves efficacious—In order that canonical crime be present, the abortion must be caused solely by the means deliberately used for this purpose, be they physical or moral, single or multiple, simple or complex, or a combination thereof. If some external cause other than the one or several designedly employed is responsible for the abortion, then there is no crime.

In order to be efficacious the means employed need not be such which of themselves *(ex natura sua)* have no other immediate effect than that of abortion. Nor is it required that the means be an infallible cause of abortion. Nor is it essential that they be effective at every stage of pregnancy, or on every woman. Thus, at certain stages during pregnancy the fetus can more readily be dislodged from its uterine site. Certain women are naturally predisposed to abortion.[10] Predispositions in these cases are occasions, not causes of abortion. They merely facilitate the abortion by enabling less potent means to secure the desired effect, and do not excuse from the canonical penalties on the grounds that the means were in themselves not efficacious.[11]

In short, the means effecting abortion need not be efficacious in an absolute sense. It is merely required, and hence it suffices, that they be relatively efficacious, i. e., in a particular case the means used actually cause the abortion. After all, the main criterion of

[10] Cf. Taussig, *Abortion,* pp. 78, 112.

[11] Cf. Heidenreich, "Dissertatio,"—*AKKR,* LXIII (1890), 387.

their efficacy is that the abortion has actually resulted from their use as an effect from an efficient cause.[12]

Article III. Further Observations Regarding the "Procuring of Abortion"

In the preceding pages of this chapter it has been pointed out that *procured* abortion, hence the crime with its consequent censure and irregularity, is constituted when the abortion (1) is actually intended (internal act); (2) results from the deliberate use of efficacious means (external act); and (3) exists as a serious sin of abortion in regard to both the internal and the external acts. That in principle is the notion of *procured* abortion. But it seems in place to make several additional observations regarding this principle as applied in practice.

Abortifacient means viewed from the aspect of physical causality alone may be called direct or indirect. The means are direct when the abortion is the immediate and primary natural result of their use—quite generally they touch the fetus itself. The means may be called indirect when the abortion is only the mediate or secondary result, i. e., the natural and primary terminus of the means or action is some organ or portion of the mother's body, but not the fetus. In accordance with this distinction of means, the abortion itself is often referred to as direct or indirect.[13] This distinction is of fundamental importance in determining the morality of abortion in a particular case. If in the sense just described, the abortion is direct, it can never be licit; if it is indirect, it may sometimes be licitly permitted in accordance with the principles of the double effect.

Simply because from the viewpoint of physical causality of the means alone the abortion is indirect, it does not follow that the

[12] Coronata, *Institutiones,* IV, 459: "Indifferens est quonam medio procurans utatur . . . dummodo tamen medium adhibitum de se sufficiens sit et de facto abortum producat."

Suffice it to state at this point that in practice it may sometimes be difficult to apply this norm. The matter of doubtful efficacy is treated under the discussion of *"Effectu Secuto," infra,* Chapter IX.

[13] See J. McCarthy, "Direct and Indirect Abortion—Ectopic Pregnancy," —*IER,* 5th series, LV (1940), 60; Merkelbach, *Quaestiones de Embryologia et de Sterilizatione* (Liège: La Pensée Catholique, 1937), p. 28.

crime of abortion will never be verified. This could possibly be concluded, although erroneously, from the statement that only a direct abortion, and not an indirect abortion, involves the canonical penalties.[14] In the question of canonical penalties the element of intention must also be considered—the *finis operantis* as well as the *finis operis*. And in the distinction discussed above only the aspect of physical causality is taken into account.

Hence the writer can not agree with Loiano's contention that the crime of abortion exists only when the means employed have no other immediate end than abortion. By "end" he must refer to the *finis operis,* for he adds that when the means have this immediate end, namely, abortion, no contrary intention *(finis operantis)* can excuse from the crime.[15] When the means or method used does not directly touch the fetus, or is such that frequently it does not cause abortion, he considers the means *per accidens* efficacious. And abortion which results from the use of such means, although employed with the intention of causing abortion, constitutes sin but not the crime of abortion, according to Loiano.[16]

It is quite true that when one places an action which he knows will *ex natura sua* directly and immediately result in abortion—the *finis operis*—he can not escape the penalties for the crime simply by pleading that he has not intended the abortion which follows. His actions give the lie to his words.

But even though the abortion may be called indirect from the aspect of physical causality on the part of the means used, yet the crime is verified also in the following case. A woman intends simply

14 Cf. *supra,* p. 82.

15 "Ad delictum abortus requiritur ut mediis procuretur *de se* et *vere efficacibus;* nempe quando nullum alium finem *immediatum* illa media habent, nisi abortus procurationem. Quando ita est, nulla alia intentio a delicto excusare potest, nisi coniuncta sit cum bona fide."—*Institutiones Theologiae Moralis,* II, n. 389, p. 468.

16 ". . . quoad indirectam abortus procurationem haberi aliquando potest peccatum non vero delictum censura punitum. Nempe habetur peccatum quando applicantur media *per accidens* tantum influentia in abortum . . . cum intentione illum procurandi. . ." ". . . si actio *directe* attingit foetum, ut incisio amnii, etc. tunc erit per se efficax, secus vero tantum per accidens."—*Op. cit.,* II, n. 389, p. 468. It should be added here that Loiano's treatment of abortion from the moral aspect appears quite satisfactory.

and solely to be rid of an unwanted child. As quasi-self-justification and for the sake of external appearances she selects means which do not directly touch the fetus. Drugs may be taken which immediately or directly affect other organs or parts of the mother's body, such as the intestines, kidneys, liver, etc. Thus certain preparations directly affect the smooth muscle of the intestine; this action may cause uterine contractions whereby the fetus is expelled. Similarly, hysterectomy may be selected. This surgical operation removes the uterus itself, and consequently also the fetus contained therein. From the viewpoint of strict physical causality, the abortion may be called indirect because the method was indirect. Yet the crime of abortion is committed, for the sinful intention is present, and the external action is efficacious and beyond doubt constitutes the serious material sin of abortion. Nothing more is required for the verification of the crime in this case.[17]

If, however, the use of these drugs or the hysterectomy had been medically indicated as necessary to safeguard the life of the mother (as quinine in case of malaria, hysterectomy in case of cancerous uterus) the crime would not be present even though the abortion had been intended. The intention would be seriously sinful, but objectively the action which effected the ejection of the fetus would have been morally licit and justifiable, as is assumed in the case; the grave *external* sin of abortion would not have been present. Hence no penalty would have been incurred.

[17] See Cipollini, *De Censuris Latae Sententiae,* pp. 173-175. It must be remembered that the present discussion deals only with *intention* and *means.* Other elements of the crime are treated later.

CHAPTER VIII

DEFINITION AND EXPLANATION OF "ABORTION"

ARTICLE I. ABORTION DEFINED

THE word "abortion" is derived from *aborior,* which in its strict etymological sense means death. The term abortion, however, has come to signify the delivery of an immature fetus.[1]

In medical circles abortion is commonly defined as "the detachment or expulsion, or a combination of both, of the pre-viable ovum,"[2] or simply as "the interruption of pregnancy before the fetus is viable, i. e., capable of extra-uterine existence."[3] The abortion may moreover be either spontaneous (non-intentional) or induced (intentional and artificial), the latter type being subdivided into therapeutic (to safeguard the life or health of the mother) and criminal (without sanction of civil law).[4]

In popular parlance the term abortion carries the implication of criminal interference, and, consequently, when it is employed it frequently is restricted to criminal abortion. Miscarriage, on the other hand, has a much wider meaning in the popular mind. It may

[1] Forcellini-Facciolati-Furlanetti, *Lexicon Totius Latinitatis* (4 vols., Patavii, 1864-1887), I, 15-16.

The matter of fetal maturity and development in relation to abortion is discussed in Article IV of this Chapter. At this point, however, it may be well to indicate the various terms employed in both ecclesiastical and medical circles to designate the stages and degrees of fetal development. The fetus is spoken of as *mature* when it has developed to the normal term of pregnancy; *premature* or *viable* when it is capable of living outside the mother, although it has not attained the normal term of gestation; *immature* or *non-viable* (also *pre-viable*) when it is incapable of extra-uterine existence. See *infra,* first paragraph of Article IV of this Chapter, p. 108.

[2] Taussig, *Abortion,* p. 480; see also p. 21.

[3] De Lee, *The Principles and Practice of Obstetrics* (7. ed., Philadelphia: W. B. Saunders Co., 1938), p. 127. See also Stander, *Williams Obstetrics* (8. ed., New York: D. Appleton-Century Co., [1941]), p. 808.

[4] Cf. Taussig, *op cit.,* pp. 22-23, 480-481.

refer to interruptions of pregnancy occurring at any time before term [5] or it may be restricted in its meaning to apply to cases terminating before viability.[6] Furthermore, it may include every termination of pregnancy, or it may be limited to cases of non-deliberate, and particularly to the so-called non-criminal terminations.[7] While the laity prefers the term miscarriage and ordinarily employs the term abortion only in its restricted sense of criminal terminations of pregnancy, medical authorities frown upon this restriction and are wont to speak of all interruptions of pregnancy before viability as abortion.[8]

In canon law, on the other hand, the abortion which is the object of the crime is defined by canonists and moralists alike as "the ejection of an immature fetus"—*eiectio fetus immaturi.*[9] This is the classical definition for abortion, and because it was employed by Pope Sixtus V, it enjoys an acknowledgment of an official character.[10] From the sixteenth century to the present day this concise statement, although sometimes expressed in slightly varying terminology, has enjoyed universal acceptation by canonists and moralists.[11] And it is altogether admissible to retain this definition for the purposes of this study, provided that it be correctly understood. The explanation of this definition will follow in three articles, which consider respectively the factors involved in the terms, "ejection," "fetus," and "immature."

[5] De Lee, *op. cit.*, p. 127.

[6] Stander, *op. cit.*, p. 808.

[7] Taussig, *op. cit.*, p. 482; O'Malley, *The Ethics of Medical Homicide and Mutilation* (New York: The Devin-Adair Co., 1922), p. 92.

[8] See De Lee, *op. cit.*, p. 474; Stander, *op. cit.*, p. 808; Taussig, *op. cit.*, p. 483.

[9] See, v. g., Vermeersch, *Theologiae Moralis Principia,* II, n. 580, 3; Chelodi, *Ius Poenale,* n. 80; Vermeersch-Creusen, *Epitome,* III, n. 551; Cerato, *Censurae Vigentes* (2. ed., Patavii: Typis Seminarii, 1921), p. 100; De Siena, *Commentarius Censurarum juxta Novum Codicem Juris Canonici* (Neapoli: Ex Typis Francisci Giannini et Filiorum, 1918), p. 53 (hereafter this work will be cited as *Commentarius Censurarum*).

[10] Const. *"Effraenatam,"* 29 oct. 1588, §1: ". . . qui . . . abortus, seu foetus immaturi . . . eiectionem procuraverint. . ."—*Fontes,* n. 165.

[11] Cf. *supra,* p. 64 and footnote 8, *ibid.*, and p. 75.

Article II. Meaning of "Ejection"

A. Refers to Entire Physical Process of Abortion

The physical process of abortion includes several stages, for example, the internal detachment of the fetus (or ovisac) from its uterine site; its passage through the cervix of the uterus into the vaginal canal; its ultimate external ejection from the vaginal canal into the outside world. The essentially lethal act in this process is the internal separation or detachment of the immature fetus from its uterine site. Once this has been effected, the external expulsion will follow, either naturally and spontaneously or with further assistance on the part of an operator.

Abortion has been defined as the ejection of an immature fetus. How is the term "ejection" to be understood? Is it to be restricted to the final ejection of the fetus, or is it to be understood as referring to the entire mechanism of abortion? In still other words, does abortion consist solely in the external ejection of the immature fetus or does it include the entire physical mechanism which results in this external ejection?

It is the writer's opinion that the term "ejection" must be referred to the entire ejective process and is not to be restricted solely to the final expulsion of the fetus from the body of the mother, this final expulsion being but one stage, albeit the final one, in the process of abortion. It is true that the abortion is not complete until the fetus is delivered externally; [12] then abortion *has taken place.* But even before the external appearance of the fetus, for example, once the detachment from the uterine site has been begun, abortion *is taking place.* Those steps which of physical necessity must precede the external expulsion are a part of the abortifacient process. It would be contrary to physical facts, therefore, to hold that abortion consists solely in the external ejection of the fetus. When abortion is said to be the ejection of a fetus, the term "ejection" is indicative and in a way descriptive of the entire process.[13] Perhaps

[12] There is no reference here to what obstetricians technically refer to as incomplete abortion. See De Lee, *The Principles and Practice of Obstetrics,* p. 482.

[13] Cf. Merkelbach, *Quaestiones de Embryologia et de Ministratione Baptismatis* (2. ed., Liège: La Pensée Catholique, 1928), p. 35.

to emphasize or at least to hint at this feature, abortion is sometimes defined as "the *separation* of a living non-viable fetus from its mother,"[14] or again as "the *detachment* or expulsion, or combination of both, of the previable ovum."[15]

It will be seen in the course of this study that not a few important observations and conclusions relative to the crime of abortion depend upon a correct appreciation of the physical process of abortion itself, which appreciation is not in evidence in many canonical treatises dealing with this crime.

B. Final Ejection Need Not Be Spontaneous

In the foregoing explanation it was stated that an operator (or accoucheur) may be at hand to assist in the final expulsion of the fetus from the mother. In actual practice such assistance is very often given in cases of deliberately induced abortion. In view of the fact that some authors seem to place great emphasis upon abortion being *ejection*,[16] it may perhaps be concluded by some that such external assistance by an accoucheur would militate against the notion of true abortion and hence the crime of abortion would not be verified.

It is unwarranted, however, to restrict abortion to such deliberate interference which merely sets the mechanism of abortion to work, and then stands idly by, as it were, to await the ultimate

[14] J. McCarthy, "Direct and Indirect Abortion—Ectopic Pregnancy,"—*Irish Ecclesiastical Record* (hereafter to be abbreviated as *IER*), 5th series, LV (1940), 59-66, especially 59. Italics above inserted.

[15] Taussig, *Abortion*, p. 480. Italics above inserted.

[16] This is frequently done in order to distinguish abortion from various forms of embryotomy. Thus authors say that abortion is *ejectio* while craniotomy is (1) *occisio* (Haine, *Theologiae Moralis Elementa* [3. ed., 4 vols., Lovanii, 1894], IV, 486), or (2) *extractio* (Berardi, *Praxis*, n. 1263), or (3) a procedure which "*per se primo* non sit eiectiva fetus sed laesiva eiusdem fetus. . ."—Iorio, *Theologia Moralis iuxta methodum Compendii Ioannis P. Gury S. I. et Raphaelis Tummolo S. I.* (6. ed., 3 vols., Neapoli: M. D'Auria, 1938-1940), II, n. 216, 4° (hereafter this work will be cited as *Theologia Moralis*).

Some authors point to *ejectio* as opposed to *egressio*, thereby distinguishing between deliberate and spontaneous abortion.—See Cappello, *De Censuris*, n. 384; Cerato, *Censurae Vigentes*, p. 100; Iorio, *Theologia Moralis*, II, n. 512.

spontaneous external ejection of the fetus. Some methods of effecting abortion are such that once the process has been set into motion, no further external assistance may be required to secure the external ejection.[17] But other methods involve the technique of digital removal of the fetus or extraction by instrument. And these methods are among those commonly employed by the more competent professional abortionist. Both classes of abortion techniques are described by medical authorities as means of inducing abortion.[18]

Even though the fetus were extracted from the womb itself, and not removed merely from the vaginal canal, the process certainly would constitute abortion. The mere technique or method employed to secure the delivery of an immature fetus is something accidental to the notion of abortion. If the removal of an immature fetus by extraction, or by any method which is strictly and precisely not an ejection, is not abortion, what is it? Certainly it is not craniotomy or one of the operations technically known as forms of embryotomy, for often the fetus will be delivered at a time when it is physically impossible to perform these operations.[19]

Hence, there should be no forced and unwarranted insistence upon the precise literal meaning of ejection when that term is in connection with abortion.[20]

[17] In general this feature is proper to the non-surgical techniques. See Taussig, *Abortion*, pp. 323-327; Stander, *Williams Obstetrics*, p. 1124. Not infrequently, however, these methods will require additional interference or assistance to finally evacuate the fetus. See Stander, *op. cit.*, p. 1118.

[18] Cf. Taussig, *op. cit.*, pp. 322-340 with 190-201; Stander, *op. cit.*, pp. 1117-1118, 1124-1134.

[19] *Cf. infra*, pp. 129-130.

[20] The following perhaps illustrates the unhappy result which will follow from too much insistence upon terms as mere words rather than as being based upon facts. Piatus Montensis (*Praelectiones Juris Regularis* [2. ed., 2 vols., Tornaci, 1898], II, 561) insists that abortion must be understood strictly as "*proprie ejectio*." Yet he says that the "*eductio*" of the fetus to the light of day by means of an operation to save the mother, e.g., by a section of the uterus, would be true abortion. Certainly "*eductio*" is not "*proprie ejectio*"; still he admits that the "*eductio*" in this case constitutes abortion. And if an "*eductio*" constitutes an abortion, why would not an "*extractio*" have the same effect? "*Eductio*" just as little as "*extractio*" can be designated "PROPRIE *ejectio*."

ARTICLE III. MEANING OF "FETUS"

It would be quite sufficient to state that the object of the process of ejection is the fetus which is immature. Nevertheless, in view of the fact that mention is sometimes made of other qualifications (qualifications which, in fact, are presupposed), this article will consider what is meant by a "fetus," and specifically, by a fetus that is "living" and "human." The element of immaturity is treated in the following article.

A. True Fetus

Medical authorities sometimes employ the term "fetus" in a restricted sense in so far as they distinguish between ovum, embryo and fetus.[21] However, the canonical definition of abortion uses the term "fetus" in a wide sense to include the developing child from the very beginning of its existence within the mother. In other words, fetus here refers to the product of conception at any and all stages of its uterine existence, hence, from the very moment of conception onward.[22]

The term "fetus" has always been employed thus in canonical jurisprudence. In the pre-Code law the product of conception was classified as a non-animated (unformed) fetus from the time of conception until the infusion of the rational soul, and as an animated (formed) fetus after the infusion of the soul. But regardless of the stage of intra-uterine existence or development, regardless of anima-

[21] The term ovum is used to designate the product of conception during the first two weeks of its existence; embryo, during the third, fourth and fifth weeks; fetus, from the beginning of the sixth week till birth.—Cf. Stander, *Williams Obstetrics*, pp. 151-154; Taussig, *Abortion*, pp. 481-482; O'Malley, *The Ethics of Medical Homicide and Mutilation*, pp. 33, 50-54. These terms, however, do not have a definitely fixed meaning even in medical circles, as may be seen by anyone who consults the citations given above. Thus in Taussig's definition of abortion (quoted, *supra*, p. 89) ovum is used in a wide sense—to include embryo and fetus as well.

[22] Conception (which is variously termed fecundation, impregnation or fertilization) may be defined as "the union of the male and female elements of procreation [i. e., spermatozoid and ovum respectively] from which union a new being is developed."—De Lee, *The Principles and Practice of Obstetrics*, p. 20. Conception therefore marks the beginning of gestation or pregnancy.

tion or non-animation, the product of conception was designated a fetus.

Today, therefore, it may be said that canonists and moralists universally affirm that no matter how soon after conception abortion is effected it involves the ejection of a fetus,[23] Augustine's opinion to the contrary notwithstanding.[24] Hence the following principle is established: Censure and irregularity result from every abortion, regardless of the stage of fetal development (of course the fetus must be immature), so long as it is established with some degree of certitude that a fetus really exists, or, in other words, that conception has taken place and thus pregnancy has begun.[25]

In actual practice it is not always easy to establish the existence of a fetus, that is, the fact of pregnancy. There is no question *post factum* when that which is expelled is observed to be a fetus. But particularly during the early stages of pregnancy this observation will be difficult and often impossible for the ordinary person and sometimes for the trained technician.[26] However, in the absence of positive indication to the contrary, that which is expelled must be considered a fetus once the fact of pregnancy has been established.[27]

The mere fact of coitus indicates only possibility, not even prob-

[23] Coronata, *Institutiones,* IV, 458; Ferreres, *Compendium Theologiae Moralis* (13. ed., 6. post codicem, 2 vols., Barcinone: Eugenius Subirana, 1925), II, n. 1268; Genicot-Salsmans, *Institutiones Theologiae Moralis* (14. ed., 7. post codicem, 2 vols., Bruxellis: L'Edition Universelle, 1939), II, nn. 607, 633; Mothon, *Institutions Canoniques* (3 vols., Paris: Desclée, 1922-1924), II, 760. See also authors cited in following footnote 25.

[24] *A Commentary on the New Code of Canon Law* (hereafter to be cited as *Commentary*), IV (3. ed., St. Louis: B. Herder Book Co., 1925), 490. But see also *op. cit.,* VIII (3. ed., St. Louis: B. Herder Book Co., 1931), 399.

[25] Cf., v. g., Vermeersch-Creusen, *Epitome,* III, n. 551; Noldin-Schönegger, *De Censuris,* n. 92, 1; Cappello, *De Censuris,* n. 385; Pistocchi, *I Canoni Penali* (Torino-Roma: Marietti, 1925), p. 171; Cavigioli, *De Censuris Latae Sententiae* (Torino: Libreria Editrice Internazionale, 1918), n. 161; Sole, *De Delictis et Poenis* (Romae: Fridericus Pustet, 1920), pp. 316-317; McHugh, "Casus Moralis—The Victim in the Crime of Abortion,"—*HPR,* XXXIV (1933-1934), 417-418.

[26] "The ovum in the first weeks . . . can be studied only with a microscope."—De Lee, *op. cit.,* p. 56. See also Stander, *op. cit.,* p. 151.

[27] Cf. Cipollini, *De Censuris Latae Sententiae,* p. 176.

ability that conception has taken place or will take place. The possibility of establishing that the coitus was fruitful and how soon thereafter conception followed depends upon many factors. Hence it is the verdict of medical authorities today that it is impossible to determine *exactly* that a particular coitus will be fruitful,[28] and how soon conception will follow fruitful coitus.[29]

There is, of course, a time when and there are means by which pregnancy can be diagnosed with certitude, and this before the expulsion of the fetus. It is beyond the scope of this study to enter into a detailed delineation of all the signs and symptoms of pregnancy. May it suffice to point out briefly that obstetricians frequently classify the signs of pregnancy into three groups: positive, probable, presumptive.[30] (1) Positive signs, which ordinarily cannot be detected until after the fourth month, establish the fact of pregnancy beyond doubt. They may be designated as unequivocal proof.[31] (2) Probable signs, some of which may be found as early as the sixth week, make the pregnancy highly probable. They can in fact make the diagnosis *morally certain.*[32] (3) Presumptive signs may be noted at any time during pregnancy; but if they alone

[28] Several of the factors that must be verified if conception is to follow, that is, if the coitus is to be fruitful, are the following: (1) presence of an ovum—ordinarily, only one is discharged from the ovary each month (Stander, *op. cit.*, p. 52); (2) fertility of this ovum—its life span is perhaps not more than one day (cf. De Lee, *op. cit.*, p. 24); (3) an active spermatozoid must reach this ovum—the sperm may live several days after coitus, although it may lose its potency sooner (cf. De Lee, *op. cit.*, p. 23; Stander, *op. cit.*, p. 88).

[29] It may be a matter of minutes; it may be a matter of hours before the active spermatozoid reaches the fertilizable ovum.—Cf. De Lee, *op. cit.*, p. 23; Stander, *op. cit.*, p. 87.

[30] Regarding the following classification, with detailed discussion, see Stander, *op. cit.*, pp. 241-251; and also De Lee, *op. cit.*, pp. 287-310.

[31] Cf. De Lee, *op. cit.*, p. 288. After giving a list of signs proper to the first trimester, De Lee says: "Taken all together, with careful exclusion of conflicting conditions, a positive diagnosis may be made toward the end of the first three months."—*Op. cit.*, p. 304. This "positive diagnosis" of De Lee is really equivalent to physical and absolute certitude. Moral certitude sometimes will be had earlier.

[32] Although termed probable signs, Stander (*op. cit.*, p. 249) admits that they can give rise to moral certitude. It may be noted here that the Ascheim-Zondek and the Friedman hormone tests for pregnancy are held to be 98 to 99 per cent accurate when properly performed. Ordinarily they can be success-

form the basis of the diagnosis, they give rise to probability at most.

The logical question which follows now is: What degree of certitude must be had that a fetus exists, that conception has really taken place? It appears unquestionable that at least moral certitude is required and that moral certitude suffices. Moral certitude excludes all prudent and positive doubt—doubt that furnishes solid probability for truth to rest on the opposite side. It is this certitude which governs the ordinary affairs of man. And it seems unreasonable to demand the presence of absolute or physical certitude—certitude which excludes not only the positive probability but even the very possibility of the opposite being true.

Hence, so long as it is morally certain that a fetus exists (that conception has taken place) the canonical notion of abortion can be verified and censure and irregularity can be incurred.

Since conception must have taken place before the crime of abortion can be committed, it is apparent that contraceptive measures are not identical with abortion.[33]

Authors sometimes illustrate this by saying that the penalties for abortion are not incurred by the expelling of the semen from the body of the woman *statim post copulam,* for then conception is not yet certain.[34] Some add that to perform such actions within twenty-four hours after coitus is not to be construed as abortion.[35]

This is true, for *statim post copulam* or within twenty-four hours no certitude can be had that conception has taken place (as has been pointed out on the immediately preceding pages) and there is, of course, no certitude that a fetus is present until the fact of conception has been certified. But since these authors do not state

fully performed from five to six weeks after the last menstrual period or from ten days to two weeks after the missed period.—Cf. Stander, *op. cit.,* pp. 251-254; De Lee, *op. cit.,* pp. 294-296; Taussig, *Abortion,* pp. 139-141.

[33] Under the present law contraceptive practices are not subjected to canonical penalties. This was not the case in former times, however, as was indicated above, p. 63.

[34] Cappello, *De Censuris,* n. 385; Noldin-Schönegger, *De Censuris,* n. 92, 1; Coronata, *Institutiones,* IV, 458; Hilarius a Sexten, *Tractatus de Censuris Ecclesiasticis,* pp. 217-218; Brys, "De Poena in Procurantes Abortum,"—*Collationes Brugenses,* XXXIV (1934), 43.

[35] Augustine, *Commentary,* VIII, 399; Coronata, *op. cit.,* p. 458.

the contrary it perhaps might be inferred that the crime of abortion must or can be considered as certain when such actions, or others undertaken with the intention of causing abortion, are performed not *statim* or within twenty-four hours, but after an interval of several days or even after a few weeks. That, however, would be an invalid and false assumption. It is of course *possible* that a true fetus be expelled by such actions at such times,[36] but, as previously shown, during the early weeks of pregnancy there is no practical way of establishing this fact with any degree of certitude. Probability at most is all that can be had.

The principle remains, however: no matter at what time abortion is brought about, if the presence of an immature fetus is morally certain, the crime is verified and the penalties are incurred.

It may be noted here that there likewise is no true abortion if that which is expelled from the mother is not a true fetus but a tumor or growth, although abortion may have been intended and a true fetus was thought to be present before the ejection was effected. If there is founded and reasonable doubt in this regard, canonical penalties are imputed to none of the parties concerned.[37]

B. Living Fetus

Sometimes it is expressly mentioned in definitions of abortion,[38] but in any event it is always understood, that the crime of abortion necessarily is performed on a *living* fetus.

[36] If a particular coitus has been fruitful, i. e., if conception does occur, it can take place in much less time than twenty-four hours; perhaps even in a few minutes.—See Stander, *Williams Obstetrics*, p. 87; De Lee, *The Principles and Practice of Obstetrics*, p. 23. But at least three to four days are required for the fertilized ovum (fetus) to negotiate the trip to the uterine cavity from the lateral portion of the Fallopian tube, where conception (fertilization) usually takes place.—See Stander, *op. cit.*, pp. 85, 88; De Lee, *op. cit.*, p. 22. It may be noted, moreover, that the ordinary douching and syringing is very unlikely to reach the uterine cavity.

[37] See Hilarius a Sexten, *Tractatus de Censuris Ecclesiasticis*, p. 218; Noldin-Schönegger, *De Censuris*, n. 92; Iorio, *Theologia Moralis*, II, n. 512; Salucci, *Il Diritto Penale*, II, 223; Brys, "De Poena in Procurantes Abortum," —*Collationes Brugenses*, XXXIV (1934), 42-46, especially 43.

[38] E. g., Prümmer, *Manuale Theologiae Moralis* (8. ed., recognita ab E. M. Münch, 2 vols., Friburgi Brisgoviae: Herder & Co., 1935-1936), II, n. 137; Beste, *Introductio in Codicem* (Collegeville, Minn.: St. John's Abbey Press

There can be no question of the crime, therefore, when the fetus is dead before the process of abortion is begun. Thus, when a physician effects the ejection of a fetus that is known to be dead, sin is not committed, much less a crime. Even though the fetus is thought to be alive, it may become evident upon the final ejection of the fetus that it had been dead before the abortion was undertaken, or at least that its death can not be attributed to the abortion. Although serious *sin* is committed in this case, the *crime* of abortion is not present; consequently the canonical penalties are not incurred.[39] The fact of pre-abortion death often can be determined only by a physician; but sometimes this fact may be apparent from the very condition and appearance of the fetus, e. g., when maceration has set in. However, as medical authorities likewise admit,[40] once it is certain that conception has taken place, the presumption is that the fetus is alive. And this presumption must maintain until there are positive and probable indications to the contrary.[41] In cases of positive doubt *post factum, reo favendum est*. That is, the canonical penalties for abortion cannot be imputed if it is positively probable that the fetus was dead before abortion was attempted.[42]

The crime of abortion is not had if the fetus continues to live after ejection from the mother, despite the fact that its ejection may have been deliberately undertaken at a time when the fetus is judged to be incapable of living independently of the mother. The very fact that the fetus continues to survive proves beyond doubt that it is not immature (i. e., not previable), but viable. Therefore,

[1938]), p. 953; Jombart, *Le Sacrament de L'Ordre* (Paris: Editions Spes, 1930), p. 78; Hilarius a Sexten, *Tractatus de Censuris Ecclesiasticis*, p. 330.

[39] Salucci, *Il Diritto Penale*, II, 223-224; Pistocchi, *I Canoni Penali*, pp. 170-171; Coronata, *Institutiones*, IV, 459; Noldin-Schönegger, *De Censuris*, n. 92, 1; Hilarius a Sexten, *Tractatus de Censuris Ecclesiasticis*, p. 118; Heidenreich, "Dissertatio,"—*AKKR*, LXIII (1890), 377.

[40] See Stander, *Williams Obstetrics*, p. 256.

[41] Cf. Iorio, *Theologia Moralis*, II, n. 512.

[42] Cf. Salucci, *op. cit.*, II, 222; Heidenreich, *art. cit.*, p. 377; Chelodi, *Ius Poenale*, n. 80, 1; Sole, (*De Delictis et Poenis*, p. 317) says that there is no censure when it can certainly be concluded that the fetus died previously. This is true, but a censure can likewise not be imputed when it is solidly probable that the death was not caused by the abortion.

there is no question of abortion, but rather of premature birth.[43] Moreover, it is inherent in the very notion of the crime that the abortion prove fatal.[44]

It has been pointed out above that if the fetus is previously dead or does not subsequently die, its delivery from the mother does not constitute the crime of abortion. An evident conclusion from this statement is the following: to have the crime of abortion, the fetus must be alive before the process of ejection is begun. But, must it still be alive when it is finally delivered, although it dies almost immediately thereafter? In other words, is the crime committed even though the fetus dies during the process and consequently is dead upon arrival into the outside world?

Most canonists do not treat this point *ex professo*. There are some authors who state that the fetus need not be living when it is finally ejected externally, but this position is naturally forced upon these authors inasmuch as they place craniotomy and its kindred destructive operations under the crime of abortion.[45] And of course a fetus subjected to these operations is not expected to be living when extracted from the maternal body.[46] Sometimes writers assume that in abortion the fetus is as a matter of actual fact always or at

[43] Lega states: "Sane ad incurrendam irregularitatem requiritur ut foetus eiectus moriatur."—*De Delictis et Poenis*, p. 419, note 1. Premature birth is discussed in the following article regarding immaturity, *infra*, Article IV of this Chapter.

[44] Cf. Vermeersch, *Theologiae Moralis Principia*, II, n. 580, 3; De Meester, *Juris Canonici et Juris Canonico-Civilis Compendium* (ed. nova, 3 vols. in 4, Brugis: Desclée, 1921-1928), Vol. III, pars 2, 259 (hereafter this work will be cited as *Compendium*); F. Bordoni, *Variae Resolutiones*, resolutio XLV, n. 2: ". . . ad ejiciendum foetum animatum mortifere. . ." Cornelisse, *Compendium Theologiae Moralis*, II, n. 488.

It is most amazing that Blat holds abortion to be verified so that irregularity would be incurred ". . . etiamsi casu supervixerit [fetus]; canon enim non distinguit. . ."—*Commentarium Textus Codicis Iuris Canonici*, 5 vols. in 6, Vol. III, pars I, *De Sacramentis* (2. ed., Romae: Collegio "Angelico," 1924), n. 349.

[45] V. g., Wernz-Vidal, *Ius Canonicum*, Vol. VII, *Ius Poenale Ecclesiasticum*, pp. 514 and 517; Göpfert, "De Excommunicatione et Irregularitate ex Abortu Oriunda,"—*ThPrQs*, XXXIX (1886), 373-375, especially 373; Wernz, *Ius Decretalium*, VI, nn. 369-370.

[46] Craniotomy is discussed in Chapter X; see especially p. 122.

least generally living at the time of external ejection—an assumption by no means justified by concrete facts, as will be pointed out shortly. Yet, these authors do not state that, if the fetus is not alive at the time of its external ejection, there is no abortion.[47] Cavigioli seems expressly to require that the fetus die only after the external expulsion from the mother.[48]

As Coronata correctly observes, it is not essential to the traditional notion of abortion that the fetus be actually living when it is finally ejected.[49] If the contrary were true, surely some authors down through the years would have called attention to so essential a feature, but this has not been done, although, as mentioned, some writers assume that the fetus is living. On the other hand, there are several authors, both before and after the Code, who expressly state that abortion (not including craniotomy, etc., under abortion) can be verified although the fetus dies during the process of expulsion and before the final ejection.[50]

The writer's position on this question is the following: It is indeed presupposed but it also suffices for the crime of abortion that the immature (previable) fetus is alive when the process of abortion is begun, and that its subsequent death be attributable to the abortion. Whether the fetus dies during the process and hence before its external ejection, or whether it is delivered alive and then dies as a result of the premature ejection is something accidental in the concept of abortion.

[47] Thus, Wernz-Vidal, *op. cit.*, p. 517; Coronata, *Institutiones*, IV, 461. In order to show that craniotomy is more malicious than abortion, these authors state that after abortion the ejected fetus can still be baptized, while after craniotomy this is impossible (since the fetus is dead).

[48] *De Censuris Latae Sententiae*, n. 161: ". . . requiritur . . . foetum ejici, i. e., extra alvum expelli, utique vi directe adhibita, et exinde foetum interire."

[49] *Institutiones*, IV, 460. Coronata, however, includes craniotomy under the crime.

[50] Heidenreich, "Dissertatio,"—*AKKR*, LXIII (1890), 377 (but note that on p. 300, footnote 1, he identifies craniotomy with abortion); Prümmer, "Zieht die Kraniotomie die Exkommunikation nach sich?"—*ThPrQs*, LXIII (1910), 587; Pistocchi, *I Canoni Penali*, p. 171; Cipollini, *De Censuris Latae Sententiae*, p. 175. The same is implied by: Hilarius a Sexten, *Tractatus de Censuris Ecclesiasticis*, p. 218; Salucci, *Il Diritto Penale*, II, 223-224.

Whether or not the immature fetus will be alive after expulsion from the mother depends both upon the degree of development it has attained before gestation is interrupted and upon the method employed to bring about the abortion.

Other things being equal, the more advanced the fetal development, the less quickly will the fetus succumb; consequently, during the latter half of the period of non-viability there is more likelihood that the fetus will survive for a short time following its expulsion. This is true theoretically at least.[51] But practically, perhaps the most decisive factor in this matter is the technique or means used to perform the abortion.

If only a casual study is undertaken of the various methods of inducing abortion which are employed by both the non-professional abortionist, including the mother herself, and by the skilled and unskilled professional abortionist, the following conclusion appears inevitable: cases in which the immature fetus is certainly alive for even a short time after external ejection constitute a minority occurrence in deliberately induced abortions.[52]

It may be recalled, moreover, that in cases of deliberately effected abortion, the destruction of the fetus is in truth the purpose of the procedure. Practically, therefore, no effort will be made to have the aborted fetus alive for even a few moments after its expulsion; rather, the contrary effect will be sought and is to be expected.

If canonical penalties were to be incurred only when the aborted fetus is still alive at its final ejection, it would be a comparatively simple matter to insure the retention of the detached fetus within the vaginal canal for a short time so as to insure its death and thus to escape the incurring of the canonical penalties. Would this procedure not be true abortion? Assuredly it would be true abortion,

[51] Cf. Stander, *Williams Obstetrics,* pp. 153-154; De Lee, *The Principles and Practice of Obstetrics,* p. 58.

[52] This conclusion was confirmed by the practicing obstetricians consulted by the writer. For a detailed description of the means employed to induce abortion, see the following: Lewin, *Die Fruchtabtreibung durch Gifte und andere Mittel* (Berlin: Stilke, 1925), the entire work; De Lee, *op. cit.,* pp. 477, 486-490, 1165-1169; Taussig, *Abortion,* pp. 190-201, 325-337, 352-357. Eschbach (*Disputationes Physiologico-Theologicae,* II, 239) very aptly says: "Neque putes abortus procurationem consueto ita fieri, ut foetus vivens edatur."

considered such by medical authorities as well as by the ordinary layman. If it is not abortion, what is it?

Therefore, when the process of ejection causes the death of the immature fetus either before or after its external expulsion, the crime of abortion exists and the censure and the irregularity are incurred.

C. Human Fetus

Before the advent of the Code of Canon Law canonical jurisprudence was not wont to employ the term "human" in reference to the fetus as the object of the crime of abortion. Canon 985, 4°, however, states that irregularity is incurred by those who procure the "abortion of a ***human*** fetus." Yet canon 2350, § 1, says nothing about a ***human*** fetus; it states simply that an excommunication is incurred by those who "procure abortion." [53] What, then, is the significance of the term "human" as employed in canon 985, 4°, and why is it not to be found in canon 2350, § 1?

It may be mentioned first of all that the use of the term "human" does not imply that the Church deemed it necessary to exclude the case of an abortion of an animal fetus. Nor does it imply that the ovum of a woman may possibly be fertilized by non-human spermatozoids. Despite the variant terminology in the respective canons, both contemplate one and the same kind of abortion.[54] It is the almost universal opinion of canonists who discuss the textual variation that the term "human" as used in canon 985, 4°, designates a change from the pre-Code law regarding irregularity, namely, the theory of delayed animation may no longer be applied as a norm relative to the incurring of the irregularity for abortion.[55]

A brief review of the papal enactments concerning the crime of

[53] It is indeed strange to find Stockums saying that the term "human" is found in both canons.—"Abortus und kirchliches Strafrecht,"—*Theologie und Glaube*, XV (1923), 97.

[54] This latter statement is questioned by no authority. See Vermeersch, *Theologiae Moralis Principia*, II, n. 584; Hilarius a Sexten, *Tractatus de Censuris Ecclesiasticis*, p. 330; Ferreres, *Compendium Theologiae Moralis*, II, 569, footnote 1: "Codex vero eodem modo intelligendus quoad abortum sive pro excommunicatione, sive pro irregularitate."

[55] Authorities are cited, *infra*, footnote 58 of this Chapter.

abortion will explain the variant wording in the pertinent canons of the Code.

Pope Gregory XIV in 1591 modified the legislation enacted three years previously by Pope Sixtus V so that the censure and the irregularity for abortion were incurred only when an animated fetus was involved. In 1869 the Constitution *"Apostolicae Sedis"* of Pope Pius IX omitted the phrase "animated fetus" of the previous law and stated simply that excommunication was incurred for "procuring abortion." And the wording of the *"Apostolicae Sedis"* regarding abortion was embodied in canon 2350, § 1. Due to the omission of any reference to the question of animation, canonists after 1869 agreed that the distinction between animated and non-animated fetus was of no practical significance with regard to the incurring of the censure; the ejection of an immature fetus, whether animated or not, gave rise to the penalty.[56]

Since the Constitution *"Apostolicae Sedis"* dealt with censures only, and was not concerned with irregularities, recognized canonists continued to hold, until the Code became obligatory, that the animation-distinction could be applied as a practical norm to determine whether or not irregularity was incurred. Thus there was no irregularity if the aborted fetus could not according to the long-standing categories of an animated and a non-animated fetus be brought within the former of these classifications.[57]

What the Constitution *"Apostolicae Sedis"* accomplished regarding the incurring of the censure, canon 985, 4°, effected for the irregularity—the elimination of the distinction between the animated and non-animated fetus as a practical norm. While the pre-Code law in reference to irregularity spoke of the "abortion of an animated fetus," canon 985, 4°, mentions "abortion of a human fetus." Thus the present-day law concerning the irregularity not only omitted "animated fetus" (as did the Constitution of Pope Pius IX, and consequently, canon 2350, § 1, which was taken from this Constitution), but substituted in its place the phrase "human fetus" (which Pius IX did not, hence, neither does canon 2350, § 1).

[56] Regarding the legislation of Popes Sixtus V and Gregory XIV, see *supra*, pp. 62-65; regarding the Constitution of Pope Pius IX, see *supra*, pp. 75-76.

[57] Cf. *supra*, pp. 68-69.

In the insertion of the phrase "human fetus" in canon 985, 4°, the authors see a definite indication of the legislator's will to eliminate the distinction between the animated and non-animated fetus. Any fetus conceived by woman, so long as it is living, is a human fetus in the sense intended by canon law. Consequently, in so far as the verification of the element *human* is concerned, irregularity and censure too are incurred for abortion effected at any time after the definitely established fact of conception.[58] In any event, the law today makes no distinction regarding animation of the fetus, and "ubi lex non distinguit, nec nos distinguere debemus." Consequently, it is to be maintained today in accordance with the almost universal agreement among theologians and canonists [59] that the animation-distinction is not applicable to the crime of abortion regarding

[58] See v. g., Cappello, *De Censuris,* n. 384, and *De Sacra Ordinatione,* n. 506, 9; Vermeersch, *Theologiae Moralis Principia,* III, n. 657; Cerato, *Censurae Vigentes,* pp. 100, 273; Vermeersch-Creusen, *Epitome,* II, n. 257; Ferreres, *Compendium Theologiae Moralis,* II, n. 898; Wernz-Vidal, *Ius Canonicum,* IV-1, 336, note 462; Salucci, *Il Diritto Penale,* II, 222; Woywod, *A Practical Commentary on the Code of Canon Law* (5. ed., 2 vols., New York: Jos. F. Wagner, 1939), I, 532 (hereafter this work will be cited as *Practical Commentary*); Prümmer, *Manuale Theologiae Moralis,* II, n. 144; Jombart, *Le Sacrement de L'Ordre,* p. 78; Bouuaert-Simenon, *Manuale Juris Canonici,* II, 181; Cavigioli, *De Censuris Latae Sententiae,* n. 161; Stockums, *"Abortus und kirchliches Strafrecht,"—Theologie und Glaube,* XV (1923), 97; "Abortion and the Embryological Theory,"—*ER,* LXXVIII (1928), 626-631, especially 630-631; Brys, "De Poena in Procurantes Abortum,"—*Collationes Brugenses,* XXXIV (1934), 43-44; see also citations in the following footnote. Regarding Augustine's opinion, cf. *infra,* footnotes 60 and 65 of this Chapter.

[59] In addition to the citations in the preceding footnote, see the following: Ferreres, *Compendium Theologiae Moralis,* II, n. 1268; Noldin-Schmitt, *Summa Theologiae Moralis* (24. ed., 3 vols., Oeniponte: F. Rauch, 1936), II, n. 342; Loiano, *Institutiones Theologiae Moralis,* II, n. 389; Iorio, *Theologia Moralis,* II, nn. 512, 519, and III, n. 962, p. 566, footnote 1; De Meester, *Compendium,* III, pars II, 310; Noldin-Schönegger, *De Censuris,* n. 92, 1; Coronata, *Institutiones,* IV, p. 458; Sipos, *Enchiridion Iuris Canonici,* p. 478; Beste, *Introductio in Codicem,* pp. 533 and 954, note 1; Pistocchi, *I Canoni Penali,* p. 171; Ayrinhac-Lydon, *Penal Legislation,* p. 241; Mothon, *Institutions Canoniques,* II, 760; Sole, *De Delictis et Poenis,* p. 317; De Siena, *Commentarius Censurarum,* p. 56; Haring, *Grundzüge des katholischen Kirchenrechtes* (3. ed., 2 vols., Graz: Verlag von Ulrich Mosers Buchhandlung, 1924), I, 153, II, 986; Bouuaert-Simenon, *Manuale Juris Canonici,* III, n. 586; Cipollini, *De*

either the censure or the irregularity, Augustine's contrary opinion notwithstanding.[60]

By this determination in the Code the Church is following the commonly accepted teaching of the present day regarding the time of animation, just as Pope Gregory XIV, by distinguishing between an animated and a non-animated fetus, followed the common opinion of the sixteenth century. It need not be concluded that through the medium of the canons dealing with penalties for abortion the Church has given a doctrinal solution to the question: "At what

Censuris Latae Sententiae, p. 174; Blat, *Commentarium Textus Codicis Iuris Canonici,* Vol. V, *De Delictis et Poenis* (Romae: Collegio "Angelico," 1924), n. 192, and *De Sacramentis,* n. 586; Eichmann, *Das Strafrecht des Codex Iuris Canonici,* p. 176; Cocchi, *Commentarium in Codicem Iuris Canonici* (8 vols., Taurinorum Augustae: Marietti), Vol. VIII, *De Delictis et Poenis* (4. ed., 1938), n. 198; Schaaf, "Abortus Foetus Inanimati,"—*ER,* XCIII (1935), 623-624; McHugh, "The Victim in the Crime of Abortion,"—*HPR,* XXXIV (1933-1934), 417-418; Gutwenger, "An Illustration of the Influence of Medical Science Upon Theological Thought,"—*The Catholic Medical Guardian,* XVII (1940), 137-143; Donovan, "Answers to Questions—At What Moment Is Soul Infused Into Fetus?"—*HPR,* XLI (1941), 1132-1133; Mair, "Absolution von Zensur und Dispens von Irregularität ex delicto,"—*ThPrQs,* LXXIII (1920), 568-577, especially 570.

[60] In the latest edition of that volume of his *Commentary* which deals with irregularities Augustine states: "Animation . . . takes place within the first week after conception. Theologians as well as canonists admit that the old theory concerning animation may still be held as far as the incurring of penalties and irregularities is concerned. This theory is that between the conception and the animation of the male fetus forty days, and of a female fetus, eighty days elapse. As long as no authentic declaration has been issued, the strict interpretation applied to penal laws may be followed here, and the period of forty, respectively eighty days may be admitted."—IV, 490. Certainly, Augustine is referring to the pre-Code teaching regarding the irregularity. As to the teaching of theologians and canonists, he evidently has not taken cognizance of the post-Code writers, for example, those enumerated in the two preceding footnotes. Woywod (+1941) in 1922 expressed the opinion that the animation-distinction perhaps might be maintained regarding penalties ("Irregularities to Ordination Arising from Crime,"—*HPR,* XXIII [1922-1923], 146), but he subsequently expressed the contrary opinion throughout the five editions of his *Practical Commentary* (see *op. cit.* [5. ed., 1939], n. 938) and in the article, "Answers to Questions—Concerning Abortion,"—*HPR,* XXXVI (1935-1936), 294-295.

moment is the rational soul infused into the human body?" [61] At least, the Church says in effect that whatever may be the speculative and academic merit of the theory of retarded animation, it can have no practical application in regard to the crime of abortion,[62] or in the matter of conferring baptism upon an aborted fetus.[63]

There is of course no true homicide unless a rational being is killed. But in the present day law of the Church her legislation concerning the procuring of an abortion may well be considered a separate juridical institute; it is a crime in its own right, independently of the crime of homicide.[64] Thus the deliberate ejection of an immature fetus constitutes the crime of abortion; whether or not true homicide is involved does not come into question so far as the verification of the crime of abortion is concerned.

In the course of this discussion regarding the term "human" it was stated that any fetus conceived by woman, so long as it is *living*, is a human fetus in the sense intended by canon law. The requirement that the fetus be living does not mean that this life necessarily is or must be derived from an intellectual principal, the rational soul.[65] According to the theory of immediate animation, the life

[61] The following proposition was condemned by Pope Innocent XI (1676-1689): "Videtur probabile, omnem foetum (quamdiu in utero est) carere anima rationali et tunc primum incipere eandem habere, cum paritur: ac consequenter dicendum erit, in nullo abortu homicidium committi." (Prop. 35)—Denzinger-Bannwart-Umberg, *Enchiridion Symbolorum* (21.-23. ed., Friburgi Brisgoviae: Herder & Co., 1937), n. 1185.

[62] See Vermeersch, *Theologiae Moralis Principia,* III, nn. 219, 657; Wernz-Vidal, *Ius Canonicum,* IV-1, 336, footnote 462; Merkelbach, *Summa Theologiae Moralis,* III (2. ed., Parisiis: Desclée [1936]), 131, footnote 3; Donovan, "Answers to Questions—At What Moment Is Soul Infused Into Fetus?"—*HPR,* XLI (1941), 1132-1133. Lanza vigorously defends the theory of delayed animation but admits that *in practice* it may not be applied to the enactments in the Code.—*La Questione del Momento in cui L'Anima Razionale è Infusa nel Corpo* (Roma: Edizioni Universitarie, 1940), pp. 192, 286-288, 293-297.

[63] Canon 747 states that every living fetus is to be baptized absolutely, no matter at what time it is brought forth.

[64] See Lanza, *op. cit.,* p. 286; Beste, *Introductio in Codicem,* pp. 535-536; Vermeersch-Creusen, *Epitome,* III, n. 138, and II, n. 255; Woywod, "Answers to Questions—Concerning Abortion,"—*HPR,* XXXVI (1935-1936), 294-295; Mahoney, "Reserved Sins,"—*The Clergy Review,* VII (1934), 431-432.

[65] Augustine (*Commentary,* IV, 489) identifies *animatus* with *living.* His

of the fetus from the very moment of conception onward is derived from the rational soul. But the protagonists of the theory of delayed animation do not deny that even before the infusion of the rational soul the fetus is certainly biologically alive and that, despite its dependence upon the mother, it is a distinct living being, not a mere part of the mother. The fetus sustains a life proper to itself, dependent upon yet distinct from that of the mother.[66]

Article IV. Meaning of "Immature" Fetus

A. *Differentiation Between Abortion and Premature Birth*

It is of fundamental importance for the verification of the crime of abortion that the fetus be immature, that is, non-viable. This presupposes, in other words, that the interruption of pregnancy take place at a time when the fetus is incapable of extra-uterine existence, when it does not possess the inherent capability of sustaining life outside the maternal body. A fetus enjoying this capability is a viable fetus, the delivery of which before the normal term of gestation constitutes not an abortion, but, as designated by medical authorities, an induction of premature labor,[67] or a premature birth,[68] or, as commonly referred to by theologians and canonists, an *acceleratio partus.*[69]

The mere fact the fetus sometimes lives for a short while after its ejection does not necessarily indicate viability. If its subsequent death is due precisely and solely to its insufficient development, then the fetus is non-viable; consequently its removal implies an abortion,

general treatment of the notion of fetus appears confused and even contradictory. See his *Commentary,* IV, 489-490, and VIII, 398-399.

[66] See Vermeersch, *Theologiae Moralis Principia,* II, n. 580, 2; Merkelbach, *Quaestiones de Embryologia et de Ministratione Baptismatis,* pp. 66-67; McHugh, "Casus Moralis—Abortion and the Natural Law,"—*HPR,* XXXIV (1933-1934), 298.

[67] Stander, *Williams Obstetrics,* p. 1120; De Lee, *The Principles and Practice of Obstetrics,* pp. 127, 474, 1163.

[68] Taussig, *Abortion,* p. 483; Antonelli, *Medicina Pastoralis* (5. ed., 4 vols., Romae: Fridericus Pustet, 1932), II, n. 75.

[69] Noldin-Schmitt, *Summa Theologiae Moralis,* II, n. 343; Prümmer, *Manuale Theologiae Moralis,* II, nn. 137, 139; Vermeersch-Creusen, *Epitome,* III, n. 551; Coronata, *Institutiones,* IV, 458; Cappello, *De Censuris,* n. 384.

not a premature delivery. On the other hand, if a fetus is ejected at a time when it is judged to be non-viable, but after delivery continues to live, this is unquestionable evidence that it is viable.[70] In this case, notwithstanding malicious will, actual abortion is not verified.

The mere fact that the fetus dies shortly after its expulsion from the maternal body does not unquestionably prove it to be non-viable. It may in itself be capable of extra-uterine existence, but dies, for example, because it received inadequate attention after delivery. In this case the fetus is viable, and its removal from the mother implies a premature birth rather than an abortion.

It cannot be questioned that an abortion is distinct from a premature birth, that is to say, from the delivery of a child that is viable although not wholly mature. Some writers are satisfied with merely calling attention to this distinction.[71] Many state simply and quite correctly that premature birth is not abortion and hence does not beget the censure and irregularity stipulated for those who are guilty of the crime of abortion.[72] Other authors explain that when for legitimate reasons the birth of a viable fetus is hastened, the crime of abortion and its penalties are not incurred.[73] This is true beyond

[70] McHugh ("Casus Moralis—The Victim in the Crime of Abortion,"—*HPR*, XXXIV [1933-1934], 418) says: "Before viability the fetus is immature and will *ordinarily* die if removed." (Italics inserted.) The very concept of immaturity (or non-viability) connotes the death of the fetus. If it actually does not die, regardless of the time when it is removed from the mother, it is certainly not immature (or non-viable) in the sense in which that term is to be understood in connection with the crime of abortion. Cf. *supra*, pp. 98-100.

[71] V. g., Bouuaert-Simenon, *Manuale Juris Canonici*, III, 381; Cocchi, *De Delictis et Poenis*, n. 198; Cipollini, *De Censuris Latae Sententiae*, p. 175.

[72] V. g., Haring, *Grundzüge des Katholischen Kirchenrechtes*, II, 986; Beste, *Introductio in Codicem*, p. 954; Noldin-Schönegger, *De Censuris*, n. 92; Chelodi, *Ius Poenale*, n. 80, 1; Lydon, *Ready Answers in Canon Law* (2. ed., New York: Benziger Brothers [1937]), pp. 5-6; Salucci, *Il Diritto Penale*, II, 222. Note, however, that the irregularity for homicide would not be escaped in this case, provided the other elements of the crime of homicide are present.

[73] Thus, Eichmann, *Des Strafrecht des Codex Iuris Canonici*, p. 176, and Wernz, *Ius Decretalium*, VI, n. 369, along with the following who give practically a repetition of Wernz's statement word for word: De Meester, *Compendium*, III, pars 2, 259; Sipos, *Enchiridion*, p. 478; Brys, "De Poena in Procurantes Abortum,"—*Collationes Brugenses*, XXXIV (1934), 43.

doubt. But these authors might have added that the following is likewise true: whether the delivery of a viable fetus is hastened for reasons either commendable or objectionable, whether it is effected only a very short while before term or immediately after the viability of the fetus, whether the fetus lives or dies after delivery, these procedures do not beget the penalties for abortion. And why not? Simply because an abortion is the ejection of an *immature*, i. e., *a non-viable* fetus; whereas all the above mentioned acts are performed after viability of the fetus has been attained. Therefore these acts cannot imply an abortion in the strict sense, regardless of how sinful they may be.[74] Of course, when a viable fetus is involved, the crime of homicide could readily be committed, for which an irregularity would be incurred precisely because homicide is involved.[75]

The element of the immaturity of the fetus was expressly mentioned in the definition of abortion given by Pope Sixtus V in his Constitution *"Effraenatam"* of 1588, and since that time has been consistently accepted by ecclesiastical jurisprudence as an essential constituent of the traditional notion of abortion.[76] Therefore, when the Code penalizes abortion, it penalizes the ejection of an immature, a non-viable fetus; a viable fetus can not be the object of the crime of abortion, and hence its ejection does not beget the penalties for abortion.

B. *Immaturity, Absolute or Relative?*

As explained above, the ejection of an immature (or non-viable) fetus constitutes the crime of abortion. But it is of no small moment

[74] Ayrinhac-Lydon, *Penal Legislation*, p. 30: "In this context abortion does not include . . . acceleration of birth without cause. . ." Heidenreich, "Dissertatio,"—*AKKR*, LXIII (1980), 376: "Item non incurri videtur censura, si mulier, ex malitia, v. g. ut infans mox moriatur, partum praematurum provocat, . . . quia hic non est abortus sensu stricto, et odia restringenda."

[75] See canon 985, 4°.

[76] Const. *"Effraenatam,"* 29 oct. 1588, §1: " . . . foetus immaturi . . . eiectionem. . ."

Prompted by the desire or conviction that craniotomy should be considered as the equivalent of abortion so as to beget the censure of canon 2350, §1, Coronata recommends a definition for abortion which would exclude the element of immaturity.—*Institutiones*, IV, 461; see *infra*, footnote 47 of Chapter X.

to know whether this immaturity is to be taken in an absolute or in a relative sense.

Absolute immaturity is had when the fetus simply could not live outside the mother, no matter how favorable the external circumstances might be; hence, even with the most expert *post-partum* care, such as hospitalization, incubation, special nursing, etc., the fetus would die. The fetus of itself, in this case, is inherently and absolutely incapable of extra-uterine existence. There is no question but that the ejection of a fetus under such conditions would constitute an abortion so far as the element of immaturity is concerned.

On the other hand, the immaturity is only relative if the fetus is of itself capable of surviving after delivery; that is, the infant could and would live provided it received extraordinary care, which in this particular case is not available. Under these circumstances the fetus is *technically* viable, but *practically* non-viable. It *de facto* will not or does not live due solely to the lack of external circumstances.[77] The question then is this: does the deliberate ejection of a fetus which is viable only in the technical sense involve the censure and irregularity for the crime of abortion? Or does this ejection imply rather an *acceleratio partus*, perhaps seriously illicit, but as such not subject to the penalties for abortion?

Creusen states in effect that the fetus is to be considered as not viable unless here and now external circumstances are such that it can live outside the mother. He thus seems to hold that mere technical viability does not suffice to make the action premature birth, and hence not free from canonical penalty.[78] However, the following statement, made by Hilarius a Sexten and Sole, certainly can be understood as favoring the opposite opinion: "To procure abortion is nothing else than deliberately to effect the ejection of a fetus from the womb of the mother while the condition of the fetus is still such that *in no way whatsoever* can it live outside the womb of the

[77] Cf. O'Malley, *The Ethics of Medical Homicide and Mutilation*, pp. 56, 116.

[78] Vermeersch-Creusen, *Epitome*, III, n. 551: " . . . *Immaturus*, i. e. qui de facto extra matrem vivere nequit. *Acceleratio partus* habetur, ubi, saltem adhibitis mediis extraordinariis quae praesto sint, fetus extra uterum maternum vivere potest."

mother." [79] Hollweck is perhaps more explicit in his statement that in order that the fetus be not considered as immature "there must be present at least the absolute possibility that the fetus can continue to live." [80] It is true that these are not clear and unequivocal statements that in such cases there can be no crime of abortion, but they can be reasonably interpreted as indicating the probability that the technical viability of the fetus is sufficient to obviate the crime of abortion.

This particular question is given no consideration *ex professo* in canonical treatises, most authors being satisfied with the statement that the fetus is immature when it *cannot live* outside the mother.[81] They do not state whether or not the crime is obviated when on the part of the fetus the possibility of surviving is merely technical, yet the assertion that the immature fetus is one which *cannot live* outside the mother may be understood in the *absolute* sense.

If the fetus really could live, but dies simply and solely because it does not receive the proper care—for although the required care be extraordinary and at present unavailable, yet as a bestowable care it remains *possible*—then this external circumstance seems to be accidental and non-essential to the strict concept of immaturity or non-viability. It must be remembered above all that the present problem is not that of determining the morality of the act, but the presence of *crime*.[82] And since the law concerning the latter is to be

[79] "Hinc procurare abortum nihil aliud est, quam *consulto* efficere, ut foetus ex utero matris eiiciatur, dum adhuc in tali statu versatur, ut extra uterum matris nullatenus vivere possit."—Hilarius a Sexten, *Tractatus de Censuris Ecclesiasticis*, p. 217, and verbatim in Sole, *De Delictis et Poenis*, p. 316.

[80] ". . . es müsste also wenigstens die absolute Möglichkeit vorhanden sein, dass das Kind am Leben bleibe. . ."—*Die kirchlichen Strafgesetze*, §163, note 7. Coronata (*Institutiones*, IV, 458) speaks of absolute viability and of relative viability, but does not expressly consider the point in question.

[81] V. g., Cappello, *De Sacra Ordinatione*, n. 506; Blat, *De Delictis et Poenis*, p. 250; Cerato, *Censurae Vigentes*, p. 100; Salucci, *Il Diritto Penale*, II, 222; Cocchi, *De Delictis et Poenis*, n. 198.

[82] The Holy Office has stated (May 4, 1898, ad 1) that the induction of premature labor is licit provided that it be effected for a sufficient reason and at a time and by the use of means which in ordinary circumstances safeguard the life of the mother and of the fetus.—Cf. *ASS*, XXX (1897-1898), 703-704; *Fontes*, n. 1199; Denzinger-Bannwart-Umberg, *Enchiridion Symbolorum*, n.

interpreted strictly,[83] there appears to be sufficient justification to maintain as probable that if the fetus is at least technically viable, the *crime* of abortion and its consequent censure and irregularity are not incurred. An irregularity could of course be incurred for the crime of homicide which may become verified in the death of this viable fetus.

C. *Practical Norm for Determining Viability*

It has been pointed out that the fetus is immature or nonviable so long as it is not capable of extra-uterine existence, and is viable once it has acquired this capability. The point under consideration at this time is this: how many days of fetal development are required before viability is attained? For all practical purposes the length of normal pregnancy is held to be approximately two hundred and eighty days or forty weeks—ten lunar or nine calendar (solar) months—this period being reckoned from the first day of the last menstrual period.[84] At what point in this forty-week period may the fetus be considered viable?

Canonists and moralists give varying estimates of the time at which the fetus ceases to be immature. Some accept one hundred and eighty days; [85] many state that after the seventh month the fetus is viable; [86] still others point out that with extraordinary care

1890b. This statement touches only the moral issue and not the question of penalties.

[83] Canons 19; 2219, §1.

[84] Since this computation counts from the first day of the last menstrual period, the actual length of pregnancy is less than two hundred and eighty days. According to obstetrical authorities conception (and this marks the beginning of pregnancy) occurs about the middle of the menstrual cycle; hence the true duration of the average pregnancy is about two hundred and sixty to two hundred and seventy days. See De Lee, *The Principles and Practice of Obstetrics,* pp. 24-25, 125; Stander, *Williams Obstetrics,* pp. 257-258; Taussig, *Abortion,* p. 481.

[85] V. g., Chelodi, *Ius Poenale,* n. 80; Haring, *Grundzüge des katholischen Kirchenrechtes,* II, 986, note 3; Coronata (*Institutiones,* IV, 458, note 3) says that the common doctrine holds to this figure.

[86] V. g., Coronata, *op. cit.,* IV, 458; Noldin-Schmitt, *Summa Theologiae Moralis,* II, n. 342; Sipos, *Enchiridion Iuris Canonici,* p. 478; Wernz-Vidal, *Ius Canonicum,* VII, 514 (on p. 516, 180 days is mentioned); Beste, *Introductio in Codicem,* pp. 533, 954.

the fetus may live after the sixth month.[87] Frequently it is not clear whether they refer to calendar or to lunar months. In the final analysis this is a matter to be determined by obstetrical authorities,[88] who commonly place the minimum age for viability between twenty-six to twenty-eight weeks, that is, after the completion of six and one-half lunar months or six calendar (solar) months. But at these stages extraordinary care and expert attention will be required if the fetus is to live.[89]

Perhaps the following will suffice as a practical rule: if a fetus ejected *before the twenty-sixth week* lives, evidently there is not the crime of abortion; if this fetus dies, it must be considered to be non-viable in the canonical sense unless there are positive indications that its death was due to external circumstances. In any event, in the presence of positive and probable doubt regarding viability, *post factum reo favendum est.*

From the preceding discussion it is evident that in individual cases it is very difficult to determine *ante factum* the precise time when the fetus is viable. Practically, however, this difficulty will occasion little trouble, for those who wish to be rid of the fetus as something wholly undesirable will interrupt the pregnancy as soon as it is ascertained, or at least before the fetus nears the time of viability. There will be other cases in which the question of inducing delivery to safeguard the life of the mother will arise. In such cases, if the judgment of competent and conscientious physicians is that the fetus is viable, there will be no question of canonical crime even though it be learned *post factum* that the fetus really was non-viable and conse-

[87] V. g., Vermeersch, *Theologiae Moralis Principia,* II, nn. 580, 584; Loiano, *Institutiones Theologiae Moralis,* II, n. 389; Ayrinhac-Lydon, *Penal Legislation,* p. 240; Cipollini, *De Censuris Latae Sententiae,* p. 175.

[88] See Heidenreich, "Dissertatio,"—*AKKR,* LXIII (1890), 376; Loiano, *Institutiones Theologiae Moralis,* II, n. 389.

[89] Cf. De Lee, *op. cit.,* pp. 58, 127, 474; Stander, *op. cit.,* pp. 154, 157, 803, 1120; Taussig, *op. cit.,* p. 483; O'Malley, *The Ethics of Medical Homicide and Mutilation,* pp. 56, 116, 109. As will be seen by consulting the reference to Stander and Taussig, there is a tendency today to determine the viability of the fetus in accordance with its weight and length, that is, from 1250 to 1500 grams in weight and 32 to 35 centimeters in length.

quently died. In this case there was no intention to cause the death of the child and the external action of inducing delivery was morally justifiable, as is supposed. Hence the requisites for "procuring" abortion are not verified, as was pointed out in a previous chapter.[90]

[90] *Supra,* Chapter VII, pp. 81-88, especially p. 86.

CHAPTER IX

EXPLANATION OF "EFFECTU SECUTO"

THE specific phrase *"effectu secuto"* appeared in the Constitution *"Apostolicae Sedis"* of Pope Pius IX [1] and now is found in both canon 985, 4°, and in canon 2350, §1. Although the phrase itself does not appear in the legislation of Pope Sixtus V, the essential notion contained in this phrase was expressed by the clause " . . . ita ut re ipsa abortus inde secutus fuerit." [2]

In virtue of the phrase *"effectu secuto"* it is required for the verification of the crime of abortion (A) that the abortion actually take place; (B) that it result from the specific means employed to bring it about; and (C) that there be certitude in this regard. The censure and the irregularity are incurred at the moment the abortion is effected.

A. Abortion Must Actually Occur

The abortion itself must certainly have taken place before the irregularity and the censure are *ipso facto* incurred. Consequently the frustrated crime (*delictum frustratum*) [3] and the attempted crime (*conatus delicti*) [4] are excluded from the canons in question, namely, canons 985, 4°, and 2350, §1. And nowhere does the Code place any other *latae sententiae* penalty, or any other specific penalty, on frustrated abortion or attempted abortion; they are not punished by the Code as offenses distinct from consummated abortion.

Regardless of how deliberate or malicious the intention to commit the crime may be, if the actual abortion does not occur, the censure and the irregularity are not contracted. Perhaps the would-be culprit has a change of heart and voluntarily desists from carrying out his intention. On the other hand, the attempt may be frus-

[1] §III, n. 2: "Procurantes abortum, effectu secuto."—*Fontes*, n. 552.

[2] Const. *"Effraenatam,"* 29 oct. 1588, §1.—*Fontes*, n. 165.

[3] Canons 2212, §§1, 3, 4, and 2213, §§1, 3.

[4] Canons 2212, §2, and 2213, §2.

trated or rendered ineffectual even against the culprit's will. Or perhaps the means or method employed, although reputed as infallibly efficacious for inducing abortion, for some reason does not produce the expected result in a particular instance. In these cases and in all other cases wherein the actual abortion is not effected, regardless of the reason for its non-occurrence, the censure and the irregularity do not come into play. The act, of course, may be seriously sinful as the result of the bad intention, and its malice may even be aggravated because of the actual attempt, but the *crime* of abortion is not present.[5]

How is it to be known that the abortion has actually taken place after efforts were made to effect it? In practice there will ordinarily be little difficulty in this regard when there is a case of abortion deliberately undertaken, and there is no concern here about spontaneous, non-intended abortion. The consummation of the abortion is not likely to occur unnoticed.

About all that one can say without considering specific and actual cases is that, if pregnancy has been established with certainty, and after deliberate actions were placed to effect abortion it is known that pregnancy has been terminated, then abortion has occurred. In the early weeks of pregnancy an examination of the expelled products may sometimes be the only way to determine the fact that abortion has taken place, and even this examination will at times prove unsatisfactory. Yet *post-factum* examination is by no means the only way to be certain that abortion has occurred. In the light of its discussion in an earlier chapter, the fact of pregnancy may be established with certitude before the product of conception is expelled and examined. If there has been deliberate interference with a certainly established pregnancy, although the actual passing of the fetus itself may not be noticed—this could be deliberately avoided—there is sufficient indication that abortion has occurred.[6]

[5] Cf. Vermeersch-Creusen, *Epitome,* III, n. 551; Cappello, *De Sacra Ordinatione,* n. 506, 9; Noldin-Schönegger, *De Censuris,* n. 92, 3; De Meester, *Compendium,* III, pars 2, 260-261; D'Annibale, *In Constitutionem A. S.,* n. 160.

[6] Cf. *supra,* Chapter VIII, Article III, pp. 94-98. See also "The Question of Abortion Under the New Canon Law,"—*ER,* LXVIII (1923), 300-301 (too much insistence is placed upon examination of the products expelled).

B. Abortion Must Result From the Means Employed

Verification of the phase *"effectu secuto"* requires not only that abortion really occur, but that it result from the specific means employed with this aim in view. Moreover, there must be certitude in this regard. If it is certain or even if it is positively probable that the abortion was not brought about by the means intentionally used, the *"effectu secuto"* element is lacking; hence the parties concerned cannot be held as contracting the censure and the irregularity.[7]

In practical cases it sometimes will be difficult to determine definitely whether the abortion was caused by the means employed with this end in mind. It is not demanded, since it is a practical impossibility, that the penitent or the confessor be acquainted with the abortifacient properties and degrees of effectiveness of every possible means which may be employed to induce abortion. Individual cases must be judged according to universally human standards, and ordinarily there will not be many cases in which a sound and reasonable judgment cannot be made regarding the efficacy of the means.[8]

In certain cases the cause of the abortion can hardly be questioned, for example, when the ejection of the fetus is preceded by deliberate dilation of the cervix of the uterus, by curettage, or by puncture of the fetal membranes,[9] which means are among those employed by physicians and by professional abortionists. In fact, there is ordinarily no reason to doubt that the abortion resulted from the means employed when a physician or a professional abortionist takes a hand in effecting the expulsion of the fetus.[10]

[7] Cf. Cappello, *De Sacra Ordinatione*, n. 506, 9, and *De Censuris*, n. 386; Noldin-Schönegger, *De Censuris*, n. 92, 3; Coronata, *Institutiones*, IV, 459, 461; De Meester, *Compendium*, III, pars 2, 260-261; Brys, "De Poena in Procurantes Abortum,"—*Collationes Brugenses*, XXXIV (1934), 44-45; Hollweck, *Die kirchlichen Strafgesetze*, §163, note 5; D'Annibale, *In Constitutionem A. S.*, n. 160.

[8] Cf. *supra*, pp. 85-88.

[9] Cf. De Lee, *The Principles and Practice of Obstetrics*, p. 1169; Stander, *Williams Obstetrics*, pp. 1117-1118.

[10] Taussig (*Abortion*, p. 252) notes the increased tendency for women to visit the professional abortionist.

When the means employed are known to possess abortifacient properties of only dubious efficacy, there is more reason to doubt that they are responsible for the abortion. Of course, if known abortifacients are employed, even though they do not possess infallible efficacy, the subsequent abortion must reasonably be attributed to these means, *provided* that there is no positive indication or reason to believe that some other cause is responsible for the abortion.

In the event however that an abortion occurs even after the deliberate use of means which are known to have only slight if any abortifacient properties, there will be reasonable and serious doubt as to the true cause of the abortion, i. e., there will be solid doubt that the abortion was effected precisely by these means.

At times it may be quite evident that the abortion did not result from the means purposely used, but came as an effect of some accidental occurrence. An example of what may be judged non-deliberate abortion—certainly a case of doubtfully efficacious means—is the following case. A woman intending abortion deliberately takes a drug of known abortifacient efficacy. Immediately thereafter, before the medication could have acted, she accidentally sustains a fall which causes serious abdominal injury to herself. Ejection of the fetus follows shortly. Although the drug would have induced abortion later on, still the ejection of the fetus may well be attributed to the fall or to the injury consequent thereto rather than to the efficacy of the drug. Therefore, although she sinned seriously because of her evil intention, the woman can not be held guilty of the crime of abortion.[11]

In the final analysis it must be certain that the abortion resulted from the specific means deliberately employed for this purpose. If there is founded doubt in this regard, the party or parties involved

[11] It may not be irrelevant to note here that according to competent medical opinion most drugs commonly vaunted to be abortifacients are by no means infallibly such. Almost all are decidedly dangerous to the mother. Not a few are valueless as abortifacients, unless they be used in connection with other methods, for example, with physical or with genital instrumentation, or at a time when the mother is naturally predisposed to abortion.—See Taussig, *Abortion*, pp. 111-116, 352-356; De Lee, *op. cit.*, p. 1169.

cannot be held to the penalties which the law connects with the crime of abortion, as will be pointed out immediately.

C. Certitude

On the foregoing pages of this chapter it is stated that the crime of abortion is not verified unless it is certain that actual abortion has taken place and moreover that the abortion was caused by the specific means used for this purpose. Similarly, throughout this commentary frequent mention has been made of certitude: sometimes this certitude has been designated as moral certitude, sometimes not. What degree of certitude must be had in any given case regarding the actualization of the various requirements for the crime of abortion?

Quite evidently at least *moral* certitude is required. But it is almost equally evident that such certitude also suffices for achieving a reasonable human judgment relative to the multiple aspects of and the many requirements pertaining to this crime. Moral certitude is that certitude which is wont to be had in human affairs, and which excludes every prudent doubt, every doubt based upon *positive* reasons. It appears unwarranted to require absolute physical certitude—that certitude which eliminates not only all positive probability on the opposite side, but even the possible existence of such a probability.[12]

The following are some of the more important factors which have been discussed on previous pages and which must stand as morally certain before anyone can be considered to have incurred the excommunication or the irregularity as a consequence which follows *ipso facto* upon abortion.

(1) True *fetus,* i. e., conception must have taken place.[13]

(2) *Living* fetus, i. e., the fetus must have been alive before the abortion-process was initiated.[14]

[12] This item of certitude is not treated *ex professo* by authors who comment upon this legislation, but see: Hilarius a Sexten, *Tractatus de Censuris Ecclesiasticis,* p. 220; Pennacchi, *De Abortu,* pp. 13, 24.

[13] Cf. *supra,* pp. 94-98.

[14] Cf. *supra,* pp. 98-103.

(3) *Non-viable* fetus, i. e., the fetus must be incapable of extra-uterine existence.[15]

(4) Abortion must be *intended,* not merely permitted.[16]

(5) There must be a *deliberate* use of apt and *efficacious* means.[17]

(6) Abortion must *actually occur.*[18]

(7) The abortion must result precisely from the means employed for this purpose.[19]

If there is a *positive* reason which makes it probable that any one of these elements is lacking in a particular case, then that case does not involve the crime of abortion.[20]

It is understood, further, that the general requirements for a crime subject to an *ipso facto* incurred censure and irregularity must be verified, for instance, the all-important item of serious sin, both internal (subjective) and external (objective) sin.[21]

[15] Cf. *supra,* pp. 108-114.
[16] Cf. *supra,* pp. 84-85, 86-88.
[17] Cf. *supra,* pp. 85-88.
[18] Cf. *supra,* pp. 116-117.
[19] Cf. *supra,* pp. 118-120.
[20] See canons 2228 and 2233.
[21] Cf. *supra,* pp. 80, 83, 88.

CHAPTER X

EMBRYOTOMY AND REMOVAL OF ECTOPIC FETUS

In preceding chapters an attempt was made to delineate the notion of abortion as subjected to the censure and irregularity. It remains to treat the relation which exists between abortion as discussed on the foregoing pages, and (1) craniotomy along with its kindred operations known as embryotomy, and (2) abortion of an ectopic fetus. In short, do these two actions beget the penalties for abortion?

Article I. Embryotomy (Craniotomy)

Craniotomy and like forms of mutilating and destructive operations, such as cephalotripsis, decapitation, exenteration, cleidotomy, spondylotomy, etc., may for the purposes of this study be included under the general term of embryotomy. The purpose and the precise technique of all these operations is to reduce the bulk of the fetal body so as to facilitate or render possible the delivery of the child.[1] And due to this mutilation these operations always cause the death of the child before its expulsion or extraction from the body of the mother.[2]

Almost all present-day canonical treatises which deal with the penalties for abortion consider the question whether embryotomy begets the censure for abortion. There is no need for concern here about the matter of irregularity, for if these operations constitute abortion, the irregularity for abortion is incurred. If they do not constitute abortion, they can readily constitute the crime of homicide and thus cause irregularity on this score, as will be seen presently.

[1] For description of these operations, see De Lee, *The Principles and Practice of Obstetrics*, pp. 1153-1162; Stander, *Williams Obstetrics*, pp. 1233-1240.

[2] In order to obviate a horrifying spectacle obstetrical texts advise the physician to make certain that the child is dead before it is ejected.—Stander, *op. cit.*, p. 1239. Cases are on record of children having survived these operations.—Cf. Moore, *Principles of Ethics* (2. ed., Philadelphia: J. B. Lippincott Co., 1937), pp. 175-181.

In so far as the writer could ascertain, the question as to whether embryotomy involves the censure for abortion was discussed for the first time in the treatises and commentaries which appeared after the Constitution *"Apostolicae Sedis"* of Pope Pius IX, which was issued in 1869. Before this time authors did not distinguish abortion from the various forms of embryotomy; at least there seems to be no mention of these operations as not begetting the censure. Before the Constitution *"Effraenatam"* was issued by Pope Sixtus V in 1588 ecclesiastical common law considered the abortion of an animated fetus as a species of homicide, and abortion was penalized in accordance with the norms governing the crime of homicide. But after the time of Popes Sixtus V and Gregory XIV (1590-1591) abortion, while still held to be true homicide, was subjected to penalties as a crime on its own specific demerits. Moreover, for the first time in ecclesiastical penal law abortion was definitely defined—the ejection of an immature, a non-viable fetus. Therefore, one might have expected to find a distinction made between abortion and embryotomy, but apparently none was made.[3]

After the Constitution *"Apostolicae Sedis"* of Pope Pius IX only a few authors held that the excommunication for abortion likewise resulted from craniotomy.[4] The great majority excluded craniotomy (while they generally spoke of craniotomy, all the similar operations were included) from this censure.[5]

[3] M. J. O'Donnell says: ". . . craniotomy and abortion are two specifically different offenses and have been *always* treated as such by writers on theology and common law."—"Craniotomy and Excommunication,"—*IER,* 4th series, XXIX (1911), 538. It appears, however, that O'Donnell's all-inclusive statement needs considerable qualification.

[4] V. g., Göpfert, "De Excommunicatione et Irregularitate ex Abortu Oriunda,"—*ThPrQs,* XXXIX (1886), 373; Heiner, *Die kirchlichen Censuren,* p. 246; Heidenreich, "Dissertation,"—*AKKR,* LXIII (1890), 298, note 1, 300, 376-377; Wernz, *Ius Decretalium,* VI, n. 370. The latter two authors admitted that in view of external authority the lenient opinion could be followed.

[5] Berardi, *Praxis,* nn. 883, 1263; Hilarius a Sexten, *Tractatus de Censuris Ecclesiasticis,* p. 218; Cornelisse, *Compendium Theologiae Moralis,* I, n. 589; Noldin, *De Poenis Ecclesiasticis,* n. 93, 1; D'Annibale, *In Constitutionem A. S.,* n. 161; Bucceroni *Institutiones,* II, n. 1204; Genicot, *Institutiones,* II, n. 608; Piatus Montensis, *Praelectiones Juris Regularis,* II, 561; O'Donnell, "Craniotomy and Excommunication,"—*IER,* 4th series, XXIX (1911), 538.

Thus, too, since the Code it is unquestionably the common and well-nigh universal opinion that embryotomy as distinct from abortion does not induce the censure of excommunication.

There are comparatively few writers since the advent of the Code who say that embryotomy begets the censure for abortion. Among these are the following, Eichmann,[6] Coronata,[7] Wernz-Vidal,[8] Felici,[9] Stockums,[10] and perhaps Augustine.[11] Stockums is the only one of this group to state that, since the matter is disputed, the lenient opinion may be followed.

Among the reasons for this position this group indicates the following. (1) The decisions of the Holy Office condemning embryotomy as morally illicit.[12] (2) Both embryotomy and abortion have the same effect, the death of the child.[13] (3) Embryotomy is a greater crime than abortion, for the former deprives the child of a chance to be baptized, which the latter does not.[14] (4) If embry-

[6] *Das Strafrecht des Codex Iuris Canonici*, pp. 176-177.

[7] *Institutiones*, IV, 460-461.

[8] *Ius Canonicum*, VII, 517.

[9] *De Poenali Iure Interpretando* (Romae: Apollinaris, 1939), 96, first column of the footnote, which begins on the preceding page.

[10] "Abortus und kirchliches Strafrecht,"—*Theologie und Glaube*, XV (1923), 97.

[11] *Commentary*, VIII, 402. His reference to the decisions of the Holy Office (see the footnote following immediately) regarding craniotomy make it appear that he includes it under the censure, unless the physician who performs the operation acts merely as a *mandatarius*.

[12] These decisions were given May 28, 1884, and August 19, 1889. For the former see *ASS*, XVII (1884), 556; *Collectanea S. C. de Prop. Fide* (2 vols., Romae, 1907), n. 1618; Denzinger-Bannwart-Umberg, *Enchiridion Symbolorum*, n. 1889; for the latter, see *ASS*, XXII (1889-1890), 748; *Collectanea S. C. de Prop. Fide*, footnote to n. 1618; Denzinger-Bannwart-Umberg, *op. cit.*, n. 1890.

Cf. Eichmann, *op. cit.*, pp. 176-177; Wernz-Vidal, *op. cit.*, II, 517; Augustine, *op. cit.*, VIII, 402. Stockums (*art. cit.*) thinks that since reference to these decisions is made in Cardinal Gasparri's footnote to canon 2350, §1, it appears that the censure has been extended by the Code to include embryotomy!

[13] Wernz-Vidal, *op. cit.*, VII, 571; Felici, *op. cit.*, p. 96, footnote.

[14] Wernz-Vidal, *op. cit.*, VII, 571; Coronata, *op. cit.*, 461. To suppose that in abortion the fetus is always or even generally alive after external ejection

otomy did not induce the censure, this would encourage the performance of a greater crime as the means with which to evade the penalty of the law.[15] (5) A law which thus encourages crime and permits evasion would be *immoralis,* would not be *iusta,*[16] and would not be *rationabilis et aequa.*[17]

Among the authors who hold that embryotomy does not induce the censure of excommunication for abortion are the following: Vermeersch,[18] Cappello,[19] Creusen,[20] Chelodi,[21] Cocchi,[22] Pistocchi,[23] Cavigioli,[24] Farrugia,[25] Salucci,[26] Bouuaert-Simenon,[27] Ayrinhac-Lydon,[28] Cipollini,[29] Sole,[30] Cerato,[31] Teodori,[32] Schaaf,[33] Noldin-

is not in accordance with actual physical facts.—See *supra,* pp. 100-102. As a matter of fact it will almost always be possible to give certain baptism to a fetus about to be subjected to embryotomy after the fashion in which this operation is performed in actual practice.

15 Wernz-Vidal, *op. cit.,* VII, 571; Coronata, *op. cit.,* 461. See also the concern expressed by Schaaf, "Canonical Notes on the Encyclical Letter of Christian Marriage,"—*ER,* LXXXIV (1931), 272-273. The writer's opinion, contrary to that of Schaaf, is that craniotomy and its kindred operations are actually becoming less frequent from year to year while abortions are increasing. This opinion is confirmed by medical journals, obstetrical texts, and by practicing physicians and obstetricians consulted by the writer.

16 Coronata, *op. cit.,* IV, 461.

17 Wernz-Vidal, *op. cit.,* VII, 517.

18 *Theologiae Moralis Principia,* II, n. 584.

19 *De Censuris,* nn. 384-385.

20 Vermeersch-Creusen, *Epitome,* III, n. 551.

21 *Ius Poenale,* n. 80, 1.

22 *De Delictis et Poenis,* n. 198.

23 *I Canoni Penila,* p. 170.

24 *De Censuris Latae Sententiae,* n. 161.

25 *Commentarium,* n. 66.

26 *Il Diritto Penale,* II, 223.

27 *Manuale Juris Canonici,* III, n. 586, IV.

28 *Penal Legislation,* pp. 30, 241. See also, Lydon, *Ready Answers in Canon Law,* pp. 5-6.

29 *De Censuris Latae Sententiae,* p. 176.

30 *De Delictis et Poenis,* p. 318.

31 *Censurae Vigentes,* p. 100.

32 "Abortus,"—*Apollinaris,* V (1932), 253.

33 "Canonical Notes on the Encyclical Letter on Christian Marriage,"—*ER,* LXXXIV (1931), 272-273.

Schönegger, [34] Ferreres,[35] Iorio,[36] Loiano,[37] Marc-Gestermann [38] and others.[39] When these authors state that craniotomy and like procedures are distinct from abortion, the principal reason given is that, while the former are directly and *per se occisiva* and *laesiva,* the latter is simply *eiectio.*[40] Sometimes it is stated merely that craniotomy, etc., are not properly or strictly abortion; [41] or that abortion is an *eiectio* while the other operations imply an *extractio;* [42] or it is stated simply that they are distinct.[43]

Before any further discussion and comment on the relation of embryotomy to the excommunication for abortion, it should be noted that those who hold that embryotomy does not induce the censure do maintain however—i. e., those who discuss the item—that the irregularity for homicide nevertheless obtains in a case of embryotomy. This contention on their part assumes, it need hardly be stated, that the other elements for the crime of homicide are verified in a particular case. Some of the authorities state simply that embryotomy, though it does not imply an abortion, constitutes homi-

[34] *De Censuris,* n. 92, 1.

[35] *Compendium Theologiae Moralis,* II, n. 1268.

[36] *Theologia Moralis,* nn. 216, 512.

[37] *Institutiones Theologiae Moralis,* II, nn. 389, 394.

[38] *Institutiones Morales Alphonsianae* (17. ed., 2 vols., Lugduni: Typis Emmanuelis Vitte, 1922-1923), I, nn. 744, 1349.

[39] Anon., "Abortion and the Embryological Theory,"—*ER,* LXXVIII (1928), 627.

[40] V. g., Bucceroni, *Institutiones,* I, n. 742; Iorio, *Theologia Moralis,* II, nn. 216, 512; Loiano, *Institutiones Theologiae Moralis,* II, 467; Cipollini, *De Censuris Latae Sententiae,* p. 176; Pistocchi, *I Canoni Penali,* p. 170; Cappello, *De Censuris,* n. 384; Cocchi, *De Delictis et Poenis,* n. 198; Chelodi, *Ius Poenale,* n. 80, 1; Teodori, "Abortus,"—*Apollinaris,* V (1932), 253.

[41] V. g., Cornelisse, *Compendium Theologiae Moralis,* I, n. 589; Hilarius a Sexten, *Tractatus de Censuris Ecclesiasticis,* p. 218; Marc-Gestermann, *Institutiones Morales Alphonsianae,* I, n. 1349; Ayrinhac-Lydon, *Penal Legislation,* p. 241.

[42] Berardi, *Praxis,* n. 1263.

[43] Sole, *De Delictis et Poenis,* p. 318; Noldin-Schönegger, *De Censuris,* n. 92, 1; O'Donnell, Craniotomy and Excommunication,"—*IER,* 4th series, XXIX (1911), 538.

cide; [44] others expressly mention that it involves the irregularity for homicide.[45]

Among the authors listed above, that is, among both those who hold that embryotomy gives rise to the excommunication for abortion and also those who maintain that it does not, the general supposition is, or seems to be, that if it is decided to terminate pregnancy embryotomy can be employed for this purpose (i. e., it is a physical possibility), whether the fetus be viable or non-viable.

In the opinion of the minority group named above, if embryotomy is performed either on a viable or on a non-viable fetus, the censure is incurred. These authors maintain that embryotomy is abortion, or at least no distinction is made so far as the incurring of the censure is concerned. The reasons for this identification have have already been mentioned. Since these authors hold that embryotomy performed upon a viable fetus begets excommunication, they must do one of two things. They must either interpret the traditional notion of abortion—the ejection of a *non-viable* fetus—to include embryotomy performed on a viable child, or they must furnish a new definition of abortion. The latter choice is made by Wernz-Vidal [46] and by Coronata, the latter expressly suggesting a new definition of abortion for the purposes of ecclesiastical penal law.[47] Thus, if embryotomy on a viable fetus is to be included under

[44] Among the pre-Code authors; Hilarius a Sexten, *Tractatus de Censuris Ecclesiasticis,* p. 218; Noldin, *De Poenis Ecclesiasticis,* n. 93, 1. Before the Code it was required, as has been pointed out earlier in this study, that for the incurring of the irregularity the fetus had to be developed to that point of time at which it was considered to be a *fetus animatus.* Among the post-Code authors: Bouuaert-Simenon, *Manuale Juris Canonici,* III, n. 586, IV, Noldin-Schönegger, *De Censuris,* n. 92, 1; Loiano, *Institutiones Theologiae Moralis,* II, n. 389; Farrugia, *Commentarium,* n. 66.

[45] Vermeersch, *Theologiae Moralis Principia,* II, n. 584; Cerato, *Censurae Vigentes,* pp. 100, 273; Cappello, *De Sacra Ordinatione,* n. 506, 4; Ferreres, *Compendium Theologiae Moralis,* II, n. 896, 6°; Iorio, *Theologia Moralis,* III, n. 962; Vermeersch-Creusen, *Epitome,* III, n. 551 (saying that craniotomy induces the penalties for homicide).

[46] *Ius Canonicum,* VII, 514.

[47] "Non obstanti igitur communiori doctrina auctorum, affirmandum censeo etiam craniotomiam, embryotomiam et alias similes operationes cadere sub

the crime of abortion, the element of fetal non-viability is ruled out of the juridical concept and definition of abortion.

What is to be thought of this opinion? In traditional ecclesiastical penal jurisprudence abortion is defined as the ejection of a non-viable fetus, a fetus which is incapable of extra-uterine existence. And on the basis of this definition, as has been indicated in the immediately foregoing chapter, once the fetus has attained viability, there can be no question of the crime of abortion as being verified, for an essential element in the crime is lacking.[48] Of course, a change in the definition could be made so as to abstract from the element of non-viability. But this radical and essential change appears to be wholly unjustified. From the time of the relevant legislation of Pope Sixtus V in 1588 until the present day, ecclesiastical jurisprudence has consistently embodied the element of non-viability as a characteristic note in the definition of abortion.[49] Medical science likewise indicates non-viability as a requisite for abortion.[50]

In view of these facts, and since penal laws are to be interpreted strictly,[51] the writer does not think it even solidly probable that under the law as it stands today abortion can legitimately be interpreted or defined so as to abstract from the notion of non-viability, and thus to include the viable fetus as a subject for the crime of abortion which would involve the excommunication. The writer believes that once the fetus is viable, abortion in the proper sense is out of question entirely. To induce premature birth and with deliberate malice to permit the delivered viable child to die of exposure, for example, or to otherwise kill the child, does not constitute abortion. Unquestionably such action is gravely illicit and concomitantly constitutes the crime of homicide in canon law. But for homicide it is an irregularity, and not a censure, that is incurred by force of the

sanctionibus contra abortum statutis et abortum melius quam immaturi foetus humani ex utero matris eiectionem definiri posse, sicut definiunt poenalistae civiles, *violentam interruptionem processus physiologici maturationis foetus.*"—*Institutiones,* IV, 461.

[48] Cf. *supra,* pp. 108-110.

[49] Cf. *supra,* pp. 64, 75, 90.

[50] Cf. *supra,* p. 89, and *infra,* p. 130.

[51] Canons 19, 2219.

common law. The same conclusion seems not only to be justified, but also to be the only admissible one regarding embryotomy when it is performed on a viable child: the irregularity for homicide is incurred, but not the excommunication for abortion.

In the opinion of the majority group of writers previously named, embryotomy never gives rise to the censure for abortion. Their principal reason, as has been seen, is that embryotomy is something different from abortion, and it is abortion not embryotomy that begets the incurring of the censure. This group must assume that craniotomy and like operations can be and are performed upon a non-viable as well as upon a viable fetus; they make no distinction as to the stage of fetal development in such cases. If they restricted these operations to a viable fetus, then surely some one of this group would have indicated this fact. Someone would have offered as a reason for his position the fact that in cases of craniotomy the fetus is viable; hence the penalty for abortion would be eliminated. But that is not the case. Therefore, they seem to consider that embryotomy, etc., are not only operations which may possibly be performed but actually are practiced upon the non-viable fetus.

And now, what is to be said about the nature of the juridical effects following upon embryotomy when it is performed upon a non-viable child? Are these effects to be identified with those of abortion, or does the embryotomy at least induce the censure of excommunication? In the estimation of the writer a solution is facilitated by a consideration, first of all, of what actually and factually constitutes craniotomy and its kindred mutilating operations. Most canonical writers seemingly have taken little cognizance of the *physical facts* regarding these surgical procedures.

Craniotomy and other like operations are procedures which as a matter of actual practice are undertaken upon the fetus only after it has attained the stage of viability. It is during the early months of pregnancy that the great majority of deliberately induced abortions are naturally expected to be and actually are undertaken. At this time the fetal body is so small that the operations technically and specifically known as embryotomy are very difficult to perform, and in most cases would be practically a physical impossibility.[52]

[52] Confirmation for this statement can be obtained from almost any physi-

Furthermore, the very purpose of these operations is to reduce the size of the fetus so as to permit delivery. Before the twenty-sixth or the twenty-eighth week—the period of viability—the child will not have developed to such a size as to require these destructive operations if its ejection is desired. And if they be not required, then it is only reasonable to suppose that, in the event the ejection of the fetus is desired, a less dangerous method will be selected, or a method more readily available, i. e., one which does not require surgical skill, in short, one of the numerous abortifacient procedures. And the latter are unquestionably more easy to obtain.

It is granted, however, that shortly before viability a particular instance of pregnancy may possibly present the rare case of a hydrocephalic child, or of unusually small pelvic measurements together with an unusually large fetus, or of an incorrigible presentation. Even in such cases it does not follow that embryotomy, for example, is medically indicated or will be performed. Caesarean section or other methods will often be employed in such cases. But let it be assumed that in an individual case, whether medically indicated or not, some form of mutilating operation is performed precisely in the way in which an embryotomy strictly so-called would be executed upon a viable child. Simply because the operative technique is similar or even identical, medical science would not label the procedure as embryotomy. Rather, the operation would be designated as *abortion,* despite the fact that the specific action is identical with that which is undertaken upon a viable child near term. And this is in accordance with the commonly accepted teaching in medical circles that any interruption of pregnancy before viability is called an abortion, no distinction being made relative to the method employed for the purpose of effecting this interruption.[58]

Among canonists, Beste rejects this identity of technique as a

cian. The truth of this statement becomes quite apparent, moreover, if the actual technique of these operations is considered.—Cf. De Lee, *The Principles and Practice of Obstetrics,* pp. 1153-1162; Stander, *Williams Obstetrics,* pp. 1233-1240.

[58] See Stander, *op. cit.,* pp. 808, 1113; De Lee, *op. cit.,* p. 474; Taussig, *Abortion,* p. 483. Every physician and obstetrician consulted said, in effect, that there is no reasonable questioning of the above conclusion.

possible escape from the censure for abortion, although he does not expressly consider the particular case outlined above. In agreement with the opinion of medical circles he makes the all-inclusive statement that any action by which the non-viable fetus is expelled is properly called abortion, regardless of whether it is previously killed in the mother's womb or whether it dies after expulsion from the body of the mother.[54] According to Beste embryotomy does not constitute a basis for the censure of excommunication, but it does induce the penalties for homicide, for embryotomy is performed on a viable fetus.[55]

De Siena, writing both before and after the Code, states that a surgeon who performs embryotomy in a case of difficult delivery is not liable to the censure of excommunication for the simple reason that the fetus is no longer non-viable, and consequently there is no abortion, even though he commits a grievous sin.[56]

Blat, in a context which points to a non-viable fetus, expressly states that an operation which kills the fetus in the womb before expulsion constitutes abortion.[57]

[54] "Ideo quaelibet actio, qua proles perdurante eo graviditatis termino [i. e., while the fetus is non-viable] eiicitur, proprio nomine vocatur abortus, sive proles antea in utero materno occidatur, sive vivus in lucem editus postea moriatur."—*Introductio in Codicem,* pp. 953-954.

[55] "Ex dictis pro praxi colligitur abortum non haberi nec proinde locum esse poenae in hoc canone [i. e., 2350, §1] statutae in sequentibus casibus. . . 4. Si infans iam vitalis in sinu materno per craniotomiam . . . occidatur et deinde extrahatur, quoniam eiusmodi interfectio foetus viabilis, etsi abortui seu eductioni foetus immaturi valde similis, proprie procuratio abortus dici nequit, sed constituit verum homicidium et ideo, attento can. 2219, §3, et firma illiceitate actus, poenis non abortus sed homicidii subiacet."—*Op. cit.,* p. 955.

[56] "Pariter eam [i. e., censuram] non incurrunt chirurgi, qui in difficili partu ad salvandam matrem in ejus utero foetum necant, et membratim extrahunt, quia in hoc casu foetus est jam maturus, et non est abortus, licet graviter peccent."—*Commentarius Censurarum juxta Novum Codicem Juris Canonici,* p. 56, and *Commentarius in Const. A. S.,* p. 164.

[57] "Ille [i. e., abortus] est proprie 'eiectio fetus immaturi,' qui proinde vivere nequibit, nec refert an prius occidatur,"—*De Delictis et Poenis,* p. 249. ". . . sic explicandus est §1. *Procurantes* . . . adhibendo media vel operationes qualitercumque, dummodo causent *abortum* proprie dictum [therefore an im-

Prümmer (+1931) indicates a like solution. Writing both before and after the Code, he points out first of all that abortion and embryotomy are distinct: abortion is the ejection of an immature fetus; embryotomy is he killing of a mature—hence, certainly a viable—fetus. Therefore, says Prümmer, he who procures abortion is excommunicated; he who performs embryotomy on a fetus, at least when it is mature, is free from excommunication.[58] The inference—if it be not more than an inference—certainly is that, in the event embryotomy is performed on a non-viable fetus, the operation either would not properly be embryotomy but abortion, or at least it would not excuse from the excommunication. Irregularity, however, would be incurred whether the fetus was viable or non-viable, though in the former case it would arise from the crime of homicide.[59]

Similarly De Meester and Brys state that craniotomy or any surgical operation which directly kills a viable fetus does not give rise to the excommunication which in the law is enacted against those who procure abortion. And the reason is that this operation constitutes a direct homicide rather than the procuring of an abortion in the proper sense of the latter crime.[60] It is true that these two

mature or non-viable fetus] . . . si occideretur praevie eius eiectio in abortum recideret."—*Op. cit.*, p. 250.

[58] ". . . cum abortus sit eiectio *immaturi* foetus, craniotomia autem occisio infantis *maturi*, aliqua adest distinctio inter procurationem abortus et craniotomiam. Unde sicut ille, qui librum haereticum legit, excommunicatur, qui vero audit legere librum talem, non censetur cadere in excommunicationem, ita, qui procurat abortum, excommunicatur; ille autem, qui craniotomiam foetus (saltem maturi) facit, liber est ab excommunicatione. Omnes enim censurae sunt stricte interpretandae."—*Manuale Theologiae Moralis*, II, n. 143. This identical quotation is to be found in the last edition before Prümmer's death; consequently it is certainly his personal opinion.—Cf. *op. cit.* (4.-5. ed., 3 vols., Friburgi Brisgoviae: Herder & Co., 1928), II, n. 143. See also his article, "Zieht die Kraniotomie die Exkommunikatio nach sich?"—*ThPrQs*, LXIII (1910), 586-588.

[59] "*Irregularitas* autem certo oritur ex craniotomiae patratione, quippe quae sit verum homicidium voluntarium."—*Op. cit.*, II, n. 143.

[60] "Ad *embryotomiam* seu *craniotomiam* quod spectat, vel aliam quamcumque operationem chirurgicam directe occisivam foetus *jam vitalis* [italics inserted], certum est eam esse graviter illicitam; sed cum haec operatio potius

authors, and also De Siena, do not expressly exclude from the proper scope of embryotomy all destructive surgical interference undertaken during the period of fetal non-viability, i. e., they do not state unequivocally that any and every interruption of pregnancy before viability is properly abortion and as such gives rise to the censure, regardless of the method employed to secure this interruption. But, although their statements are less clear perhaps in this respect than the affirmations of Beste and Prümmer, taken at face value they nevertheless seem to warrant the same conclusion which Prümmer and Beste propose in a more forthright manner.

The writer's opinion is that *any* procedure performed to secure the ejection or expulsion of a *non-viable* fetus constitutes abortion in the sense envisioned by the penal law of the Church, and hence gives rise to the censure of excommunication and to the irregularity *ex delicto*. It is assumed, of course, that the other requisites, as previously indicated with reference to the crime of abortion, are verified in the case.

Whether the abortionist employs hysterotomy, instrumental dilation of the cervix, tamponade, forceps, curette, cranioclast, drugs, x-ray, or any other means whatsoever seems quite irrelevant. All these various means are merely variant physical techniques which may be employed to effect the ejection of the non-viable fetus.

No matter what technique is used, it is *occisiva* and *laesiva* to the fetus. Is it to be maintained that, because the cranioclast and often the forceps and the curette attack the very body of the fetus, this procedure constitutes an *occisio*—hence not an *eiectio*—and consequently not an abortion? Is it to be maintained that, when some admittedly abortifacient technique is employed, as tamponade for

directum homicidium dicendum sit quam proprie dicta procuratio abortus, non plectitur excommunicatione qua feriuntur procurantes abortum."—De Meester, *Compendium*, III, pars 2, 259. The above quotation is repeated verbatim by Brys, "De Poena in Procurantes Abortum,"—*Collationes Brugenses*, XXXIV (1934), 43. In a previous article Brys stated simply that embryotomy does not induce excommunication, for the word abortion is to be understood strictly.—"De Poenis Latae Sententiae,"—*Collationes Brugenses*, XXXIII (1933), 187-188.

example, which loosens the fetus from the uterine site and thereby really *strangles* the fetus, this is not an *occisio*—hence an *eiectio*—and therefore an abortion? In the latter example there is no room for the contention that this "strangling" technique merely permits the fetus to die, and therefore is not directly *occisiva*. Such a contention, it appears to the writer, constitutes mere quibbling, a play on words, rather than a consideration of facts. Whether the physical technique "knifes" the fetus or "strangles" the fetus, both methods are directly *occisivae* and *laesivae* to the fetus. If the procedure of tamponade for example, which actually strangles the fetus, constitutes an abortion—and no one denies that—then the former technique likewise constitutes an abortion.

The reasonable norm in this matter is afforded by the condition of viability or non-viability. Consequently, it may be repeated that once the fetus is viable then abortion is out of the question. If the fetus is non-viable and the other elements for the crime of abortion are present, then the interruption of pregnancy constitutes an abortion regardless of the technique employed.

Article II. Removal of an Ectopic Fetus

It happens at times that the fertilized ovum does not reach the uterine cavity, the usual and normal site of development, but lodges in the ovary or in some portion of the fallopian tube or in the abdominal cavity. When gestation does not take place in the uterus, then there is the case of ectopic or extra-uterine pregnancy, of which tubal pregnancy is the most common.[61] Does the removal of a non-viable ectopic fetus constitute the crime of abortion so as to give rise to the censure and the irregularity?

Perhaps other writers have proposed an answer, but the present writer has found only two authors who consider this question. Both Barrett and Beste hold it to be probable, *"salvo meliori,"* that in this case the crime of abortion is not verified. As reason for this position Barrett states that in the case of the ectopic fetus there is

[61] Cf. De Lee, *The Principles and Practice of Obstetrics*, pp. 830 ff; Stander, *Williams Obstetrics*, pp. 436 ff.

no *procuratio abortus,* inasmuch as that presupposes the *ejectio foetus immaturi ex utero matris.*[62] Beste indicates the following reason: abortion is the expulsion of a uterine fetus, and of course the ectopic fetus is extra-uterine.[63]

To be sure, many if not most of the definitions speak of abortion as the ejection of an immature fetus from the *womb* of the mother.[64] But other definitions state simply that abortion is the ejection of an immature fetus, no *locus a quo* being mentioned.[65] The texts of ecclesiastical penal statutes against abortion have not exclusively connected the crime of abortion with the case of uterine pregnancy. As a matter of fact the law of Pope Sixtus V, upon which subsequent definitions are based, defined abortion simply as "the ejection of an immature fetus." [66] And an "immature fetus" includes the immature *ectopic* fetus as well as the immature *uterine* fetus.

Since uterine pregnancy is the ordinary and normal occurrence, it is quite natural that canonists treat and speak of the ejection from the *womb* when they discuss canonical penalties for abortion. They simply do not discuss the matter of extra-uterine pregnancy

[62] ". . . probabile est, salvo meliori, extractionem foetus in casu praegnantiae extrauterinae non esse procurationem abortus; quia haec, secus ac illa, est ejectio foetus immaturi ex utero matris."—Sabetti-Barrett, *Compendium Theologiae Moralis* (34. ed., 8. post codicem, New York: Frederick Pustet Co., Inc., 1939), n. 998, q. 1.

[63] "Ex dictis pro praxi colligitur abortum non haberi nec proinde locum esse poenae in hoc canone [i. e., 2350, §1] statutae in sequentibus casibus: . . . 5. Si quis, salvo meliori, foetum ectopicum extrahat in casu praegnationis extrauterinae, quia abortus est expulsio foetus uterini."—*Introductio in Codicem,* p. 955.

[64] V. g., Beste, *op. cit.,* p. 953; Coronata, *Institutiones,* IV, 458; Ayrinhac-Lydon, *Penal Legislation,* p. 240; Pistocchi, *I Canoni Penali,* p. 169; Cipollini, *De Censuris Latae Sententiae,* p. 176.

[65] V. g., Vermeersch, *Theologiae Moralis Principia,* II, n. 580; Chelodi, *Ius Poenale,* n. 80, 1; Bouuaert-Simenon, *Manuale Juris Canonici,* III, n. 586 IV; De Siena, *Commentarius Censurarum juxta Novum C. J. C.,* p. 55; Vermeersch-Creusen, *Epitome,* III, n. 551; Iorio, *Theologia Moralis,* III, n. 962; Bucceroni, *Institutiones Theologiae Moralis,* II, n. 1204.

[66] Const. "*Effraenatam,*" 29 oct. 1588, §1—*Fontes,* n. 165.

in relation to penalties for abortion. Ectopic pregnancy, however was not something unknown to ecclesiastical writers, for the Holy Office issued a statement in 1898 regarding the morality of the removal of an ectopic fetus.[67] And canonists unfailingly point out numerous cases and circumstances in which the canonical notion of abortion is *not* verified. Perhaps their non-inclusion of the case of the removal of a non-viable ectopic fetus among the non-abortion cases may well indicate that they regarded the case as giving rise to the penalties for abortion.

If the fact that the pregnancy is extra-uterine is the sole reason that can be assigned as a cause that excuses from the incurring of the canonical penalties, then the present writer considers that cause as insufficient for excusing anyone from incurring the penalties. The very essence of abortion seems to consist in the *lethal* removal or expulsion of a *non-viable* fetus; the precise *place from which* the fetus is removed within the mother appears to be a factor that is quite accidental.

Hence, the other presuppositions for the constitution of the crime being verified, the writer holds that the removal of a non-viable fetus from the tube, or the excision of the pregnant tube itself, is in itself a true abortion and therefore gives rise to the censure of excommunication and to the irregularity.

In practice, however, there will in all likelihood be little occasion for concern about the canonical penalties for the removal of an ectopic fetus. For this the following may be assigned as the reason. An essential requisite for the constitution of a crime is an external action which objectively is seriously sinful. And almost every ectopic pregnancy will, sooner or later, engender a pathological condition which then, independently of the pregnancy itself, constitutes a serious danger to the mother's life. In accordance with the accepted principles of moral theology, the excision of the pathological tube

[67] S. C. S. Off., 4 maii 1898 ad 3—*ASS,* XXX (1897-1898), 703-704; *Collectanae S. C. de Prop. Fide,* n. 1997; Denzinger-Bannwart-Umberg, *Enchiridion Symbolorum,* n. 1890b. Another decision was given by the Holy Office on March 5, 1902—*Collectanea S. C. de Prop. Fide,* n. 2131; Denzinger-Bannwart-Umberg, *op. cit.,* n. 1890c.

containing the fetus will in most cases be justifiable. And in that event there is no question of canonical crime, for the external action is not objectively a serious sin, but a justified mode of procedure in safeguarding the health and the life of the mother.[68]

[68] For a detailed treatment of the medical and moral aspects with relation to the removal of an ectopic fetus, see the following: Bouscaren, *Ethics of Ectopic Operations* (Chicago: Loyola University Press, 1933) ; Davis, *Moral and Pastoral Theology* (3. ed., 4 vols., New York: Sheed & Ward, Inc., 1938), II, 171-182; Bonnar, *The Catholic Doctor* (London: Burns, Oates & Washbourne, Ltd., 1938), pp. 88-90; Schlueter, "Ectopic Gestation—Medical Aspects,"—*ER*, CV (1941), 81-94, and the companion article, O'Brien, "Ectopic Gestation—Moral Aspects,"—*ER*, CV (1941), 95-103; for a rejoinder to O'Brien's article, see Davis, "Ectopic Gestation—A Rejoinder,"—*ER*, CVI (1942), 122-126; and for a reply to the latter, see O'Brien, "Ectopic Gestation,"—*ER*, CVI (1942), 282-284.

CHAPTER XI

PERSONS INVOLVED IN THE CRIME OF ABORTION

In preceding chapters an attempt has been made to indicate the essential elements proper to the crime of abortion. It remains to indicate summarily what persons can be and are involved in the procuring of abortion and hence incur the excommunication and the irregularity.

The abortion may be effected by one party, for example, by the mother herself, or by some other individual who administers drugs or performs some action even without the mother's knowledge or against her will. The actual perpetrator of the abortion of course incurs the penalties. Frequently more than one person is substantially and immediately implicated in effecting the abortion. Before any discussion in general of the classes of persons who may incur the penalties, it is to be noted that the mother can no longer by the very fact that she is the mother plead an excuse from incurring the censure, since the Code expressly states *"matre non excepta."* This phrase in canon 2350, §1, settles a dispute of centuries' standing. In view of the fact that this was so celebrated a controversy, it may be of historical and academic interest to outline the salient features of the pre-Code problem: does the mother herself incur the censure for abortion?

Article I. Pre-Code Controversy Regarding the Mother

A. From Pope Sixtus V to Pope Pius IX

In the years intervening between the legislation of Pope Sixtus V in 1588 and that of Pope Pius IX in 1869, principally the following reasons were advanced by those who considered the mother subject to the censure for abortion. (1) The wide scope and general tenor of the Constitution of Pope Sixtus V is evidence that the mother is to be included. (2) The reason or purpose of the law and the requisites for incurring the penalty are verified in the mother as well as in others. (3) She is, in fact, mentioned in §1 of the Sixtine Constitution. (4) The mother is naturally to be included under the term *principales* employed by Pope Sixtus in §7 of his Constitution.[1]

Authors who held that the mother was excused offered the following arguments. (1) Since the mother is not clearly included in the law of Pope Sixtus she is excused. (2) Pope Sixtus expressly refers to her by using the term *mulier* in relation to the penalties for homicide in vogue before his time (§1), and in relation to the penalties for the procuring of sterility (§5), but when levying the censure he employs no particular term to single her out. (3) The *principales* who certainly incur the censure (§7) are a class of co-operators, and the mother cannot be said to cooperate with herself.[2]

The generally accepted opinion was that the mother incurred the excommunication. This was held by De Graffiis (+1620)[3] and by Bonacina (+1631), the latter saying that this opinion was the one followed in practice.[4] In accepting this teaching Diana (+1663) claimed to follow Filliucius (+1622) and Dicastillus (+1653).[5] Sporer (+1714) called this view the common one and expressed his conviction that thus Pope Sixtus intended the law, but admitted

[1] Thus enumerated by De Lugo (*Responsiones Morales,* lib. II, dubium IV, n. 3—*Disputationes,* tom. VIII, 106-107) and by St. Alphonsus (*Theologia Moralis,* lib. III, n. 395), both of whom, however, accepted the contrary opinion. It may be noted here that Leech is incorrect in stating that Pope Gregory XIV excused the mother from the excommunication.—Cf. Leech, *A Comparative Study of the Constitution "Apostolicae Sedis" and the Codex Juris Canonici,* The Catholic University of America Canon Law Studies, No. 15 (Washington, D. C.: The Catholic University of America, 1922), pp. 83-84. The modification made by Pope Gregory in the Sixtine legislation in no way pertained to the question of the mother's incurring or being immune from the censure for abortion.—Cf. *supra,* pp. 62-63.

[2] De Lugo, *Responsiones Morales,* lib. II, dubium IV, nn. 4, 8—*Disputationes,* tom. VIII, 107-108; St. Alphonsus, *Theologia Moralis,* lib. III, n. 395; Salmanticenses, *Cursus Theologiae Moralis,* tom. III, tract. XIII *de restitutione,* cap. II, punct. IV, § III, nn. 70-71.

[3] *Decisiones Aureae Casuum Conscientiae,* lib. II, cap. 63, nn. 10-11.

[4] *Opera de Morali Theologia,* tom. II, disp. II, q. ult., punct. 10, n. 6, and tom. III, disp. II, q. II, n. 13.

[5] *Omnium Resolutionum Moralium Tomi Decem,* tom. V, tract. VI, resolut. 35, n. 5.

that grave fear would excuse the mother from the censure.[6] Pauwels (+ after 1759) also accepted the more comprehensive opinion[7] and Gury (+1866) recognized no valid reason in substantiation of the lenient viewpoint which held the mother to be excused.[8]

While admitting the comprehensive view to be the more common one, Cardinal De Lugo (+1645) preferred to follow Avila (+1601) and Naldus (+1645), holding the mother to be excused from incurring the censure. The Cardinal maintained that the text of the Sixtine Constitution gave this opinion sufficient probability, but added that if the contrary teaching were followed in practice it should be observed by all.[9] The Salmanticenses (1665-1724) excused the mother.[10] St. Alphonsus Liguori (+1787) likewise accepted as very probable the opinion that the mother did not incur the censure, particularly since the matter was doubtful.[11] In subscribing to the lenient teaching the Barbielliani Editors (1784) added that there was a predominant reason to hold the mother excused when grave fear moved her to commit the abortion.[12] Scavini (+1869) likewise excused the mother from the censure.[13]

B. From Pope Pius IX to the Code of Canon Law

When Pope Pius IX issued his Constitution "*Apostolicae Sedis,*" the law regarding the censure for abortion was stated very simply: Excommunication reserved to the ordinary is incurred *ipso facto* by "*procurantes abortum, effectu secuto.*"[14] The controversy regarding the mother continued.

[6] *Theologia Moralis,* tom. III, pars IV, n. 718.

[7] *Tractatus Theologicus de Casibus Reservatis,* tom. I, n. 153—*MTCC,* XVIII, 989.

[8] *Compendium Theologiae Moralis,* p. 901, col. 2, note 2.

[9] *Responsiones Morales,* lib. II, dubium IV, nn. 4, 8—*Disputationes,* tom. VIII, 107-108.

[10] *Cursus Theologiae Moralis,* tom. III, tract. XIII *de restitutione,* cap. II, punct. IV, § III, n. 70.

[11] *Theologia Moralis,* lib. III, n. 395.

[12] *Additiones recentiores ex editionibus barbiellianis* in Ferraris, *Bibliotheca,* v. *abortus,* n. 35.

[13] *Theologia Moralis Universa* (13. ed., 4 vols., Mediolani, 1882), I, n. 905.

[14] § III, n. 2—*Fontes,* n. 552.

After this Constitution the principal reasons assigned for not excusing the mother from the censure were the following. (1) The law of Pope Pius IX is general, making no distinction to favor the mother. (2) The purpose of the law—the preventing of abortion—is served very substantially by potentially including the mother under the excommunication, for she certainly can be and frequently is the principal cause of the abortion. (3) Since co-operators are not included in the legislation of Pope Pius (as was almost universally admitted)[15] the law could be violated with impunity and would be rendered useless if the mothers themselves were exempted. (4) The mother was subject to the censure under the former law.[16]

Many leading theologians and canonists accepted these arguments and considered the mother as coming under the designation *procurantes,* and thereby as being subject to the censure. D'Annibale (+1892),[17] De Varceno (+1893),[18] Genicot (+1900),[19] Wernz (+1914)[20] and Hollweck (+1926)[21] accepted the opinion, but also stated expressly that grave fear on the part of the mother excused her from incurring the censure. Bucceroni (+1918)[22] saw no valid basis for any of the reasons which were advanced by those who excused the mother, and Lega (+1935) thought that the opinion which exempted the mother could not be followed in practice.[23]

[15] Cf. *supra,* pp. 74-75.

[16] Thus summarized by Pennacchi (*De Abortu,* pp. 19-20), who personally held the contrary opinion and offered a detailed refutation of the above arguments (*op. cit.,* pp. 21-23).

[17] *In Constitutionem A. S.,* n. 161.

[18] *Compendium Theologiae Moralis,* II, 495-496.

[19] *Theologiae Moralis Institutiones,* II, n. 608.

[20] *Ius Decretalium,* VI, n. 370 II.

[21] *Die kirchlichen Strafgesetze,* § 163, note 2.

[22] *Institutiones Theologiae Moralis,* II, n. 1204.

[23] *Praelectiones de Iudiciis,* n. 55. Others holding the mother subject to the censure were: Hinschius, *Das Kirchenrecht de Katholiken und Protestanten in Deutschland,* V, 799, footnote 1; Ernestus Müller, *Theologia Moralis* (3 vols., Vindobonae, 1876), III, 538; Avanzini, in Pennacchi, *Commentarium in Constitutionem "Apostolicae Sedis" qua Censurae Latae Sententiae Limitantur* (2 vols., Romae, 1883), I, 30, footnote 1; Heiner, *Die kirchlichen Censuren,* p. 246. Téphany (*Constitution "Apostolicae Sedis" Commentaire,* n. 407) and Heidenreich ("Dissertatio,"—*AKKR,* LXIII [1890], 379-380) expressly admitted the probability of the opposite opinion.

The reasons advanced by the proponents of the lenient opinion were these. (1) The term *procurantes* is admittedly taken by Pope Pius IX from the Constitution of Pope Sixtus V; and the latter did not include mothers under the censure. (2) The intention of Pius IX was to restrict, not to extend, censures. (3) Since the matter is at least doubtful, the mother cannot in practice be held subject to the censure until an authentic declaration so states.[24]

Among those who subscribed to the view which exempts the mother were the following authors: Ballerini (+1881),[25] Pennacchi (+1898),[26] Mocchegiani (+1905),[27] Lehmkuhl (+1917),[28] Noldin (+1922),[29] and others.[30]

Thus the question remained unsettled until the Code of Canon Law expressly included the mother as subject to the censure for procuring abortion. Of course the mother may still be excused on the grounds of fear, ignorance, etc., factors which apply also to other persons involved in procuring abortion, and for that matter, involved in other canonical crimes.[31]

Article II. Complicity and Co-operation in Abortion

A. Regarding the Censure

Canon 2350, §1, which establishes the censure of excommunication for the procuring of abortion, makes no mention of complicity and co-operation. But the Code provides special canons apropos of complicity and co-operation in crime in general, and in virtue of

[24] Cf. Pennacchi, *De Abortu,* p. 20; Heidenreich, "Dissertatio,"—*AKKR,* LXIII (1890), 379; citation in the following footnotes regarding this discussion.

[25] Ballerini-Palmieri, *Opus Theologicum Morale,* VII, n. 320.

[26] *De Abortu,* p. 20.

[27] *Iurisprudentia Ecclesiastica,* II, n. 529.

[28] *Theologia Moralis,* II, n. 1247.

[29] *De Poenis Ecclesiasticis,* n. 93, 2.

[30] Cornelisse (+1923), *Compendium Theologiae Moralis,* I, 589; De Siena, *Commentarius in Constitutionem Apostolicae Sedis,* p. 165; *NRT,* XI (1879), 320.

[31] See canons 2201 to 2206. Regarding ignorance, see Swoboda, *Ignorance in Relation to the Imputability of Delicts,* The Catholic University of America Canon Law Studies, No. 143 (Washington, D. C.: The Catholic University of America Press, 1941).

these canons certain kinds of participation in abortion will involve excommunication. In accordance with the provisions of canon 2231 [32] and canon 2209, §1 and §3, the censure of excommunication is incurred *ipso facto* by those who participate in abortion either (1) as co-agents, or (2) as necessary co-operators.[33] It is apparent from canon 2231 that the censure is not incurred by those who merely facilitate the abortion (canon 2209, §4) or by those who are mere negative co-operators (canon 2209, §6)—those who do nothing to prevent the abortion, although perhaps they are morally bound to do so.[34]

1. *Co-Agents Incur the Censure*

Co-agents in the procuring of abortion are all those who conspire by common intention and at the same time physically participate in the specific action or procedure which effects the abortion. Such participants place executive acts, acts which precisely effect the ejection of the fetus, and not those acts which are only preparatory or facilitating to the abortion itself. The mother and the abortionist are co-agents in this sense, and as such they both incur the penalty of excommunication.[35] Even though the abortion be done for the

[32] Si plures ad delictum perpetrandum concurrerint, licet unus tantum in lege nominetur, ii quoque de quibus in can. 2209, §§1-3, tenentur, nisi lex aliud caverit, eadem poena; ceteri vero non item, sed alia iusta poena prudenti Superioris arbitrio puniendi sunt, nisi lex peculiarem poenam in ipsos constituat.

[33] Regarding co-agents, canon 2209, §1: Qui communi delinquendi consilio simul physice concurrunt in delictum, omnes eodem modo rei habentur, nisi adiuncta alicuius culpabilitatem augeant vel minuant.

Regarding necessary co-operators, canon 2209, §3: Non solum mandans qui est principalis delicti auctor, sed etiam qui ad delicti consummationem inducunt vel in hanc quoquo modo concurrunt, non minorem, ceteris paribus, imputabilitatem contrahunt, quam ipse delicti executor, si delictum sine eorum opera commissum non fuisset.

[34] Ayrinhac-Lydon, *Penal Legislation*, pp. 241-242; Noldin-Schönegger, *De Censuris*, n. 92, 2.

[35] Canon 2209, §1. For detailed treatment of co-agents in crime, see Eltz, *Co-operation in Crime*, The Catholic University of America Canon Law Studies, No. 156, Chapter IX. The writer consulted this work in manuscript form; it is to appear in print shortly.

advantage of or at the command of another, the party or parties who actually perform it incur the censure.[36]

Persons who prepare or sell drugs, sterilize the instruments, counsel the abortion, etc., perform acts that are in themselves indifferent in so far as the execution of abortion is concerned. Such actions do not constitute the specific physical procedure which effects the abortion, but are rather preparatory and facilitating acts. Persons performing such and similar actions are not co-agents of but co-operators in the abortion. In practice it frequently will be difficult to establish this distinction, but the distinction must be sought by considering the nature of the specific concrete acts which were directed to the commission of the abortion in question.[37]

2. *Necessary Co-operators Incur the Censure*

If a person who performs a certain action that is directed toward the effecting of abortion cannot be established as a true co-agent or executor, this does not necessarily mean that he escapes the incurring of the censure. He may well be a *necessary* co-operator. As such he will incur the censure, as will be explained immediately.

The Code designates the *mandans,* who shares no physical participation at all, the *principalis delicti auctor.*[38] A most effective participant in the crime is the *mandans*—one who by command, threat, hire, etc., secures another to perform the criminal action. The *mandans,* in a certain sense, performs the abortion, not *per se* but *per alium,* and as such unquestionably incurs the censure for abortion.[39] It is presumed, of course, that the mandate was actually carried out, and that the one who performed the abortion had not

[36] Cf. Ayrinhac-Lydon, *op. cit.,* p. 241; Cerato, *Censurae Vigentes,* p. 101; Cappello, *De Censuris,* n. 387; Vermeersch, *Theologiae Moralis Principia,* II, n. 584; Brys, "De Poena in Procurantes Abortum,"—*Collationes Brugenses,* XXXIV (1934), 45.

[37] Cf. Eltz, *op. cit.,* Chapter IX.

[38] Canon 2209, §3, quoted in footnote 33 of this Chapter.

[39] See v. g., Michiels, *De Delictis et Poenis,* Vol. I (Lublin-Polonia: Universitas Catholica, 1934), 311-312; Cappello, *De Censuris,* n. 387; Noldin-Schönegger, *De Censuris,* n. 92, 2; Prümmer, *Manuale Theologiae Moralis,* II, n. 131; Cerato, *Censurae Vigentes,* p. 101.

previously determined to do so. In short, the mandate must be a true mandate.[40]

Effective co-operators in abortion may be those who by counsel, material assistance, or by any other means induce or concur in the commission of the crime, provided however that their co-operation was *necessary* for the commission of the *abortion in question*. The *abortion in question:* the condition expressed in canon 2209, §3—"si delictum sine eorum opera commissum non fuisset"—must be referred to a specific instance of abortion, not to the crime of abortion in general. It is apparent therefore that the necessity of the co-operation can be determined only after a consideration of the various circumstances which attend the perpetration of abortion in a particular concrete instance.[41] And in actual practice even with concrete cases at hand it will often be difficult to evaluate the necessity or non-necessity of co-operation, for example, of druggists, nurses, advisers, etc. Each case will have to be considered on its own merits.[42]

It is indisputable that excommunication is entailed by only such co-operation which was *necessary* for the effecting of abortion in a particular concrete case. But is this co-operation to be understood as necessary in the sense that without it this particular abortion *would* not *de facto* have been committed, or *could* not have been committed? The answer depends upon the interpretation of the clause in canon 2209, §3, "si delictum sine eorum opera commissum non fuisset." Contrary to what apparently is the commonly accepted interpretation of "commissum non fuisset," several authors venture the opinion that physical co-operation is to be judged necessary only then when without it the particular crime in given circumstances *could not* have been committed. This is proposed as at least

[40] Cf. Coronata, *Institutiones*, IV, 118; Cappello, *De Censuris*, n. 28.

[41] Wernz-Vidal, *Ius Canonicum*, VII, 144; Eltz, *op. cit.*, Chapter XI.

[42] Compare, for example, the various opinions regarding the co-operation of druggists: Cappello, *De Censuris*, n. 387; Vermeersch, *Theologiae Moralis Principia*, II, n. 584; Beste, *Introductio in Codicem*, p. 984; Prümmer, *Manuale Theologiae Moralis*, II, n. 142; Vermeersch-Creusen, *Epitome*, III, nn. 392, 495; Stockums, "Abortus und kirchliches Strafrecht,"—*Theologie und Glaube*, XV (1923), 98.

a probable opinion by Heimberger (+1933),[43] Michiels,[44] and Eltz,[45] who appear to be the only authors who *ex professo* give this particular question any consideration. However, as Eltz points out, this same interpretation seems to be implied and insinuated by others.[46] Until the opinion advanced by these authors has been refuted, or until the matter has been decided by an official decision, there appears to be a founded *dubium iuris*. Consequently that interpretation of canon 2209, §3, which affords more leniency in a particular case of co-operation in abortion may be followed in practice—in accordance with the general principles of interpretation.[47]

In any event, as long as there is positive doubt about the necessity of co-operation in a particular case of abortion, the censure of excommunication cannot be attributed to the person thus co-operating.[48]

3. *Untenable Opinions Regarding Co-operation*

Several writers since the advent of the present Code express opinions relative to complicity and co-operation in the crime of abortion that are untenable in the light of the present-day law. Contrary to the present law, before the Code there was no general statute in law by which co-operators in crime were penalized in case they were not mentioned in the statute penalizing a definite crime. If they were not mentioned in the latter individual law, they did not incur the penalty stipulated in that law.[49] Thus, after the Constitution *"Apostolicae Sedis"* of Pope Pius IX and until the advent of the Code, co-operators were excused from the censure for abortion

[43] *Aus dem Strafrecht des Codex J. C.*, Sonderabdruck aus der Bonner Festgabe für Ernst Zitelmann (München-Leipzig, 1923), pp. 68-71. Quoted and cited by Michiels, *op. cit.*, pp. 322-323.

[44] *De Delictis et Poenis*, I, 322-324.

[45] *Co-operation in Crime*, Chapter XI, Article III.

[46] See Eltz, *op. cit.*, Chapter XI, Article III; Roberti, *De Delictis et Poenis*, I, n. 188.

[47] See canons 15; 19; 2219, §1.

[48] See Oesterle, "Mitwirkung zur procuratio abortus,"—*ThPrQs*, LXXXIX (1936), 354-355 and 584.

[49] See Wernz, *Ius Decretalium*, VI, n. 44.

simply because they were not included in the statute relative to abortion enacted by Pope Pius IX.[50]

Several post-Code authors neglect to take cognizance of the special norms in the Code regarding complicity and co-operation in crime in general, notably in canons 2231 and 2209. In their opinions regarding co-operation in abortion they appear to be guided solely by the pre-Code jurisprudence in this regard.

Thus, Augustine and De Siena maintain that the person who actually performs the abortion is to be excused from censure when he acts as a *mandatarius*—i. e., when he performs the abortion solely in the name of and because of the commission given him by some other party. The reason alleged by Augustine is that "the question is controverted." [51] More correctly, the question *was* controverted before the Code. As has been indicated in the historical part of this study, before the Code many authors considered the *mandatarius*, although executing the abortion, to be a mere co-operator. And co-operators were not included in the penal statute of Pope Pius IX. Moreover, it is evident that Augustine reflects the former teaching in this regard, for as authorities he cites only pre-Code authors, and does not even allude to canons 2231 and 2209.[52] De Siena's post-Code work [53] gives practically a repetition verbatim of his statement regarding the pre-Code law.[54]

Cipollini excuses even the *mandans*,[55] the statement of canon 2209, §3, notwithstanding!

Some writers make the express and simple statement that co-operators in abortion do not incur the censure because co-operators are not mentioned in canon 2350, §1. The exemption is thus stated by Bargilliat (+1926) [56] and De Siena.[57] According to Cipollini, if the

[50] Cf. *supra*, pp. 74-75.

[51] *Commentary*, VIII, 400-401, see also 402.

[52] *Commentary*, VIII, *loc. cit.*

[53] *Commentarius Censurarum*, pp. 55-56. This work appeared in 1918.

[54] *Commentarius in Constitutionem Apostolicae Sedis*, p. 163. This work appeared in its third edition in 1902.

[55] *De Censuris Latae Sententiae*, p. 175.

[56] *Praelectiones Juris Canonici* (37. ed., 2 vols., Parisiis: Apud Baston, Berche et Pagis, 1923-1924), I, n. 386.

[57] *Commentarius Censurarum*, pp. 55-56.

co-operator does not participate in the precise physical action which executes the abortion—hence, even though his co-operation may have been necessary for the crime—he is excused from censure.[58]

These opinions, although occasionally repeated by others [59] cannot be accepted today on their face value. There is no general exemption for co-operators. All cases involving the censure for abortion must be determined according to the principles that govern the factor of co-operation in crime in general, as has been indicated in this chapter.[60]

B. Regarding the Irregularity

Canon 985, 4°, states that an irregularity *ex delicto* is incurred by those who procure and by all who co-operate in abortion.[61]

The one who performs or participates in the very act which induces abortion beyond all question incurs the irregularity. It is here understood of course that the other requisites for the crime are verified in the case.

Apparently because the Code uses the expression *all co-operators* some few authors, as Cerato for example, hold that the irregularity is incurred as a result of negative co-operation.[62] But by far the great majority of canonists maintains that mere negative co-operators are not included among those who incur the irregularity in question, but that *positive* co-operation is required as a basis for the incurring of the irregularity.[63] Mere negative co-operation is in

[58] *De Censuris Latae Sententiae*, p. 176.

[59] V. g., McHugh, "Casus Moralis—Canonical Penalties for Abortion,"—*HPR*, XXXIV (1933-1934), 522-524.

[60] See Woywod, "Answers to Questions—What Persons Come Under 'Procurantes Abortum'?"—*HPR*, XL (1939-1940), 324-325.

[61] Canon 985. Sunt irregulares ex delicto: . . . 4° Qui voluntarium homicidium perpetrarunt aut fetus humani abortum procuraverunt, effectu secuto, omnesque cooperantes.

[62] *Censurae Vigentes*, p. 229.

[63] V. g., Woywod, *Practical Commentary*, I, 532-533; Bouuaert-Simenon, *Manuale Juris Canonici*, II, n. 203, 4; Vermeersch-Creusen, *Epitome*, II, n. 257; Blat, *De Sacramentis*, n. 349; Cappello, *De Sacra Ordinatione*, n. 506, 7-8; Noldin-Schmitt, *Summa Theologia Moralis*, III, n. 495; Wernz-Vidal, *Ius Canonicum*, IV-1, 335-336.

the strict sense not true co-operation,[64] and the pre-Code jurisprudence moreover held negative co-operators excused.[65]

Consequently, it may be safely held that at least *positive* co-operation is required for the incurring of the irregularity. But the question arises: is the irregularity incurred only by those whose co-operation is *necessary* for the commission of the abortion, or is it incurred also by those whose co-operation merely *facilitates* the abortion?

Practically all the post-Code authors are satisfied to say simply that an efficacious positive co-operation is demanded in order that the irregularity be incurred. They do not require that the participation be *necessary* to the abortion here and now committed, as is the case regarding the censure of excommunication. In fact, quite the contrary is implied.[66]

Beste, however, states that the phrase "*omnesque cooperatores*" of canon 985, 4°, is to be understood as designating simply those of whom mention is made in canon 2209, §§1-3; he offers no additional comment or explanation. Consequently, in accordance with this opinion the irregularity is incurred by only those co-operators whose contribution, whether moral (e. g., by counsel) or physical (e. g., by providing the required instruments) was *necessary* for the commission of the abortion.[67] Jombart says that it *seems* the co-operators mentioned in 985, 4°, are to be restricted to those mentioned in canon 2209, §§1-3.[68] Lydon expresses the same opinion, i. e., the irregularity for co-operation in abortion is incurred by "all necessary co-operators."[69] While Beste and Jombart expressly restrict the irregu-

[64] Vermeersch, *Theologiae Moralis Principia*, III, n. 657; Wernz, *Ius Decretalium*, VI, n. 42.

[65] Cf. *supra*, pp. 66-67. See also Vermeersch-Creusen, *Epitome*, II, n. 257.

[66] See also in addition to the authors cited in footnote 63, the following: Augustine, *Commentary*, IV, 491; Prümmer, *Manuale Theologiae Moralis*, II, n. 142, and especially n. 144; Iorio, *Theologia Moralis*, II, n. 962.

[67] Beste, *Introductio in Codicem*, p. 533; see also *ibid.*, p. 883.

[68] "Même parmi les coopérateurs positifs, il faut, semble-t-il, restreindre l'irrégularité à ceux dont la coopération fut pro chaine et efficace, tels qu'ils sont mentionnés à propos des délits dans les troit premiers paragraphes du c. 2209."—*Le Sacrament De L'Ordre*, p. 79.

[69] *Ready Answers in Canon Law*, p. 322.

larity to necessary co-operators, Lydon's statement implies the same.

The writer is inclined to disagree with the acceptance of this restrictive meaning for the phrase *"omnesque cooperatores"* of canon 985, 4°. The above named authors indicate no reason for this restriction in meaning. It is true that canon 2209, §4, states expressly that co-operation which merely facilitated the commission of a crime and which was not essential to its commission involves less imputability.[70] It appears, however, that this diminished imputability need not immediately be ruled out as incapable of begetting the irregularity. So long as the positive co-operation because of its relation to the abortion is objectively a seriously sinful external act, the irregularity can be incurred.[71]

In the pre-Code jurisprudence which dealt specifically with the irregularity incurred for the crime of abortion there did not appear to be any restriction of the factor of co-operation in such a manner that there was contemplated only that co-operation or participation which was necessary for the commission of the abortion. The Constitution of Sixtus V in its enactment of an irregularity for abortion continued as binding law down to the advent of the present Code. And this Constitution was understood by pre-Code authors as having enacted an irregularity for those who co-operated in procuring abortion, with no restriction being made for the purpose of exempting those whose contribution to the crime was not essential to its execution.[72]

It may be recalled, moreover, that an irregularity, even an irregularity which arises *ex delicto,* is not primarily a juridical penalty; it is not so much meant to punish a delinquent as it is intended to safeguard the dignity of the clerical state.[73] Consequently the writ-

[70] Si vero eorum concursus facilius tantum reddidit delictum, quod etiam sine eorundem concursu commissum fuisset, minorem imputabilitatem secumfert.

[71] Cf. canon 986.

[72] See *supra,* pp. 66-67; also Lega, *Praelectiones de Iudiciis,* IV, n. 55; Lehmkuhl, *Theologia Moralis,* II, n. 1294; De Angelis, *Praelectiones Iuris Canonici,* IV, 222; Bargilliat, *Praelectiones Juris Canonici* (24. ed., 2 vols., Parisiis: Apud Berche et Tralin, 1907), I, n. 335, b.

[73] See Cappello, *De Sacra Ordinatione,* n. 435; Woywod, *Practical Commentary,* I, 522.

er's opinion is that, other requirements being verified, the irregularity for co-operating in the crime of abortion is incurred by one whose *positive* co-operation by reason of its relation to the abortion in question constitutes an objectively seriously sinful act.

In practice very often those whose co-operation is not necessary to the commission of the abortion will escape the irregularity even according to this more comprehensive viewpoint, simply because their material participation does not constitute serious external, objective sin. In cases of doubt supported by positive reason, the irregularity cannot be attributed to such co-operators.

CHAPTER XII

THE RESULTS WHICH *IPSO FACTO* FOLLOW UPON THE CRIME OF ABORTION

SINCE the purpose of this commentary is to indicate what specifically constitutes the crime of abortion, this final chapter points out only summarily the results which *ipso facto* follow upon the crime. These results are twofold: (1) excommunication reserved to the ordinary,[1] and (2) irregularity *ex delicto*.[2]

Absolution from the censure of excommunication is reserved "to the ordinary," that is, not specifically to the proper ordinary of the person incurring the censure. Consequently, in accordance with a general provision regarding censures thus reserved, absolution or the faculties to absolve from this excommunication may be given by any ordinary for his own subjects, and by any local ordinary also for *peregrini*.[3] The major superior of a clerical exempt religious institute, as a true ordinary,[4] can absolve and can delegate other priests to absolve those and only those who are his subjects.

Only for the cases of people who are in danger of death,[5] or also in the more urgent cases as defined by the law,[6] does the simple confessor have faculties in virtue of the Code to absolve from this censure. But since the faculty of the ordinaries, both local and religious, is *ex potestate ordinaria*, the power to absolve from the excommunication incurred for abortion can be and frequently is delegated even habitually to other confessors.[7]

[1] Canon 2350, §1. This canon adds that a cleric is in addition to be deposed. Regarding the *ferendae sententiae* penalty of deposition, see Findlay, *Canonical Norms Governing the Deposition and Degradation of Clerics,* The Catholic University of America Canon Law Studies, No. 130 (Washington, D. C.: The Catholic University of America Press, 1941).

[2] Canon 985, 4°.

[3] Canon 2253, 3°.

[4] Cf. canons 198, §1, and 488, 8°.

[5] Canon 2252.

[6] Canon 2254.

[7] Cf. canon 199, §1. Not infrequently this concession is made by local ordinaries in the usual diocesan faculties.

Those confessors who are members of clerical exempt religious institutes and who enjoy the "privileges of regulars" can absolve from this excommunication by reason of these privileges, and they can moreover do so without the necessity of a recourse to higher superiors for the *mandata*.[8]

The irregularity incurred for this crime is a permanent impediment to the licit reception of orders and to the licit exercise of orders already received.[9] The irregularity can be removed only by dispensation.

The irregularity arising from the crime of abortion is expressly excluded from the faculty which the Code of Canon Law gives to all ordinaries, both local and religious, to permit them to dispense their subjects from the irregularities which have arisen from occult crimes. This particular irregularity is likewise excluded from the similar faculty conceded to all confessors under certain circumstances and in cases specified in the law.[10] Ordinarily, therefore, recourse must be made to the Holy See for a dispensation. But sometimes the Holy See gives to certain ecclesiastical superiors, and even to simple confessors, special faculties whereby a dispensation may be granted under specified conditions, usually in order to permit the exercise of orders already received.[11] Likewise, authors list special faculties relative to the dispensation from the irregularity for abortion, which faculties may be exercised by certain clerical exempt religious who enjoy the "privileges of regulars." [12]

[8] Regarding these privileges, see Vermeersch-Creusen, *Epitome*, I, n. 785, 5; Coronata, *Institutiones*, I, 819-820; Noldin-Schönegger, *De Censuris*, n. 95; Lyszczarczyk, *Compendium Privilegiorum Regularium praesertim Ordinis Fratrum Minorum* (Leopoli, 1906), p. 146.

[9] Cf. canons 968, 983. For a detailed consideration of the effects of irregularity, see Cappello, *De Sacra Ordinatione*, nn. 444-448.

[10] Cf. canon 990.

[11] See, v. g., *Quinquennial Faculties of Ordinaries:* Latest Formula for the United States—Faculties from the Sacred Penitentiary, n. 9—Bouscaren, *The Canon Law Digest* (2 vols. and *Supplement—1941*, Milwaukee: The Bruce Publishing Co., 1934-1941), *Supplement—1941*, p. 36.

[12] See, v. g., Vermeersch-Creusen, *Epitome*, I, n. 785, 5, and II, n. 261; Coronata, *Institutiones*, I, 819; Burkhard von Wolfenschiessen, "Das Franziskanische Privilegienrecht,"—*Collectanea Franciscana*, IV (1934), 337-362, especially 354-355.

CONCLUSIONS

1. The canon of the Council of Ancyra (314) which demanded ten years of public penance for abortion appears to have been basic for ecclesiastical legislation in the punishment of abortion up to the time of Gratian.

2. The Council of Lerida (524) was the first to apply the penalties for abortion to *men*. Furthermore, the canons of this Council contain the first reference to *clerics* in connection with this crime.

3. The prevention of conception was for the first time subjected to canonical punishment by the legislation of St. Martin of Braga (+c.580).

4. Ecclesiastical law has always viewed the abortion of an animated fetus as murder, and although the Councils before the Middle Ages enacted penalties specifically against abortion, from the time of the *Decretum* of Gratian (c.1140) to Pope Sixtus V (1585-1590) the penalty of the general ecclesiastical law was simply the penalty for murder. From Pope Sixtus V to the present day, both the irregularity and the censure of excommunication have been applied specifically to abortion.

5. The distinction between an animated and a non-animated (formed and non-formed) fetus, although admitted by several of the early Fathers, was not accepted by the ecclesiastical legislation which punished abortion until after the time of Gratian. Except for the short interval of three years (between the Constitutions of Popes Sixtus V and Gregory XIV [1590-1591]) the theory of delayed animation was used as a juridical norm from the twelfth century onward to the Code of Canon Law with regard to the irregularity, and from the twelfth century to the Constitution *"Apostolicae Sedis"* (1869) with regard to the censure of excommunication.

6. The essential notion of *procurare* in relation to abortion is that the abortion be intended and be a result of the means deliberately used for this specific purpose. It is not required that the *finis operis* of these means be solely *abortifacient*.

7. The definition of abortion as employed in ecclesiastical jurisprudence today was first used by Pope Sixtus V in 1588. And in ac-

cordance with the jurisprudence of the following four centuries and until the Holy See determines otherwise, the element of fetal non-viability must be retained in the canonical definition of abortion.

8. This definition of abortion as *eiectio foetus immaturi* does not imply that the fetus be alive after delivery, but only that it be living when the abortion procedure is started.

9. It is probable that the censure of excommunication is not incurred if the fetus which is ejected has attained absolute, i. e., technical, viability. The irregularity for homicide, however, is incurred, provided of course that the various other factors essential to the constitution of crime are verified in the case.

10. As long as it is a non-viable fetus which is affected, the crime of abortion is verified even though the particular technique employed involves first the killing of the fetus and then its detachment and expulsion from the body of the mother.

11. Craniotomy and any method of killing the *viable* fetus in the womb is not abortion. Illicit and even malicious premature delivery which results in the death of a *viable* child is not abortion. Consequently the excommunication for abortion is not incurred in either of these cases, but the irregularity for homicide is involved.

12. An ectopic or extra-uterine pregnancy does not of itself preclude the crime of abortion.

13. Co-operators in the crime of abortion incur the censure of excommunication only when their co-operation was necessary for the perpetration of the particular abortion in question. They incur the irregularity, however, even when their co-operation in the crime was only such that the abortion could and would have been perpetrated without their help. Naturally, it is presupposed that the co-operation carries the note of serious sin, both subjectively and objectively.

BIBLIOGRAPHY

Sources

Acta Sanctae Sedis, 41 vols., Romae, 1865-1908.

Agapios & Nicodemus, Πηδάλιον, ἤτοι ἅπαντες οἱ ἱεροὶ καὶ θεῖοι κανόνες, 5. ed., Athens: J. N. Kesisoglou, 1908.

Alvizatos, A. S., Οἱ ἱεροὶ κανόνες, Athens: "O Prometheus," 1923.

Augustinus, Antonius, *Antiquae Collectiones Decretalium cum Antonii Augustini Episcopi Ilerdensis Notis*, Ilerdae, 1576.

Beveregius, Guglielmus, *Synodicon sive Pandectae Canonum et Conciliorum*, 2 vols., Oxford, 1672.

Biblia Sacra Polyglotta, ed. Brian Walton, 6 vols., London, 1657.

Canones et Decreta Sacrosancti Oecumenici Concilii Tridentini, Romae: Ex Typographia Polyglotta S. C. de Prop. Fide, 1882.

Codex Iuris Canonici Pii X Pontificis Maximi iussu digestus Benedicti XV auctoritate promulgatus, Romae: Typis Polyglottis Vaticanis, 1917.

Codicis Iuris Canonici Fontes cura Emi. Petri Card. Gasparri Editi, 9 vols., Romae (postea Civitate Vaticana): Typis Polyglottis Vaticanis, 1923-1939. (Vols. VII, VIIII, IX ed. cura et studio Emi. Iustiniani Card. Serédi.)

Collectanea S. Congregationis de Propaganda Fide, 2 vols., Romae: Ex Typographia Polyglotta S. C. de Prop. Fide, 1907.

Corpus Iuris Canonici, ed. Lipsiensis 2. post Aemilii Ludovici Richteri curas . . . instruxit Aemilius Friedberg, 2 vols., Lipsiae: Ex Officina Bernhardi Tauchnitz, 1879-1881. Editio anastatice repetita, Lipsiae: Tauchnitz, 1928.

Corpus Iuris Civilis, 3 vols., Berolini: Apud Weidmannos, 1928-1929; Vol. I, ed. stereotypa 15., *Institutiones*, recognovit P. Krueger, *Digesta*, recognovit T. Mommsen, retractavit P. Krueger; Vol. II, ed. stereotypa 10., *Codex Iustinianus*, recognovit et retractavit P. Krueger; Vol. III, ed. stereotypa 5., *Novellae Constitutiones*, recognovit R. Schoell et absolvit G. Kroll.

Decretales D. Gregorii Papae IX, una cum Glossis Restitutae, Romae, 1582.

Decretum Gratiani Emendatum et Notationibus Illustratum una cum Glossis, Romae, 1582.

Denzinger, H.-Bannwart, C.-Umberg, J., *Enchiridion Symbolorum, Definitionum, et Declarationum de Rebus Fidei et Morum*, 21.-23. ed., Friburgi Brisgoviae: Herder & Co., 1937.

Friedberg, Aemilius, *Quinque Compilationes Antiquae*, Lipsiae, 1882.

Funk, F. X., *Didascalia et Constitutiones Apostolorum*, 2 vols., Paderborn, 1905.

———, *Patres Apostolici*, 2. ed., 2 vols., Tubingae, 1901 and 1913.

Ghilardi, Joannes T., *Pontificiae Constitutiones in Bullariis Magno et Romano Contentae et aliunde desumptae ex Epitome Aloysii Guerra selectae*, editio novissima, Monteregali, 1870.

Hartzheim, Joseph, *Concilia Germaniae,* 11 vols., Coloniae Augustae Agrippinensium, 1759-1790.

Hinschius, Paulus, *Decretales Pseudo-Isidorianae et Capitula Angilramni,* Lipsiae, 1863.

Jaffé, Philippus, *Regesta Pontificum Romanorum ab condita Ecclesia ad annum post Christum natum MCXCVIII, Berolini,* 1851.

Liber Sextus Decretalium D. Bonifacii Papae VIII suae integritati una cum Clementinis et Extravagantibus earumque Glossis Restitutus, Romae, 1582.

Mansi, Joannes D., *Sacrorum Conciliorum Nova et Amplissima Collectio,* 53 vols. in 60, Parisiis, 1901-1927.

Monumenta Germaniae Historica, Legum Sectio II, Capitularia Regum Francorum, tom. II, pars I, ed. Alfredus Boretius et Victor Krause, Hannoverae, 1890.

Pallottini, Salvator, *Collectio Omnium Conclusionum et Resolutionum quae in causis praepositis apud Sacram Congregationem Cardinalium S. Concilii Tridentini Interpretum Prodierunt ab eius Institutione anno MDLXIV ad MXCCCLX, distinctis titulis alphabetico ordine per materias digestas,* 18 vols., Romae, 1868-1895.

Pitra, I. B., *Iuris Ecclesiastici Graecorum Historia et Monumenta,* 2 vols., Romae, 1864-1868.

Potthast, A., *Regesta Pontificum Romanorum inde ab a. post Christum natum MCXCVIII ad a. MCCCIV,* 2 vols., Berolini, 1874-1875.

Thesaurus Resolutionum Sacrae Congregationis Concilii, 167 vols., Romae, 1718-1908.

Wasserschleben, F. G. A., *Reginonis Abbatis Prumiensis Libri Duo de Synodalibus Causis et Disciplinis Ecclesiasticis,* Lipsiae, 1840.

Reference Works

Acta Congressus Iuridici Internationalis, 5 vols., Romae: Libraria Pont. Instituti Utriusque Iuris, 1935-1937.

Alphonsus Liguori, St., *Theologia Moralis,* ed. L. Gaudé, 4 vols., Romae, 1905-1912.

Antonelli, Joannes, *Tractatus Posthumus de Juribus et Oneribus Clericorum,* Romae, 1669.

Antonelli, Ioseph, *Medicina Pastoralis,* 5. ed., 4 vols., Romae: Fridericus Pustet, 1932.

Aristotle, *The Politics,* translated by H. Rackham, Loeb Classical Library, New York: G. P. Putnam's Sons, 1932.

———, *The Works of Aristotle,* 11 vols., Oxford edition, Oxford, 1908-1931.

Ayrinhac, H. A., and Lydon, P. J., *Penal Legislation in the New Code of Canon Law,* New York: Benziger Brothers, 1936.

[Bachofen], Charles Augustine, *A Commentary on the New Code of Canon Law,* 8 vols., Vol. IV, 3. ed., 1925; Vol. VIII, 3. ed., 1931; St. Louis: B. Herder Book Co.

Ballerini, A.-Palmieri, D., *Opus Theologicum Morale,* 3. ed., 7 vols., Prati, 1898-1901.

Barbosa, Augustinus, *Collectanea Doctorum tam Veterum quam Recentiorum in Ius Pontificium Universum,* 6 vols. in 3, Lugduni, 1716.

——, *De Officio et Potestate Episcopi,* Lugduni, 1628.

——, *Vota Decisiva et Consultativa Canonica,* Venetiis, 1710.

Bargilliat, M., *Praelectiones Juris Canonici,* 24. ed., 2 vols., Parisiis: Apud Berche et Tralin, 1907.

——, *Praelectiones Juris Canonici,* 37. ed., ad canones novi codicis, 2 vols., Parisiis: Apud Baston, Berche et Pagis, 1923-1924.

Baronius, *Annales Ecclesiastici,* 37 vols., reprint, Vols. I-XXVIII, Bar-le-Duc, 1864-1875, Vols. XXIX-XXXVII, Paris, 1876-1883.

Beck, Alexander, *Römisches Recht bei Tertullian und Cyprian,* Eine Studie zur frühen Kirchenrechtsgeschichte, Schriften der Königsberger gelehrten Gesellschaft: Geisteswissenschaftliche Klasse, 7 Jahr, Heft 2, Halle: Max Niemeyer Verlag, 1930.

Belkin, Samuel, *Philo and the Oral Law,* Harvard Semitic Series, Vol. XI, Cambridge, Mass.: Harvard University Press, 1940.

Berardi, Aemilius, *Praxis Confessariorum seu Universae Theologiae Moralis et Pastoralis Tractatus Theoricus-Practicus,* Faventiae, 1884.

Berardi, Carolus S., *Gratiani Canones Genuini ab Apocryphis Discreti,* 2. ed. Veneta, 3 vols. in 4, Venetiis, 1783.

Beste, Udalricus, *Introductio in Codicem,* Collegeville, Minn.: St. John's Abbey Press, [1938].

Binterim, A. J., *Pragmatische Geschichte der deutschen Concilien,* 7 vols., Mainz, 1851-1852.

Blat, Albertus, *Commentarium Textus Codicis Iuris Canonici,* 5 vols. in 6, Vol. III, pars I, *De Sacramentis,* 2. ed.; Vol. V, *De Delictis et Poenis*; Romae: Collegio Angelico, 1924.

Blundus, Franciscus A., *Opus de Censuris et Irregularitate,* Romae, 1636.

Boenninghausen, E., *Tractatus Iuridico-Canonicus de Irregularitatibus,* 3 fasc. in 1 vol., Monasterii, 1863-1864.

Bonacina, Martinus, *Opera de Morali Theologia,* 3 vols., Venetiis, 1687.

Bonnar, A., *The Catholic Doctor,* London: Burns, Oates & Washbourne, Ltd., 1938.

Bordoni, Francesco, *Variae Resolutiones seu Consilia Regularia,* Venetiis, 1641.

Borgasius, Paulus, *Tractatus de Irregularitatibus et Impedimentis Ordinum, Officiorum, et Beneficiorum Ecclesiasticorum et Censuris Ecclesiasticis et Dispensationibus super Eis,* Venetiis, 1574.

Bouscaren, T. Lincoln, *Ethics of Ectopic Operations,* Chicago: Loyola University Press, 1933.

——, *The Canon Law Digest,* 2 vols. and *Supplement—1941,* Milwaukee: The Bruce Publishing Co., 1934-1941.

Bouuaert, F. Claeys et Simenon, G., *Manuale Juris Canonici,* 3 vols., Vols. I, III, 3. ed., Gandae et Leodi: Dessain, 1931.

Bucceroni, Ianuarius, *Institutiones Theologiae Moralis,* 2. ed., 2 vols., Romae, 1893.

Cappello, Felix M., *Tractatus Canonico-Moralis de Censuris iuxta Codicem Iuris Canonici,* 3. ed., Taurinorum Augustae: Marietti, 1933.

———, *Tractatus Canonico-Moralis de Sacramentis,* 3 vols. in 6, Vol. II, pars III, *De Sacra Ordinatione,* Taurinorum Augustae: Marietti, 1939.

Cavigioli, Joannes, *De Censuris Latae Sententiae,* Torino: Libreria Editrice Internazionale, 1918.

Cerato, Prosdocimus, *Censurae Vigentes Ipso Facto a Codice Iuris Canonici Excerptae,* 2. ed., Patavii: Typis Seminarii, 1921.

Chelodi, Ioannes, *Ius Poenale et Ordo Procedendi in Iudiciis Criminalibus,* 4. ed. recognita et aucta a Vigilio Dalpiaz, Tridenti: Ardesi, 1935.

Cicero, The Speeches, translated by H. Grose Hodge, Loeb Classical Library, New York: G. P. Putnam's Sons, 1927.

Cicognani, Amleto G., *Canon Law,* authorized English version by J. M. O'Hara and F. Brennan, 2. ed., Philadelphia: The Dolphin Press, 1935.

Cipollini, Albertus, *De Censuris Latae Sententiae Iuxta Codicem Iuris Canonici,* Taurini: Marietti, 1925.

Clement of Alexandria, edit. Stählin, Die griechischen christlichen Schriftsteller, 3 vols., Leipzig, 1905-1909.

Clericatus, Joannes, *Erotemata Ecclesiastica,* 4. ed., Venetiis, 1710.

Cocchi, Guidus, *Commentarium in Codicem Iuris Canonici,* 8 vols., Taurinorum Augustae: Marietti, Vol. VIII, *De Delictis et Poenis,* 4. ed., 1938.

Cornelisse, Eugenius, *Compendium Theologiae Moralis,* 3 vols., Quaracchi, 1908-1909.

Coronata, Matthaeus Conte a, *Institutiones Iuris Canonici,* 5 vols., Vols. I, II, 2. ed., 1939; Vols. III, IV, V, 1933-1936, Taurini: Marietti.

Corpus Scriptorum Ecclesiasticorum Latinorum, editum consilio et impensis Academiae Litterarum Caesareae Vindobonensis, Vindobonae, 1866—

D'Alès, A., *L'Edit de Calliste, Etude sur les origines de la pénitence chrétienne,* Paris, 1914.

D'Annibale, Ios., *In Constitutionem Apostolicae Sedis qua Censurae Limitantur Commentarii,* 5. ed., Romae, 1909.

Davis, Henry, *Moral and Pastoral Theology,* 3. ed., 4 vols., New York: Sheed & Ward, Inc., 1938.

De Angelis, Philippus, *Praelectiones Iuris Canonici ad Methodum Decretalium Gregorii IX Exactae,* persequi curavit Nazareno Gentilini, 5 tomes in 8 vols., Romae, 1877-1891.

De Graffiis, Jacobus, *Decisiones Aureae Casuum Conscientiae,* Venetiis, 1596.

De Lee, Joseph B., *The Principles and Practice of Obstetrics,* 7. ed., Philadelphia: W. B. Saunders Co., 1938.

De Lugo, Ioan., *Disputationes Scholasticae et Morales,* 8 vols., Parisiis, 1891-1894.

De Meester, Alphonsus, *Juris Canonici et Juris Canonico-Civilis Compendium,* ed. nova, 3 vols. in 4, Brugis: Desclée, 1921-1928.

De Siena, Paschalis, *Commentarius in Constitutionem Apostolicae Sedis,* 3. ed., Romae, 1902.

———, *Commentarius Censurarum juxta Novum Codicem Juris Canonici,* Neapoli: Ex Typis Francisci Giannini et Filiorum, 1918.

De Varceno, *Compendium Theologiae Moralis,* 4. ed., 2 vols., Augustae Taurinorum, 1876.

Diana, Antonius, *Omnium Resolutionum Moralium Tomi Decem,* 10 vols. in 5, Venetiis, 1728.

Dictionnaire de Droit Canonique, Paris: Librairie Letouzey et Ané, 1924—

Dictionnaire de Théologie Catholique, Paris: Librairie Letouzey et Ané, 1903—

Döllinger, J., *The Gentile and the Jew in the Courts of the Temple of Christ,* translated by N. Darnell, 2. ed., 2 vols., London, 1906.

Eichmann, Eduard, *Das Strafrecht des Codex Iuris Canonici,* Paderborn: Ferdinand Schöningh, 1920.

Elbel, Benjamin, *Theologia Moralis per Modum Conferentiarum,* ed. Irenaeus Bierbaum, 2. ed., 3 vols., Paderbornae, 1895.

Enciclopedia Italiana di Scienze, Lettere ed Arti, 36 vols. and Appendix, Milano: Istituto Giovanni Treccani, 1929-1939.

Eschbach, Alphonse, *Disputationes Physiologico-Theologicae,* 3. ed., 3 fasc. in 1 vol., Romae: Desclée et Socii, 1913.

Falchi, Giuseppino Ferruccio, *Diritto Penale Romano,* Padova: R. Zannoni, 1932.

Farrugia, Nicolaus, *Commentarium in Censuras Latae Sententiae Codicis Juris Canonici,* 2. ed., Melitae: Ex Typographia "Malta" Fortunati Mizzi, 1921.

Felici, Pericles, *De Poenali Iure Interpretando,* Romae: Apollinaris, 1939.

Ferraris, Lucius, *Bibliotheca Canonica, Juridica, Moralis, Theologica, necnon Ascetica, Polemica, Rubristica, Historica,* 9 vols., Romae, 1885-1899.

Ferreres, Ioan. B., *Compendium Theologiae Moralis,* 13. ed., 6. post codicem, 2 vols., Barcinone: Eugenius Subirana, 1925.

Findlay, Stephen W., *Canonical Norms Governing the Deposition and Degradation of Clerics,* The Catholic University of America Canon Law Studies, No. 130, Washington, D. C.: The Catholic University of America Press, 1941.

Fournier, Paul-Le Bras, Gabriel, *Histoire des Collections Canoniques en Occident depuis les Fausses Decretales jusqu'au Decret de Gratien,* 2 vols., Paris: Recueil Sirey, 1931-1932.

Forcellini-Facciolati-Furlanetti, *Lexicon Totius Latinitatis,* 4 vols., Patavii, 1864-1887.

Galenus [Pesudo], *Omnia Quae Exstant Opera,* 7 vols., Venetiis, 1572.

Gasparri, P., *Tractatus Canonicus de Sacra Ordinatione,* 2 vols., Parisiis, 1893-1894.

Geffcken, J., *Zwei griechische Apologeten,* Leipzig-Berlin, 1907.

Genicot, Eduardus, *Theologiae Moralis Institutiones,* 2. ed., 2 vols., Lovanii, 1898.

Genicot, Eduardus-Salsmans, I., *Institutiones Theologiae Moralis,* 14. ed., 7. post codicem, 2 vols., Bruxellis: L'Edition Universelle, 1939.

Giraldi, Ubaldus, *Expositio Juris Pontificii iuxta Recentiorem Ecclesiae Disciplinam,* 3 vols. in 2, Romae, 1829-1830.

Goodenough, Erwin R., *The Jurisprudence of the Jewish Courts in Egypt,* New Haven, Conn.: Yale University Press, 1929.

Gury, Joan. P., *Compendium Theologiae Moralis,* 5. ed. in Germania, Ratisbonae, 1874.

Haine, A. J. J. F., *Theologiae Moralis Elementa,* 3. ed., 4 vols., Lovanii, 1894.

Haring, Johann B., *Grundzüge des katholischen Kirchenrechtes,* 3. ed. nach dem Codex, 2 vols., Graz: Verlag von Ulrich Mosers Buchhandlung, 1924.

Hefele, Carl Joseph von, *Conciliengeschichte,* 2. ed., 9 vols., Freiburg im Breisgau, 1873-1890.

———, *A History of the Councils of the Church from the Original Documents,* translated by H. N. Oxenham and William R. Clark, 4 vols., Edinburgh, 1876-1895.

——— -Leclercq, H., *Histoire des Conciles,* 10 vols. in 19, Paris, 1907-1938.

Heiner, F., *Die kirchlichen Censuren,* Paderborn, 1884.

Hickey, John J., *Irregularities and Simple Impediments in the New Code of Canon Law,* The Catholic University of America Canon Law Studies, No. 7, Washington, D. C.: The Catholic University of America, 1920.

Hilarius a Sexten, *Tractatus de Censuris Ecclesiasticis,* Moguntiae, 1898.

Hinschius, Paulus, *Das Kirchenrecht der Katholiken und Protestanten in Deutschland,* 6 vols., Berlin, 1869-1897.

Hippolytus, Die griechischen christlichen Schriftsteller, 3 vols., Leipzig, 1916.

Hollweck, Joseph, *Die kirchlichen Strafgesetze,* Mainz, 1899.

Hostiensis, Cardinalis (Henricus de Segusio), *Commentaria in Quinque Decretalium Libros,* 5 vols. in 3, Venetiis, 1581.

———, *Summa Aurea,* Venetiis, 1570.

Ioannes Andreae, *In sex Decretalium Libros Novella Commentaria,* 6 vols. in 5, Venetiis, 1587.

Iorio, Thomas A., *Theologia Moralis iuxta Methodum Compendii Ioannis P. Gury S. I. et Raphaelis Tummolo S. I.,* 6. ed., 3 vols., Neapoli: D'Auria, 1938-1940.

Jombart, Emile, *Le Sacrement De L'Ordre,* Paris: Editiones Spes, 1930.

Josephus, Loeb Classical Library, 6 of 9 vols. published; Vols. 1-4, New York: G. P. Putnam's Sons, 1926-1930; Vols. 5-6, Cambridge, Mass.: Harvard University Press, 1934—

Kober, F., *Die Deposition und Degradation nach den Grundsätzen des kirchlichen Rechts,* Tübingen, 1867.

Kuttner, Stephan, *Kanonistische Schuldlehre von Gratian bis auf die Dekretalen Gregors IX,* Studi e Testi, n. 64, Città del Vaticano: Biblioteca Apostolica Vaticana, 1935.

Lanza, Antonio, *La Questione del Momento in Cui L'Anima Razionale è Infusa nel Corpo,* Roma: Edizioni Universitarie, 1940.

Laspeyres, E. A. Th., *Bernardi Papiensis Summa Decretalium,* Ratisbonae, 1860.

Laymann, Paulus, *Theologia Moralis,* 2 vols., Venetiis, 1719.

Lecky, W. E. H., *History of European Morals from Augustus to Charlemagne,* 4. ed., 2 vols., London, 1880.

Leech, George L., *A Comparative Study of the Constitution "Apostolicae Sedis" and the Codex Juris Canonici,* The Catholic University of America Canon Law Studies, No. 15, Washington, D. C.: The Catholic University of America, 1922.

Lega, Michael, *Praelectiones in Textum Iuris Canonici de Delictis et Poenis,* 2. ed., Romae, 1910.

———, *Praelectiones in Textum Iuris Canonici de Iudiciis Ecclesiasticis,* 2 vols. in 4, Romae, 1896-1901.

Lehmkuhl, Augustinus, *Theologia Moralis,* 12. ed., 2 vols., Friburgi Brisgoviae, 1914.

Lewin, F., *Die Fruchtabtreibung durch Gifte und andere Mittel,* Berlin: Stilke, 1925.

Lijdsman, Bernardus, *Introductio in Jus Canonicum,* 2 vols., Helversum in Hollandia, 1924-1929.

Loiano, Seraphinus a, *Institutiones Theologiae Moralis ad Normam Iuris Canonici,* 4 vols., Vol. II, 1935, Taurini: Marietti.

Lydon, P. J., *Ready Answers in Canon Law,* 2. ed. revised, New York: Benziger Bros, [1937].

Lyszczarczyk, Venantius, *Compendium Privilegiorum Regularium praesertim Ordinis Fratrum Minorum,* Leopoli, 1906.

Marc-Gestermann, *Institutiones Morales Alphonsianae,* 17. ed., 2 vols., Lugduni: Typis Emmanuelis Vitte, 1922-1923.

Maassen, Friedrich, *Geschichte der Quellen und der Literatur des canonischen Rechts im Abenlande bis zum Ausgang des Mittelalters,* Gratz, 1870.

Mai, A., *Scriptorum Veterum Nova Collectio,* 10 vols., Romae, 1825-1838.

Maiolus, S., *Tractatus de Irregularitate et aliis Canonicis Impedimentis,* Romae, 1619.

Meisner, Brunno, *Babylonien und Assyrien,* 2 vols., Heidelberg: Carl Winters Universitätsbuchhandlung, 1920-1925.

Merkelbach, Benedictus H., *Quaestiones de Embryologia et de Ministratione Baptismatis,* 2. ed., Liège: La Pensée Catholique, 1928.

———, *Quaestiones de Embryologia et de Sterilizatione,* Liège: La Pensée Catholique, 1937.

———, *Summa Theologiae Moralis,* 3 vols., Vol. III, 2. ed., Parisiis: Desclée, [1936].

Michiels, Gommarus, *De Delictis et Poenis,* Vol. I, *De Delictis,* Lublin-Polonia: Universitas Catholica, 1934.

Migne, J. P., *Patrologiae Cursus Completus,* series graeca, 161 vols., Parisiis, 1856-1866.

———, *Patrologiae Cursus Completus,* series latina, 221 vols., Parisiis, 1858-1864.

———, *Theologiae Cursus Completus,* 28 vols., Parisiis, 1837-1845.

Minucius Felix, translated by G. H. Rendall, Loeb Classical Library, New York: G. P. Putnam's Sons, 1931.

Mocchegiani, P., *Iurisprudentia Ecclesiastica ad Usum et Commoditatem Utriusque Cleri,* 3 vols., Quaracchi, 1905.

Mommsen, Theodorus, *La Droit Pénal Romain,* translated by J. Duquesne, 4 vols., Paris, 1907.

Montensis, Piatus, *Praelectiones Juris Regularis,* 2. ed., 2 vols., Tornaci, 1898.

Moore, Thomas Vernon, *Principles of Ethics,* 2. ed., Philadelphia: J. B. Lippincott Co., 1937.

Moriarty, Francis E., *The Extraordinary Absolution from Censures,* The Catholic University of America Canon Law Studies, No. 113, Washington, D. C.: The Catholic University of America, 1938.

Mothon, Joseph P., *Institutions Canoniques,* 3 vols., Paris: Desclée, 1922-1924.

Müller, Ernestus, *Theologia Moralis,* 3 vols., Vindobonae, 1876.

Noldin, H., *De Poenis Ecclesiasticis,* 6. ed., Oeniponte, 1907.

——— -Schmitt, A., *Summa Theologiae Moralis,* 24. ed., 3 vols., Oeniponte: F. Rauch, 1936.

——— -Schönegger, A., *De Censuris,* 30. ed., (CIC adaptata 18), Oeniponte: F. Rauch, 1936.

O'Malley, Austin, *The Ethics of Medical Homicide and Mutilation,* New York: The Devin-Adair Company, 1922.

Panormitanus, Abbas (Nicholaus de Tudeschis), *Commentaria in Quinque Libros Decretalium,* 5 vols. in 7, Venetiis, 1588.

Pauwels, Ios., *Tractatus Theologicus de Casibus Reservatis,* Lovanii, 1751-1752.

Pennacchi, Ios., *Commentarium in Constitutionem "Apostolicae Sedis" qua Censurae Latae Sententiae Limitantur,* 2 vols., Romae, 1883.

———, *De Abortu et Embryotomia seu Commentarium in Caput II. Sect. III. Const. "Apostolicae Sedis" Procurantes Abortum Effectu Sequuto,* Romae, 1884.

Perozzi, Silvio, *Istituzioni di Diritto Romano,* 2. ed., 2 vols., Roma: Athenaeum, 1928.

Philo, Loeb Classical Library, 8 of 10 vols. published, Cambridge, Mass.: Harvard University Press, 1929—

Pistocchi, Mario, *I Canoni Penali del Codice Ecclesiastico Espositi e Commentati*, Torino-Roma: Marietti, 1925.

Plato, *The Republic*, translated by Paul Shorey, 2 vols., Loeb Classical Library, New York: G. P. Putnam's Sons, 1930-1935.

Plutarch Lives, translated by Bernadotte Perrin, 11 vols., Loeb Classical Library, New York: The Macmillan Co., and G. P. Putnam's Sons, 1914-1926.

Porpora, A., *Theologia Moralis*, 2 vols., Neapoli, 1855.

Potestas, Felix, *Examen Ecclesiasticum*, Venetiis, 1751.

Prümmer, Dominicus M., *Manuale Theologiae Moralis*, 8. ed. recognita ab E. M. Münch, 3 vols., Friburgi Brisgoviae: Herder & Co., 1935-1936.

Raymundus Pennafort, St., *Summa*, 2. ed., Avenione, 1715.

Reiffenstuel, Anacletus, *Ius Canonicum Universum*, 7 vols., Parisiis, 1864-1870.

———, *Theologia Moralis*, Mutinae, 1737.

Roberti, Franciscus, *De Delictis et Poenis*, Vol. I, altera impressio, Romae: Libraria Pontificii Instituti Utriusque Iuris, 1938.

Routh, Martinus J., *Reliquiae Sacrae*, 2. ed., 5 vols., Oxonii, 1846-1848.

Sabetti, Aloysius-Barrett, Timotheus, *Compendium Theologiae Moralis*, 34. ed., 8. post codicem, Neo Eboraci: Frederick Pustet Co., Inc., 1939.

Sacred Books and Early Literature of the East, The, Charles F. Horne et al. editors, 14 vols., New York and London: Austin & Lipscomb, Inc., 1914.

Sägmüller, Johannes B., *Lehrbuch des katholischen Kirchenrechts*, 3. ed., 2 vols., Freiburg im Breisgau: Herdersche Verlagshandlung, 1914.

St. Basil, The Letters, translated by Roy J. Deferrari, Loeb Classical Library, 4 vols., New York: G. P. Putnam's Sons, 1926-1934.

Salmanticenses, *Cursus Theologiae Moralis*, 6 vols. in 4, Venetiis, 1728.

Salucci, Raffaele, *Il Diritto Penale secundo il Codice di Diritto Canonico*, 2 vols., Subiaco: Tipographia dei Monasterii, 1926-1930.

Sanchez, Thomas, *Disputationum de Sancto Matrimonii Sacramento Tomi Tres*, 3 vols., Antverpiae, 1607.

Scavini, P., *Theologia Moralis Universa*, 13. ed., 4 vols., Mediolani, 1882.

Schaff, P., *Teaching of the Twelve Apostles*, 3. ed., New York, 1890.

Schmalzgrueber, Franciscus, *Ius Ecclesiasticum Universum*, 5 vols. in 12, Romae, 1843-1845.

Schmitz, H. I., *Die Bussbücher und die Bussdisciplin der Kirche*, Mainz, 1883.

Schroeder, H. J., *Disciplinary Decrees of the General Councils, Text, Translation, and Commentary*, St. Louis: B. Herder Book Co., 1937.

Schulte, J. F. von, *Die Summa des Paucapalea*, Giessen, 1890.

———, *Die Summa des Stephanus Tornacensis*, Giessen, 1891.

Sherman, Charles P., *Roman Law in the Modern World*, 2. ed., 3 vols., New York: Voorhis & Co., 1924.

Singer, Heinrich, *Die Summa Decretorum des Magister Rufinus*, Paderborn, 1902.

Sinistrari, Ludovicus, *De Delictis et Poenis Tractatus Absolutissimus*, Romae, 1754.

Sipos, Stephanus, *Enchiridion Iuris Canonici*, 4. ed., Pécs: "Haladás R. T.," 1940.

Smith, J. M. P., *The Origin and History of Hebrew Law*, Chicago: The University of Chicago Press, 1931.

Sole, Jacobus, *De Delictis et Poenis*, Romae: Fridericus Pustet, 1920.

Sporer, Patritius, *Theologia Moralis*, Supplementa by K. Kazenberger, 3 vols., Venetiis, 1731.

Stander, H. J., *Williams Obstetrics*, 8. ed., New York: D. Appleton-Century Co., [1941].

Strachan-Davidson, *Problems of the Roman Criminal Law*, 2 vols., Oxford, 1912.

Sturtevant, Edgar H., and Bechtel, George, *A Hittite Chrestomathy*, Philadelphia: University of Pennsylvania, 1935.

Suarez, Franciscus, *Opera Omnia*, ed. nova a Carole Berton, 26 vols., Parisiis, 1856-1866.

Swoboda, Innocent R., *Ignorance in Relation of the Imputability of Delicts*, The Catholic University of America Canon Law Studies, No. 143, Washington, D. C.: The Catholic University of America Press, 1941.

Taussig, F. J., *Abortion, Spontaneous and Induced, Medical and Social Aspects*, St. Louis: The C. V. Mosby Co., 1936.

Téphany, Joseph-Marie, *Constitution "Apostolicae Sedis" de sa Saintete le Pape Pie IX Limitant les Censures "Latae Sententiae" Commentaire*, Tours, 1883.

Tertullian, translated by T. R. Glover, Loeb Classical Library, New York: G. P. Putnam's Sons, 1931.

Thaner, Fredericus, *Die Summa Magistri Rolandi nachmals Papstes Alexander III*, Innsbruck, 1874.

Thesaurus, Carolus, *De Poenis Ecclesiasticis Praxis Absoluta et Universalis*, ed. U. Giraldi, Romae, 1831.

Van Hove, A., *Commentarium Lovaniense in Codicem Iuris Canonici*, Vol. I, Tom. I, *Prolegomena*, Mechliniae: H. Dessain, 1928.

Vermeersch, A., *Theologiae Moralis Principia, Responsa, Concilia*, 3. ed., 4 vols., Romae: Università Gregoriana, 1933-1937.

——— -Creusen, J., *Epitome Iuris Canonici*, Vol. I, 6. ed., 1937; Vols. II, III, 5. ed., 1934-1936; Mechliniae: H. Dessain.

Wernz, Franciscus, *Ius Decretalium*, 6 vols., Romae et Prati, 1906-1913.

——— -Vidal, Petrus, *Ius Canonicum*, 7 vols. in 8, Romae: Universitas Gregoriana, 1923-1938.

Wasserschleben, H., *Beitraege zur Geschichte der vorgratianischen Kirchenrechtsquellen,* Leipzig, 1839.

Woywod, Stanislaus, *A Practical Commentary on the Code of Canon Law,* 5. ed., 2 vols., New York: Jos. F. Wagner, 1939.

Zeiger, Ivo A., *Historia Iuris Canonici,* 2 vols., Romae: Apud Aedes Universitatis Gregorianae, 1939-1940.

Articles

"Abortion and the Embryological Theory,"—*ER,* LXXVIII (1928), 626-631.

Aptowitzer, V., "Observations on the Criminal Law of the Jews: 5: The Status of the Embryo in Criminal Law,"—*The Jewish Quarterly Review,* new series, XV (1924-1925), 85-118.

Beugnet, A., "Avortement,"—*Dictionnaire de Théologie Catholique,* I, part 2, 2644-2652.

Brys, J., "De Poena in Procurantes Abortum,"—*Collationes Brugenses,* XXXIV (1934), 42-46.

———, "De Poenis Latae Sententiae,"—*Collationes Brugenses,* XXXIII (1933), 185-188.

Chollet, A., "Animation,"—*Dictionnaire de Théologie Catholique,* I, part 2, 1305-1320.

"Commentaire sur la Constitution *Apostolicae Sedis* de Pie IX,"—*NRT,* XL (1879), 307-332.

Davis, Henry, "Ectopic Gestation—A Rejoinder,"—*ER,* CVI (1942), 122-126.

Delmaille, M., "Avortement,"—*Dictionnaire de Droit Canonique,* I, 1536-1561.

Dölger, Franz J., "Das Lebensrecht des ungeborenen Kindes und die Fruchtabtreibung in der Bewertung der heidnischen und christlichen Antike,"—*Antike und Christentum,* IV (1933), 1-61.

Donovan, Joseph P., "Answers to Questions—At What Moment Is Soul Infused Into Fetus?"—*HPR,* XLI (1941), 1132-1133.

Florentinus, Hieronymus, "Disputatio de Ministrando Baptismo Humanis Fetibus Abortivorum,"—*Analecta Juris Pontificii,* VI (1863), 1280-1339.

Foote, John A., "Child Care in the Church,"—*The Catholic Historical Review,* XI (1925-1926), 56-74.

Gillmann, F., "Zur Geschichte des Gebrauchs der Ausdrücke 'irregularis' und 'irregularitas,' "—*AKKR,* XCI (1911), 49-86.

Göpfert, Franz A., "De excommuncatione et irregularitate ex abortu oriunda," —*ThPrQs,* XXXIX (1886), 373-375.

Gutwenger, Engelbert, "An Illustration of the Influence of Medical Science Upon Theological Thought,"—*The Catholic Medical Guardian,* XVII (1940), 137-143.

Harty, J. M., "The Church and the Unborn Child,"—*Irish Theological Quarterly,* I (1906), 171-182.

Heidenreich, Joannes, "Dissertatio in casum alterum Constitutionis Pii P. IX. d. d. 12 octob. 1869,"—*AKKR,* LXIII (1890), 289-390.

Jastrow, Jr., Morris, "An Assyrian Law Code,"—*Journal of the American Oriental Society,* XLI (1921), 20 ff.

Kuttner, Stephan, "The Father of the Science of Canon Law,"—*The Jurist,* I (1941), 2-19.

Mahoney, E. J., "Reserved Sins,"—*The Clergy Review,* VII (1934), 431-432.

Mair, Franz, "Absolution von Zensur und Dispens von Irregularität ex delicto,"—*ThPrQs,* LXXIII (1920), 568-577.

McCarthy, J., "Direct and Indirect Abortion—Ectopic Pregnancy,"—*IER,* 5th series, LV (1940), 58-66.

McHugh, J. A., "Casus Moralis—Abortion and the Natural Law,"—*HPR,* XXXIV (1933-1934), 297-302.

———, "Casus Moralis—The Victim in the Crime of Abortion,"—*HPR,* XXXIV (1933-1934), 417-418.

———, "Casus Moralis—Canonical Penalties for Abortion,"—*HPR,* XXXIV (1933-1934), 522-524.

O'Brien, James W., "Ectopic Gestation—Moral Aspects,"—*ER,* CV (1941), 95-103.

———, "Ectopic Gestation,"—*ER,* CVI (1942), 282-284.

O'Donnell, M. J., "Craniotomy and Excommunication,"—*IER,* 4th series, XXIX (1911), 537-538.

Oesterle, G., "Mitwirkung zur procuratio abortus,"—*ThPrQs,* LXXXIX (1936), 354-355, 584.

Perla, L., "Aborto,"—*Enciclopedia Italiana di Scienze, Lettere ed Arti,* I, 111.

Prümmer, Dominicus, "Zieht die Kraniotomie die Exkommunikation nach sich?"—*ThPrQs,* LXIII (1910), 586-588.

"Question of Abortion Under the New Canon Law, The,"—*ER,* LXVIII (1923), 300-301.

Roberti, Melchoir, "Nasciturus pro iam nato habetur,"—*Christianesimo e Diritto Romano,* Pubblicazioni della Università Cattolica del Sacro Cuore, serie seconda: Scienze Giuridiche, Vol. XLIII, pp. 66-84, Milano: Società Editrice "Vita E Pensiero," 1935.

Schaaf, Valentine, "Abortus Foetus Inanimati,"—*ER,* XCIII (1935), 623-624.

———, "Canonical Notes on the Encyclical Letter on Christian Marriage,"—*ER,* LXXXIV (1931), 272-273.

Scherer, Rudulf Ritter von, "Die Irregularitas ex delicto homicidii,"—*AKKR,* XLIX (1883), 37-73.

Schlueter, Elmer A., "Ectopic Gestation—Medical Aspects,"—*ER,* CV (1941), 81-94.

Stockums, W., "Abortus und kirchliches Strafrecht,"—*Theologie und Glaube,* XV (1923), 93-100.

———, "Historisch-Kritisches über die Frage: 'Wann entsteht die geistige Seele'?"—*Philosophisches Jahrbuch,* XXXVII (1924), 225-252.

Teodori, I., "Abortus,"—*Apollinaris,* V (1932), 251-254.

Wolfenschiessen, Burkhard von, "Das Franziskanische Privilegienrecht,"—*Collectanea Franciscana,* IV (1934), 337-362.
Woywod, Stanislaus, "Answers to Questions—Concerning Abortion,"—*HPR,* XXXVI (1935-1936), 294-295.
———, "Irregularities to Ordination Arising from Crime,"—*HPR,* XXIII (1922-1923), 142-149.
———, "Penal Law of the Code—The Crime of Abortion,"—*HPR,* XXXVIII (1937-1938), 385-394.
———, "Answers to Questions—What Persons Come Under 'Procurantes Abortum'?"—*HPR,* XL (1939-1940), 324-325.

PERIODICALS

Analecta Juris Pontificii, Romae: 1855-1868; Parisiis, 1869-1890.
Antike und Christentum, Münster in Westfalen, 1830—
Apollinaris, Romae, 1928—
Archiv für katholisches Kirchenrecht, Innsbruck, 1857-1861; Mainz, 1862—
Catholic Historical Review, The, Philadelphia, Pa., 1915—
Catholic Medical Guardian, London, 1924—
Clergy Review, The, London, 1931—
Collationes Brugenses, Bruges, 1896—
Collectanea Franciscana, Assisi, 1931—
Ecclesiastical Review, The (formerly *The American Ecclesiastical Review*), Philadelphia, Pa., 1889—
Homiletic and Pastoral Review, The, New York, 1900—
Irish Ecclesiastical Record, The, Dublin, 1864—
Irish Theological Quarterly, The, Dublin, 1906-1922.
Jurist, The, Washington, D. C., 1941—
Nouvelle Revue Théologique, Tournai, 1869—
Philosophisches Jahrbuch, Fulda, 1888—
Theologie und Glaube, Paderborn, 1909—
Theologisch-praktische Quartalschrift, Linz, 1832—

ABBREVIATIONS

AJP—*Analecta Juris Pontificii.*
AKKR—*Archiv für katholisches Kirchenrecht.*
ASS—*Acta Sanctae Sedis.*
AuC—*Antike und Christentum.*
C.—*Codex* (Justinianus).
CSEL—*Corpus Scriptorum Ecclesiasticorum Latinorum.*
D.—*Digestum* (Justinianum).
ER—*The Ecclesiastical Review.*
Fontes—*Codicis Iuris Canonici Fontes.*
HPR—*The Homiletic and Pastoral Review.*
IER—*The Irish Ecclesiastical Record.*
LCL—*Loeb Classical Library.*
Mansi—*Sacrorum Conciliorum Nova et Amplissima Collectio.*
MPG—Migne, *Patrologiae Cursus Completus, series graeca.*
MPL—Migne, *Patrologiae Cursus Completus, series latina.*
MTCC—Migne, *Theologiae Cursus Completus.*
N.—*Novellae* (Justinianae).
NRT—*Nouvelle Revue Théologique.*
ThPrQs—*Theologisch-praktische Quartalschrift* (Linz).

ALPHABETICAL INDEX

BIOGRAPHICAL NOTE

Roger John Huser was born at Spades, Indiana, August 25, 1909. His elementary education was received at Holy Family School, Oldenburg, Indiana. After attending Oldenburg High School for two years, he spent a year at Jasper Academy, Jasper, Indiana, and graduated from East Night High School, Cincinnati, Ohio, June, 1927. After one year at Indiana University, Bloomington, Indiana, he entered the Cincinnati Province of the Order of Friars Minor, August 15, 1930. He received the A.B. degree in 1934 from Duns Scotus College, Detroit, Michigan, where he made his seminary course in philosophy. His theological course completed, he was ordained to the priesthood at Holy Family Monastery, Oldenburg, Indiana, June 11, 1938. In September, 1939 he entered the School of Canon Law at the Catholic University of America, where he received the Baccalaureate in Canon Law in June, 1940, and the Licentiate in Canon Law in June, 1941.

CANON LAW STUDIES *

1. Freriks, Rev. Celestine A., C.PP.S., J.C.D., Religious Congregations in Their External Relations, 121 pp., 1916.
2. Galliher, Rev. Daniel M., O.P., J.C.D., Canonical Elections, 117 pp., 1917.
3. Borkowski, Rev. Aurelius L., O.F.M., J.C.D., De Confraternitatibus Ecclesiasticis, 136 pp., 1918.
4. Castillo, Rev. Cayo, J.C.D., Disertacion Historico-Canonica sobre la Potestad del Cabildo en Sede Vacante o Impedida del Vicario Capitular, 99 pp., 1919 (1918).
5. Kubelbeck, Rev. William J., S.T.B., J.C.D., The Sacred Penitentiaria and Its Relation to Faculties of Ordinaries and Priests, 129 pp., 1918.
6. Petrovits, Rev. Joseph, J.C., S.T.D., J.C.D., The New Church Law on Matrimony, X-461 pp., 1919.
7. Hickey, Rev. John J., S.T.B., J.C.D., Irregularities and Simple Impediments in the New Code of Canon Law, 100 pp., 1920.
8. Klekotka, Rev. Peter J., S.T.B., J.C.D., Diocesan Consultors, 179 pp., 1920.
9. Wanenmacher, Rev. Francis, J.C.D., The Evidence in Ecclesiastical Procedure Affecting the Marriage Bond, 1920 (Printed 1935).
10. Golden, Rev. Henry Francis, J.C.D., Parochial Benefices in the New Code, IV-119 pp., 1921 (Printed 1925).
11. Koudelka, Rev. Charles J., J.C.D., Pastors, Their Rights and Duties According to the New Code of Canon Law, 211 pp., 1921.
12. Melo, Rev. Antonius, O.F.M., J.C.D., De Exemptione Regularium, X-188 pp., 1921.
13. Schaaf, Rev. Valentine Theodore, O.F.M., S.T.B., J.C.D., The Cloister, X-180 pp., 1921.
14. Burke, Rev. Thomas Joseph, S.T.D., J.C.D., Competence in Ecclesiastical Tribunals, IV-117 pp., 1922.
15. Leech, Rev. George Leo, J.C.D., A Comparative Study of the Constitution "Apostolicae Sedis" and the "Codex Juris Canonici," 179 pp., 1922.
16. Motry, Rev. Hubert Louis, S.T.D., J.C.D., Diocesan Faculties According to the Code of Canon Law, II-167 pp., 1922.
17. Murphy, Rev. George Lawrence, J.C.D., Delinquencies and Penalties in the Administration and the Reception of the Sacraments, IV-121 pp., 1923.
18. O'Reilly, Rev. John Anthony, S.T.B., J.C.D., Ecclesiastical Sepulture in the New Code of Canon Law, II-129 pp., 1923.

* Below n. 100 only the following numbers are still available: Nn. 3, 4, 9, 25, 34, 57 and 75. Beginning with n. 100 only the following are unavailable: Nn. 100, 101, 102, 104, 105, 107, 108, 109, 111 and 113.

19. MICHALICKA, REV. WENCESLAS CYRILL, O.S.B., J.C.D., Judicial Procedure in Dismissal of Clerical Exempt Religious, 107 pp., 1923.
20. DARGIN, REV. EDWARD VINCENT, S.T.B., J.C.D., Reserved Cases According to the Code of Canon Law, IV-103 pp., 1924.
21. GODFREY, REV. JOHN A., S.T.B., J.C.D., The Right of Patronage According to the Code of Canon Law, 153 pp., 1924.
22. HAGEDORN, REV. FRANCIS EDWARD, J.C.D., General Legislation on Indulgences, II-154 pp., 1924.
23. KING, REV. JAMES IGNATIUS, J.C.D., The Administration of the Sacraments to Dying Non-Catholics, V-141 pp., 1924.
24. WINSLOW, REV. FRANCIS JOSEPH, O.F.M., J.C.D., Vicars and Prefects Apostolic, IV-149 pp., 1924.
25. CORREA, REV. JOSE SERVELION, S.T.L., J.C.D., La Potestad Legislativa de la Iglesia Catolica, IV-127 pp., 1925.
26. DUGAN, REV. HENRY FRANCIS, A.M., J.C.D., The Judiciary Department of the Diocesan Curia, 87 pp., 1925.
27. KELLER, REV. CHARLES FREDERICK, S.T.B., J.C.D., Mass Stipends, 167 pp., 1925.
28. PASCHANG, REV. JOHN LINUS, J.C.D., The Sacramentals According to the Code of Canon Law, 129 pp., 1925.
29. PIONTEK, REV. CYRILLUS, O.F.M., S.T.B., J.C.D., De Indulto Exclaustrationis necnon Saecularizationis, XIII-289 pp., 1925.
30. KEARNEY, REV. RICHARD JOSEPH, S.T.B., J.C.D., Sponsors at Baptism According to the Code of Canon Law, IV-127 pp., 1925.
31. BARTLETT, REV. CHESTER JOSEPH, A.M., LL.B., J.C.D., The Tenure of Parochial Property in the United States of America, V-108 pp., 1926.
32. KILKER, REV. ADRIAN JEROME, J.C.D., Extreme Unction, V-425 pp., 1926.
33. MCCORMICK, REV. ROBERT EMMETT, J.C.D., Confessors of Religious, VIII-266 pp., 1926.
34. MILLER, REV. NEWTON THOMAS, J.C.D., Founded Masses According to the Code of Canon Law, VII-93 pp., 1926.
35. ROELKER, REV. EDWARD G., S.T.D., J.C.D., Principles of Privilege According to the Code of Canon Law, XI-166 pp., 1926.
36. BAKALARCZYK, REV. RICHARDUS, M.I.C., J.U.D., De Novitiatu, VIII-208 pp., 1927.
37. PIZZUTI, REV. LAWRENCE, O.F.M., J.U.L., De Parochis Religiosis, 1927. (Not Printed.)
38. BLILEY, REV. NICHOLAS MARTIN, O.S.B., J.C.D., Altars According to the Code of Canon Law, XIX-132 pp., 1927.
39. BROWN, MR. BRENDAN FRANCIS, A.B., LL.M., J.U.D., The Canonical Juristic Personality with Special Reference to its Status in the United States of America, V-212 pp., 1927.
40. CAVANAUGH, REV. WILLIAM THOMAS, C.P., J.U.D., The Reservation of the Blessed Sacrament, VIII-101 pp., 1927.

41. DOHENY, REV. WILLIAM J., C.S.C., A.B., J.U.D., Church Property: Modes of Acquisition, X-118 pp., 1927.
42. FELDHAUS, REV. ALOYSIUS H., C.PP.S., J.C.D., Oratories, IX-141 pp., 1927.
43. KELLY, REV. JAMES PATRICK, A.B., J.C.D., The Jurisdiction of the Simple Confessor, X-208 pp., 1927.
44. NEUBERGER, REV. NICHOLAS J., J.C.D., Canon 6 or the Relation of the Codex Juris Canonici to the Preceding Legislation, V-95 pp., 1927.
45. O'KEEFE, REV. GERALD MICHAEL, J.C.D., Matrimonial Dispensations, Powers of Bishops, Priests, and Confessors, VIII-232 pp., 1927.
46. QUIGLEY, REV. JOSEPH A. M., A.B., J.C.D., Condemned Societies, 139 pp., 1927.
47. ZAPLOTNIK, REV. JOHANNES LEO, J.C.D., De Vicariis Foraneis, X-142 pp., 1927.
48. DUSKIE, REV. JOHN ALOYSIUS, A.B., J.C.D., The Canonical Status of the Orientals in the United States, VIII-196 pp., 1928.
49. HYLAND, REV. FRANCIS EDWARD, J.C.D., Excommunciation, Its Nature, Historical Development and Effects, VIII-181 pp., 1928.
50. REINMANN, REV. GERALD JOSEPH, O.M.C., J.C.D., The Third Order Secular of Saint Francis, 201 pp., 1928.
51. SCHENK, REV. FRANCIS J., J.C.D., The Matrimonial Impediments of Mixed Religion and Disparity of Cult, XVI-318 pp., 1929.
52. COADY, REV. JOHN JOSEPH, S.T.D., J.U.D., A.M., The Appointment of Pastors, VIII-150 pp., 1929.
53. KAY, REV. THOMAS HENRY, J.C.D., Competence in Matrimonial Procedure, VIII-164 pp., 1929.
54. TURNER, REV. SIDNEY JOSEPH, C.P., J.U.D., The Vow of Poverty, XLIX-217 pp., 1929.
55. KEARNEY, REV. RAYMOND A., A.B., S.T.D., J.C.D., The Principles of Delegation, VII-149 pp., 1929.
56. CONRAN, REV. EDWARD JAMES, A.B., J.C.D., The Interdict, V-163 pp., 1930.
57. O'NEILL, REV. WILLIAM H., J.C.D., Papal Rescripts of Favor, VII-218 pp., 1930.
58. BASTNAGEL, REV. CLEMENT VINCENT, J.U.D., The Appointment of Parochial Adjutants and Assistants, XV-257 pp., 1930.
59. FERRY, REV. WILLIAM A., A.B., J.C.D., Stole Fees, V-136 pp., 1930.
60. COSTELLO, REV. JOHN MICHAEL, A.B., J.C.D., Domicile and Quasi-Domicile, VII-201 pp., 1930.
61. KREMER, REV. MICHAEL NICHOLAS, A.B., S.T.B., J.C.D., Church Support in the United States, VI-136 pp., 1930.
62. ANGULO, REV. LUIS, C.M., J.C.D., Legislation de la Iglesia sobre la intencion en la application de la Santa Misa, VII-104 pp., 1931.
63. FREY, REV. WOLFGANG NORBERT, O.S.B., A.B., J.C.D., The Act of Religious Profession, VIII-174 pp., 1931.

64. Roberts, Rev. James Brendan, A.B., J.C.D., The Banns of Marriage, XIV-140 pp., 1931.
65. Ryder, Rev. Raymond Aloysius, A.B., J.C.D., Simony, IX-151 pp., 1931.
66. Campagna, Rev. Angelo, Ph.D., J.U.D., Il Vicario Generale del Vescovo, VII-205 pp., 1931.
67. Cox, Rev. Joseph Godfrey, A.B., J.C.D., The Administration of Seminaries, VI-124 pp., 1931.
68. Gregory, Rev. Donald J., J.U.D., The Pauline Privilege, XV-165 pp., 1931.
69. Donohue, Rev. John F., J.C.D., The Impediment of Crime, VII-110 pp., 1931.
70. Dooley, Rev. Eugene A., O.M.I., J.C.D., Church Law on Sacred Relics, IX-143 pp., 1931.
71. Orth, Rev. Clement Raymond, O.M.C., J.C.D., The Approbation of Religious Institutes, 171 pp., 1931.
72. Pernicone, Rev. Joseph M., A.B., J.C.D., The Ecclesiastical Prohibition of Books, XII-267 pp., 1932.
73. Clinton, Rev. Connell, A.B., J.C.D., The Paschal Precept, IX-108 pp., 1932.
74. Donnelly, Rev. Francis B., A.M., S.T.L., J.C.D., The Diocesan Synod, VIII-125 pp., 1932.
75. Torrente, Rev. Camilo, C.M.F., J.C.D., Las Processiones Sagradas, V-145 pp., 1932.
76. Murphy, Rev. Edwin J., C.PP.S., J.C.D., Suspension Ex Informata Conscientia, XI-122 pp., 1932.
77. MacKenzie, Rev. Eric F., A.M., S.T.L., J.C.D., The Delict of Heresy in its Commission, Penalization, Absolution, VII-124 pp., 1932.
78. Lyons, Rev. Avitus E., S.T.B., J.C.D., The Collegiate Tribunal of First Instance, XI-147 pp., 1932.
79. Connolly, Rev. Thomas A., J.C.D., Appeals, XI-195 pp., 1932.
80. Sangmeister, Rev. Joseph V., A.B., J.C.D., Force and Fear as Precluding Matrimonial Consent, V-211 pp., 1932.
81. Jaeger, Rev. Leo A., A.B., J.C.D., The Administration of Vacant and Quasi-Vacant Episcopal Sees in the United States, IX-229 pp., 1932.
82. Rimlinger, Rev. Herbert T., J.C.D., Error Invalidating Matrimonial Consent, VII-79 pp., 1932.
83. Barrett, Rev. John D. M., S.S., J.C.D., A Comparative Study of the Third Plenary Council of Baltimore and the Code, IX-221 pp., 1932.
84. Carberry, Rev. John J., Ph.D., S.T.D., J.C.D., The Juridical Form of Marriage, X-177 pp., 1934.
85. Dolan, Rev. John L., A.B., J.C.D., The Defensor Vinculi, XII-157 pp., 1934.
86. Hannan, Rev. Jerome D., A.M., S.T.D., LL.B., J.C.D., The Canon Law of Wills, IX-517 pp., 1934.

87. LEMIEUX, REV. DELISE A., A.M., J.C.D., The Sentence in Ecclesiastical Procedure, IX-131 pp., 1934.
88. O'ROURKE, REV. JAMES J., A.B., J.C.D., Parish Registers, VII-109 pp., 1934.
89. TIMLIN, REV. BARTHOLOMEW, O.F.M., A.M., J.C.D., Conditional Matrimonial Consent, X-381 pp., 1934.
90. WAHL, REV. FRANCIS X., A.B., J.C.D., The Matrimonial Impediments of Consanguinity and Affinity, VI-125 pp., 1934.
91. WHITE, REV. ROBERT J., A.B., LL.B., S.T.B., J.C.D., Canonical Ante-Nuptial Promises and the Civil Law, VI-152 pp., 1934.
92. HERRERA, REV. ANTONIO PARRA, O.C.D., J.C.D., Legislacion Ecclesiastica sobra el Ayuno y la Abstinencia, XI-191 pp., 1935.
93. KENNEDY, REV. EDWIN J., J.C.D., The Special Matrimonial Process in Cases of Evident Nullity, X-165 pp., 1935.
94. MANNING, REV. JOHN J., A.B., J.C.D., Presumption of Law in Matrimonial Procedure, XI-111 pp., 1935.
95. MOEDER, REV. JOHN M., J.C.D., The Proper Bishop for Ordination and Dimissorial Letters, VII-135 pp., 1935.
96. O'MARA, REV. WILLIAM A., A.B., J.C.D., Canonical Causes for Matrimonial Dispensations, IX-155 pp., 1935.
97. REILLY, REV. PETER, J.C.D., Residence of Pastors, IX-81 pp., 1935.
98. SMITH, REV. MARINER T., O.P., S.T.Lr., J.C.D., The Penal Law for Religious, VII-169 pp., 1935.
99. WHALEN, REV. DONALD W., A.M., J.C.D., The Value of Testimonial Evidence in Matrimonial Procedure, XIII-297 pp., 1935.
100. CLEARY, REV. JOSEPH F., J.C.D., Canonical Limitations on the Alienation of Church Property, VIII-141 pp., 1936.
101. GLYNN, REV. JOHN C., J.C.D., The Promoter of Justice, XX-337 pp., 1936.
102. BRENNAN, REV. JAMES H., S.S., M.A., S.T.B., J.C.D., The Simple Convalidation of Marriage, VI-135 pp., 1937.
103. BRUNINI, REV. JOSEPH BERNARD, J.C.D., The Clerical Obligations of Canons 139 and 142, X-121 pp., 1937.
104. CONNOR, REV. MAURICE, A.B., J.C.D., The Administrative Removal of Pastors, VIII-159 pp., 1937.
105. GUILFOYLE, REV. MERLIN JOSEPH, J.C.D., Custom, XI-144 pp., 1937.
106. HUGHES, REV. JAMES AUSTIN, A.B., A.M., J.C.D., Witnesses in Criminal Trials of Clerics, IX-140 pp., 1937.
107. JANSEN, REV. RAYMOND J., A.B., S.T.L., J.C.D., Canonical Provisions for Catechetical Instruction, VII-153 pp., 1937.
108. KEALY, REV. JOHN JAMES, A.B., J.C.D., The Introductory Libellus in Church Court Procedure, XI-121 pp., 1937.
109. MCMANUS, REV. JAMES EDWARD, C.SS.R., J.C.D., The Administration of Temporal Goods in Religious Institutes, XVI-196 pp., 1937.

110. Moriarty, Rev. Eugene James, J.C.D., Oaths in Ecclesiastical Courts, X-115 pp., 1937.
111. Rainer, Rev. Eligius George, C.SS.R., J.C.D., Suspension of Clerics, XVII-249 pp., 1937.
112. Reilly, Rev. Thomas F., C.SS.R., J.C.D., Visitation of Religious, VI-195 pp., 1938.
113. Moriarty, Rev. Francis E., C.SS.R., J.C.D., The Extraordinary Absolution from Censures, XV-334 pp., 1938.
114. Connolly, Rev. Nicholas P., J.C.D., The Canonical Erection of Parishes, X-132 pp., 1938.
115. Donovan, Rev. James Joseph, J.C.D., The Pastor's Obligation in Prenuptial Investigation, XII-322 pp., 1938.
116. Harrigan, Rev. Robert J., M.A., S.T.B., J.C.D., The Radical Sanation of Invalid Marriages, VIII-208 pp., 1938.
117. Boffa, Rev. Conrad Humbert, J.C.D., Canonical Provisions for Catholic Schools, VII-211 pp., 1939.
118. Parsons, Rev. Anscar John, O.M.Cap., J.C.D., Canonical Elections, XII-236 pp., 1939.
119. Reilly, Rev. Edward Michael, A.B., J.C.D., The General Norms of Dispensation, XII-156 pp., 1939.
120. Ryan, Rev. Gerald Aloysius, A.B., J.C.D., Principles of Episcopal Jurisdiction, XII-172 pp., 1939.
121. Burton, Rev. Francis James, C.S.C., A.B., J.C.D., A Commentary on Canon 1125, X-222 pp., 1940.
122. Miaskiewicz, Rev. Francis Sigismund, J.C.D., Supplied Jurisdiction According to Canon 209, XII-340 pp., 1940.
123. Rice, Rev. Patrick William, A.B., J.C.D., Proof of Death in Prenuptial Investigation, VIII-156 pp., 1940.
124. Anglin, Rev. Thomas Francis, M.S., J.C.D., The Eucharistic Fast, VIII-183 pp., 1941.
125. Coleman, Rev. John Jerome, J.C.D., The Minister of Confirmation, VI-153 pp., 1941.
126. Downs, Rev. Joseph Emmanuel, A.B., J.C.D., The Concept of Clerical Immunity, XI-163 pp., 1941.
127. Esswein, Rev. Anthony Albert, J.C.D., Extrajudicial Penal Powers of Ecclesiastical Superiors, X-144 pp., 1941.
128. Farrell, Rev. Benjamin Francis, M.A., S.T.L., J.C.D., The Rights and Duties of the Local Ordinary Regarding Congregations of Women Religious of Pontifical Approval, V-195 pp., 1941.
129. Feeney, Rev. Thomas John, A.B., S.T.L., J.C.D., Restitutio in Integrum, VI-169 pp., 1941.
130. Findlay, Rev. Stephen William, O.S.B., A.B., J.C.D., Canonical Norms Governing the Deposition and Degradation of Clerics, XVII-279 pp., 1941.

131. Goodwine, Rev. John, A.B., S.T.L., J.C.D., The Right of the Church to Acquire Property, VIII-119 pp., 1941.
132. Heston, Rev. Edward Louis, C.S.C., Ph.D., S.T.D., J.C.D., The Alienation of Church Property in the United States, XII-222 pp., 1941.
133. Hogan, Rev. James John, A.B., S.T.L., J.C.D., Judicial Advocates and Procurators, XIII-200 pp., 1941.
134. Kealy, Rev. Thomas M., A.B., Litt.B., J.C.D., Dowry of Women Religious, IX-152 pp., 1941.
135. Keene, Rev. Michael James, O.S.B., J.C.D., Religious Ordinaries and Canon 198, V-164 pp., 1942.
136. Kerin, Rev. Charles A., S.S., M.A., S.T.B., J.C.D., The Privation of Christian Burial, XVI-279 pp., 1941.
137. Louis, Rev. William Francis, M.A., J.C.D., Diocesan Archives, X-101 pp., 1941.
138. McDevitt, Rev. Gilbert Joseph, A.B., J.C.D., Legitimacy and Legitimation, X-247 pp., 1941.
139. McDonough, Rev. Thomas Joseph, A.B., J.C.D., Apostolic Administrators, X-217 pp., 1941.
140. Meier, Rev. Carl Anthony, A.B., J.C.D., Penal Administration Procedure Against Negligent Pastors, XI-240 pp., 1941.
141. Schmidt, Rev. John Rogg, A.B., J.C.D., The Principles of Authentic Interpretation in Canon 17 of the Code of Canon Law, XII-331 pp., 1941.
142. Slafkosky, Rev. Andrew Leonard, A.B., J.C.D., The Canonical Episcopal Visitation of the Diocese, X-197 pp., 1941.
143. Swoboda, Rev. Innocent Robert, O.F.M., J.C.D., Ignorance in Relation to the Imputability of Delicts, IX-271 pp., 1941.
144. Dubé, Rev. Arthur Joseph, A.B., J.C.D., The General Principles for the Reckoning of Time in Canon Law, VIII-299 pp., 1941.
145. McBride, Rev. James T., A.B., J.C.D., Incardination and Excardination of Seculars, XX-585 pp., 1941.
146. Król, Rev. John T., J.C.D., The Defendant in Ecclesiastical Trials, XII-207 pp., 1942.
147. Comyns, Rev. Joseph J., C.SS.R., A.B., J.C.D., Papal and Episcopal Administration of Church Property, XIV-155 pp., 1942.
148. Barry, Rev. Garrett Francis, O.M.I., J.J.D., Violation of the Cloister, XII-260 pp,, 1942.
149. Bolduc, Rev. Gatien, C.S.V., A.B., S.T.L., J.C.D., Les Études dans les Religions Cléricales.
150. Boyle, Rev. David John, M.A., J.C.D., The Juridic Effects of Moral Certitude on Pre-Nuptial Guarantees, XII-188 pp., 1942.
151. Canavan, Rev. Walter Joseph, M.A., Litt.D., J.C.D., The Profession of Faith, XII-143 pp., 1942.
152. Desrochers, Rev. Bruno, A.B., Ph.L., S.T.B., J.C.D., Le Premier Concile Plénier de Québec et le Code de Droit Canonique, XIV-186 pp., 1942.

153. Dillon, Rev. Robert Edward, A.B., J.C.D., Common Law Marriage, X-148 pp., 1942.
154. Dodwell, Rev. Edward John, Ph.D., S.T.B., J.C.L., The Time and Place for the Celebration of Marriage.
155. Donnellan, Rev. Thomas Andrew, A.B., J.C.D., The Obligation of the Missa pro Populo, VII-131 pp., 1942.
156. Eltz, Rev. Louis Anthony, A.B., J.C.L., Cooperation in Crime.
157. Gass, Rev. Sylvester Francis, M.A., J.C.L., Ecclesiastical Pensions, XI-206 pp., 1942.
158. Guiniven, Rev. John Joseph, C.SS.R., J.C.D., The Precept of Hearing Mass, XIV-188 pp., 1942.
159. Gulczynski, Rev. John Theophilus, J.C.L., The Desecration and Violation of Churches.
160. Hammill, Rev. John Leo, M.A., J.C.D., The Obligations of the Traveler According to Canon 14, VIII-204 pp., 1942.
161. Haydt, Rev. John Joseph, A.B., J.C.D., Reserved Benefices, XI-148 pp., 1942.
162. Huser, Rev. Roger John, O.F.M., A.B., J.C.L., The Crime of Abortion in Canon Law.
163. Kearney, Rev. Francis Patrick, A.B., S.T.L., J.C.L., The Principles of Canon 1127.
164. Linahen, Rev. Leo James, S.T.L., J.C.D., De Absolutione Complicis In Peccato Turpi, 114 pp., 1942.
165. McCloskey, Rev. Joseph Aloysius, A.B., J.C.D., The Subject of Ecclesiastical Law According to Canon 12, XVII-246 pp., 1942.
166. O'Neill, Rev. Francis Joseph, C.SS.R., J.C.D., The Dismissal of Religious in Temporary Vows, XIII-220 pp., 1942.
167. Prince, Rev. John Edward, A.B., S.T.B., J.C.D., The Diocesan Chancellor, X-136 pp., 1942.
168. Riesner, Rev. Albert Joseph, C.SS.R., J.C.D., Apostates and Fugitives from Religious Institutes, IX-168 pp., 1942.
169. Stenger, Rev. Joseph Bernard, J.C.D., The Mortgaging of Church Property, 186 pp., 1942.
170. Waldron, Rev. Joseph Francis, A.B., J.C.D., The Minister of Baptism, XII-197 pp., 1942.
171. Willett, Rev. Robert Albert, J.C.D., The Probative Value of Documents in Ecclesiastical Trials, X-124 pp., 1942.
172. Woeber, Rev. Edward Martin, M.A., J.C.D., The Interpellations, XII-161 pp., 1942.
173. Benko, Rev. Matthew Aloysius, O.S.B., M.A., J.C.L., The Abbot *Nullius*.
174. Christ, Rev. Joseph James, M.A., S.T.L., J.C.L., Dispensation from Vindicative Penalties.
175. Clancy, Rev. Patrick M. J., O.P., A.B., S.T.Lr., J.C.L., The Local Religious Superior.

176. Clarke, Rev. Thomas James, J.C.L., Parish Societies.
177. Connolly, Rev. John Patrick, S.T.L., J.C.L., Synodal Examiners and Parish Priest Consultors.
178. Drumm, Rev. William Martin, A.B., J.C.L., Hospital Chaplains.
179. Flanagan, Rev. Bernard Joseph, A.B., S.T.L., J.C.L., The Canonical Erection of Religious Houses.
180. Kelleher, Rev. Stephen Joseph, A.B., S.T.B., J.C.L., Discussions with non-Catholics: Canonical Legislation.
181. Lewis, Rev. Gordian, C.P., J.C.L., Chapters in Religious Institutes.
182. Marx, Rev. Adolph, J.C.L., The Declaration of Nullity of Marriages Contracted Outside the Church.
183. Matulenas, Rev. Raymond Anthony, O.S.B., A.B., J.C.L., Communication, a Source of Privileges.
184. O'Leary, Rev. Charles Gerard, C.SS.R., Religious Dismissed After Perpetual Profession.
185. Power, Rev. Cornelius Michael, J.C.L., The Blessing of Cemeteries.
186. Shuhler, Rev. Ralph Vincent, O.S.A., J.C.L., Privileges of Religious to Absolve and Dispense.
187. Ziolkowski, Rev. Thaddeus Stanislaus, A.B., J.C.L., The Consecration and Blessing of Churches.

www.ingramcontent.com/pod-product-compliance
Lightning Source LLC
LaVergne TN
LVHW041116090826
844660LV00060B/545